Animalkind

Blackwell Public Philosophy

Edited by Michael Boylan, Marymount University

In a world of 24-hour news cycles and increasingly specialized knowledge, the Blackwell Public Philosophy series takes seriously the idea that there is a need and demand for engaging and thoughtful discussion of topics of broad public importance. Philosophy itself is historically grounded in the public square, bringing people together to try to understand the various issues that shape their lives and give them meaning. This "love of wisdom" – the essence of philosophy – lies at the heart of the series. Written in an accessible, jargon-free manner by internationally renowned authors, each book is an invitation to the world beyond newsflashes and soundbites and into public wisdom.

Forthcoming

For further information about individual titles in the series, supplementary material, and regular updates, visit www.wiley.com/go/bpp

Animalkind

What We Owe to Animals

Jean Kazez

WILEY-BLACKWELL

A John Wiley & Sons, Ltd., Publication

Registered Office
John Wiley & Sons Ltd, The Atrium, Southern Gate, Chichester, West Sussex, PO19 8SQ, United Kingdom

Editorial Offices
350 Main Street, Malden, MA 02148-5020, USA
9600 Garsington Road, Oxford, OX4 2DQ, UK
The Atrium, Southern Gate, Chichester, West Sussex, PO19 8SQ, UK

For details of our global editorial offices, for customer services, and for information about how to apply for permission to reuse the copyright material in this book please see our website at www.wiley.com/wiley-blackwell.

Library of Congress Cataloging-in-Publication Data
Kazez, Jean.
  Animalkind : what we owe to animals / Jean Kazez.
     p.   cm. – (Blackwell public philosophy)
  Includes bibliographical references and index.
     ISBN 978-1-4051-9937-7 (hardcover : alk. paper) – ISBN 978-1-4051-9938-4 (pbk. : alk. paper)
     1. Animal rights. 2.   Animal welfare–Moral and ethical aspects. I.   Title.
HV4701.K39 2010
179′.3–dc22
                                                                    2009018562

A catalogue record for this book is available from the British Library.

Set in 10.5/13pt Minion by SPi Publisher Services, Pondicherry, India
Printed in Singapore by Ho Printing Singapore Pte Ltd

1   2010

With thanks to Peter, Becky, Sammy, and my parents

Contents

Contents

Introduction: Wondering in Alaska

On a recent trip to Alaska I took a tour of Resurrection Bay, at the southern end of the Kenai Peninsula, on a particularly lucky day. It was grey and windy and the water was rough, but the wildlife was spectacular. Our captain pointed out one pod of humpback whales after another, puffins bobbing on the water, porpoises dancing about at the boat's bow, sea lions on a rocky shore, and further off on the hills, baby eagles in a huge nest, two bears, and a sprinkling of Dall sheep. Everyone on board rushed around gleefully, clambering to get the best view. That was actually part of the fun: we were all in it together.

Seeing animals in the wild reminds us that there are many radically different ways to live a life. We humans do it with our two feet planted on solid ground, with words constantly tumbling out of our mouths. A whale's life is almost unimaginably different. Is it joy that a breaching whale feels as she bounds out of the water? Do whales have any sense of tomorrow? Do they enjoy mating and love their young? Are their songs meaningful, like our words?

After the boat tour, we stopped at the Sea Life Center in Seward, and got a closer look at crabs, shrimp, puffins, sea otters, and many other local creatures. Facts and figures captured the glory of Alaskan sea life. But as we walked through the museum, a different side of the human–animal relationship started to surface. Alaska's giant seafood industry was the subject of a large, colorful exhibit that detailed the commercially valuable species of the Bering Sea. The shift of gears reminded us that we can look at animals in two very different ways. The crab is a fascinating alien with a different way of life, but crabs are also protein, not just edible but delicious.

Wandering around the vast state of Alaska with my husband and my two animal-loving kids, there was plenty of time and occasion to think about "the animal conundrum" – who or what animals are, what we owe to them, and how these two questions are connected. From Seward we made our way north to Whittier, and from there we took a boat across Prince William Sound to Valdez, the town made infamous by the oil spill in 1989. From Valdez we drove north through a stunning landscape of valleys, rivers, and glaciers and huge snow-covered mountains. This is the un-Switzerland, a starkly beautiful landscape not warmed by a steeple in the distance, a wisp of smoke coming from a chimney, a herd of cows, or fences separating fields.

Four hundred miles up the road, Fairbanks is home to the University of Alaska and the Institute of Arctic Biology's Large Animal Research Station. There you can observe a herd of muskoxen, members of a stocky, long-haired species that look like holdovers from the last ice age. These mellow beasts were hunted nearly to extinction in the 1800s. In 1930 a small number were captured in Greenland and put on airplanes to Fairbanks and then sent on to Nunivak Island, where the herd grew from 31 members to 750 over the next 30 years. Muskoxen have been released in many parts of Alaska and now their survival seems assured. So assured, in fact, that the sport of killing them has made a comeback. A Google search of "muskox" will turn up pictures of a grinning Caucasian hunter kneeling in the snow on Nunivak Island, a bow in one hand and a dead muskox at his side. The accompanying story is all about the marvel of these beasts, until the very end, when the author describes the inevitable conclusion – an arrow in the animal's lungs – as an "incredible thrill." Our desire to preserve the species raises one question – why? What is the good of the diversity of animal species? The hunter's desire to kill raises another: are animals really so far different from human beings that we can even end their lives just for the fun of it?

We all know our relationship with animals is a little strange. Denali National Park affords the visitor splendid animal-viewing opportunities. The animals in the park are so accustomed to the hoards of visitors (none with guns) that they let themselves be seen up close. Forced to pile into a crowded school bus at the periphery of the car-free park, we were driven over a vertiginous route through stunning mountain scenery. Our driver pointed out caribou, foxes, rabbits, eagles, bears, sheep, and other creatures, telling us interesting things about their habits and habitats. At the end of the tour he boasted that he'd observed 125 species of birds in Denali, adding, with perfect comic timing, that he'd eaten 30 of them. The big laugh he got shows that most of us do see something incongruous there. We admire. We devour. Sometimes in quick succession.

We can easily find our relationship with animals odd, but for many people it takes additional factors to find it seriously thought-provoking.

The whales of Resurrection Bay are protected by law, but in the Arctic Ocean it's another story. A battle has been raging for many years because native peoples want to continue the centuries-old tradition of hunting the bowhead whale. The problem is that the number of these whales is dwindling. The International Whaling Commission estimates there are only about 10,500 left in the seas off northern Alaska, down from as many as 50,000 before commercial whaling began in the nineteenth century.

An extensive display at the Museum of History and Art in Anchorage, our final destination, told the native side of the story. For centuries the whale and other marine mammals were a critical resource for traditional Eskimos, the linchpin of their survival. A culture of whale hunting evolved, complete with specific types of boats and gear and methods as well as stories and rituals. To abandon the practice is to lose something central to native identity, and so native ecologists have pressed their case before the International Whaling Commission, which banned commercial whaling in 1982. In a special allowance for aboriginal subsistence hunting, the Commission gave Eskimos permission to kill 280 bowhead whales every five years in 2002, and renewed that quota in 2007 (with additional allowances for other northern aboriginal peoples). The museum provides a photo record of the traditional hunt, leaving the viewer caught between two responses. With the dignity of the hunt captured in evocative black and white photographs, cultural continuity starts to seem worth a lot. But anyone fresh off a tour of Resurrection Bay will think whales are worth a lot too.

Here two things we're immediately inclined to value come into conflict – the survival of a species, and the survival of a culture. Each represents a way of life, and we find our world more rich and interesting the more that it is filled with diverse ways of life. We are for native customs, but we are also for the bowhead lifestyle, which can't go on existing if bowhead whales become extinct; thus, our confusion.

Some of our wonderings are pure pleasure. We can stand back and marvel at the way of life of the humpback whale, and how it diverges from the bowhead, and how whales are like and unlike ourselves, and we are entirely the better for it. Our world seems more interesting and our lives are enriched. Wondering about our relationship with animals is equally pleasant, if the relationship is that between a boy and his dog, or a girl and her cat; or we are studying the subtle ways of the horse whisperer. When we start wondering about using animals as our resources, it's another matter. Now we get uncomfortable, especially if it's our own way of life – not someone else's – that is in question.

These wonderings must take us beyond the coastal waters and pristine forests of Alaska to much uglier places in the lower 48. In the bizarre world of modern factory farming, animals are packed tightly into giant barns like cars in a parking lot. For the whole duration of their lives, they never see the blue sky, amble across a pasture, or obey their own instincts. In animal laboratories we'd like to think there's proper deference for animal welfare, that every experiment has a compelling justification, but it isn't always true. The subject of our relationship with animals quickly becomes disturbing.

Wondering about the way we use animals isn't guaranteed to be a passive thing, like gazing at the stars, but may be the beginning of a changed way of life. Most of us, deep down, will guard against a total upheaval. And that can hold us back from wondering. If an Eskimo teen can't imagine not participating in the community whale hunt, then he won't let himself think, if thought must immediately lead to change. If you eat lobster on special occasions, and reflection looks like it may threaten that custom, you may just have to hold back from any wondering. Even the horrifying facts about factory farms and slaughter houses can just provoke a defensive reaction if new eating habits aren't in a person's immediate plans.

Rethinking the human–animal relationship is daunting because we are worried about what we might have to give up, but also because we fear being drawn toward extremes. A step in the direction of taking animals more seriously appears to be a step right off a cliff; the old way of thinking that sees animals as "just animals" seems in jeopardy of being replaced with notions of equality that go too far. We feel, in our hearts, that we can't go along with anyone who thinks "cats are people too" – almost literally. But that's where we're going to find ourselves, if we don't put up enough resistance at the very start. Let's just not wonder at all, if that's where wonder is going to lead!

I'm not going to tell you what to wear and eat in this book. In fact, I'll be confessing my own inconsistencies and practical dilemmas. I also won't be arguing that cats are people too. They obviously aren't people, but the question is how they are different, and what ethical differences arise because of the factual differences.

We spent our last few hours in Alaska at the zoo in Anchorage, and got a second look at our favorite prehistoric beast, the muskox. Zoos are all about differences. That's the whole point – to see, in quick succession, a flamingo, a tiger, a crocodile. Implicit in the zooscape, but not behind bars, is another animal: us. It's never far from our minds how different *we* are from all of them. Zoos can't possibly do justice to the drama of diversity. The muskoxen on display had the characteristic stocky bodies and long hair and horns we expect from the species, but exhibited little of the instinctive behavior. Captive muskoxen don't use their foraging skills to find lichen to eat, the males don't enjoy a rambunctious rutting season, they don't arrange themselves like the spokes of a wheel to ward off predators. Most animals at a zoo just wander around bored. The body of an exotic animal can be put on display at a zoo, but not the ways of the animal.

Differences will be the focus of many chapters of this book. We will see what has been said about the human/animal divide in ancient religion and indigenous myth (Chapter 1), and in the writings of philosophers West and East (Chapter 2). And we'll check all of that against what we can learn about the human/animal divide from animal psychologists and ethologists (Chapters 3 and 4). That's all "lead up" to the central question of the book. What do differences matter, ethically speaking? Are humans and animals on two different moral planes, or on the same plane, or does diversity actually count, morally speaking? Are there as many moral planes as there are different animals in the zoo (Chapters 5 and 6)?

We've been thinking about animals since the proverbial dawn of time, but also using animals in myriad ways. In the beginning we killed them in order to survive, for food, warmth, and building materials; later we killed them to make ivory baubles and fancy fur coats, and for their taste (Chapter 7); still later, researchers killed them to develop vaccines against deadly diseases (Chapter 8) and sport hunters killed them to reenact the elemental life and death struggles of our ancestors. With a better grip on species differences, and how they matter, we should be in a better position to sort it all out and decide how to look at this history. Is this a story of ingenuity, with humans developing an ever more impressive ability to exploit animals? Or is it a story of gradual decline, starting innocently enough but eventually going downhill? Or is it a story of wickedness, from beginning to end – despite the assumptions made almost everywhere, by almost everyone?

The need to look at the animal conundrum is more urgent today than it's ever been. A 2006 UN report called *Livestock's Long Shadow* paints a frightening portrait of proliferating domesticated animals. With the Western taste for animal products spreading to every society, 30 percent of the total land surface of the earth is now occupied by livestock and feedcrops. In the storied war between wild and domesticated animals, it was the fox that broke into the chicken coop, the wolf that made away with the lamb, but in population terms, it's definitely the mild animals, not the wild animals, that are winning. All the choice real estate is going to the animals that satisfy human appetites, with wild habitats drastically reduced and fragmented. To understand what's happening to animals in our world, we will need to come to grips with both the plight of the veal calf, and the fate of his disappearing animal brethren in the wild (Chapter 9).

We each stand in a force field of culture, instinct, personal habits, social pressures, identifications and allegiances. As hard as we try to free ourselves and look at animal questions dispassionately, we must remain uncertain how well we've succeeded (Chapter 10). Our way of life has always included hunting, killing, eating, wearing, and harnessing animals. How much of that can stay the same, and what must we change? What should be our ultimate destination, and how soon can we hope to arrive there?

Part I

Before

Perplexity about other species is nothing new. It's visible in every culture, and especially in those with the closest contact with animals. Philosophers have always dealt with the question of the "brutes," typically giving them a status far beneath human beings.

1

The Myth of Consent

What do you see when you look at an animal? A kindred spirit, a creature much like you; but possibly, the very next moment, a beast, a stranger, *just* an animal. Animals are like those pictures that we see as one thing and then another; the duck that suddenly becomes a rabbit; the wine glass that's also an old woman in profile. Now the pig is a fellow creature, like Wilbur in *Charlotte's Web*. Now he's pork.

The gestalt switch produced by a picture is no special problem, but our double vision of animals has to concern us. If Wilbur is a friend, then he shouldn't be treated as bacon. If he's bacon, then we're kidding ourselves when we regard him as a friend. What's the right way to look at animals?

There are loud voices coming from animal rights organizations that tell us this is a good question to ask. Those voices seem to come from outside the mainstream. Most of us are animal lovers in the sense that we love our pets, we like to go to zoos, and we'd hate to see endangered species disappear. That animals may be used for multiple purposes is something we don't question. The animal people who want us to think twice about these things seem faintly ridiculous – like they've lost all sense of proportion.

But confusion about our relationship with animals isn't a recent invention. Our ancestors lived their lives in closer proximity to animals than most of us do, experiencing both fondness and the need to exploit them more intensely. There were plenty of signs of ambivalence way before animal rights organizations came on the scene.

Animal Spirits

Indigenous, pre-European peoples are sometimes credited with a deep and respectful relationship to nature. Perhaps that image involves a certain amount of exaggeration and wishful thinking. The very first wave of immigrants to the Americas, those who crossed the Bering land bridge around 11,000 BCE, eventually hunted the big mammal species to extinction (at least on one theory). Gone were American horses, camels, elephants, giant ground sloths. In *Guns, Germs, and Steel,* Jared Diamond hypothesizes that these animals had evolved without any exposure to dangerous human hunters and were thus easy prey. By contrast, he writes, the mammals of Africa had evolved alongside human beings and earlier hominids, and learned to fear them.

Much later, all was not peaceful coexistence either. The Blackfoot Indians of Montana couldn't have been too soft-hearted toward the animal world. Their preferred method of hunting buffalo involved corralling them on the top of a cliff and then scaring them into throwing themselves, en masse, off the edge. One can only imagine the tumult of injured, howling animals below.

Still, native cultures do show particularly clear signs of wrestling with the two ways we can look at animals. A sign of this is found, surprisingly, in a comforting story. Joseph Campbell says the Blackfoot Indians believed the buffaloes voluntarily plunged to their deaths, obeying the command of their "animal master" – a sort of archetypal buffalo. Thus, "the animal is a willing victim, giving its flesh to be the food of the people." If only it were true! The wish for the buffalo's consent seems to reveal a desire to stay friends, to show respect, even as the animal meets a violent end. The hunters seem to want their victims' approval.

An even more thorough form of exoneration is implicit in a Blackfoot legend of a maiden who brings her father back to life under the tutelage of the lead buffalo, the animal master. With that lesson, she also learns how to bring the buffalo back to life. That was the goal behind the ritual dances that were performed by the hunters, wearing animal heads and skins. As Campbell interprets it, "The buffalo dance, properly performed, insures that the creatures slaughtered shall be giving only their bodies, not their essence, not their lives." If the buffalo don't really die, then there's a limitless supply of them, and the next hunt will meet with success. The legend and rituals are attractive for that reason, but I'm inclined to interpret the story as a symptom of unease about the carnage at the base of the cliff. It reassures the hunters that no serious violation has taken place.

Arctic Eskimos grappled with the problem of killing in a similar way. Before contact with Europeans and Americans in the eighteenth and nineteenth centuries, arctic peoples depended almost completely on hunting animals for the fulfillment of their basic needs. With killing being so critical to survival, we might expect there to be complete indifference to the problems of animals. But that's not what the stories and practices of the various Eskimo cultures suggest.

The whale played a vital role as food, fuel, building materials, clothing, and so on, but it was never regarded as "nothing but" all of the above. Whales were taken to have spirits, like people do, and their spirits had to be treated with respect. Only then would the whale "give itself" to the people. This is an interpretation of whale behavior that's difficult to sustain – whales do try to avoid their deaths. Even Charles Wohlforth, a sympathetic observer of Eskimo (or more precisely, Iñupiat) customs, reports that a whale will dive away from hunters. Sometimes a whale will be harpooned six to ten times before finally becoming too exhausted to try to escape. Occasionally the whales win the contest, and swim away with their wounds. Oddly, recalcitrant whales have given something else to the people – evidence of the astonishing lifespan of bowhead whales: in 1992, a bowhead was butchered and discovered to have a stone spearhead embedded in his or her flesh, though stone hasn't been in use since the 1880s. The natural lifespan of a bowhead is now thought to be 130–150 years. It's natural to ask what drew Eskimos to the notion that whales offer themselves to hunters.

Part of the answer surely lies in the natural anxiety of a people so totally reliant on an unpredictable hunt for survival. If whales give themselves to humans now, then they can be expected to do so again in the future. In fact, the very same whale might make a second gift; Eskimos, like the Blackfoot Indians, believe in the recycling of animal spirits. But the consent of the whale is a reassuring notion for another reason. If the whale says Yes, then the hunter doesn't need to have any compunction about the hunt. And mixed feelings do seem inevitable for a people that lived in close proximity with animals, appreciating not just their abundant usefulness, but their majesty, beauty, and intelligence.

If being killed doesn't harm an animal's inner essence, could it even be *good* for the animal? One can't help but suspect an element of spin in the myths of the Ainu, the aboriginal people of the northern islands of Japan. Traditionally, a black bear cub was captured in the mountains and brought to the village, where he or she became a beloved member of a family, even being nursed by the mother. When he got older and more ferocious, he was placed in a wooden cage and fattened up for two years. The time finally had come to eat the bear, but that was good news for all, even the bear.

In a festival called "the sending away," the bear was actually now "returned" to his mountain home. Campbell reports that "the whole spirit of the feast is of a joyous send-off, and the bear is supposed to be extremely happy." The bear was secured by ropes and released from the cage, then paraded in a circle. At that point the people threw little bamboo arrows at him until he worked himself into a frenzy. He was then tied to a stake, skewered, and strangled. But not to be left out of the fun, the bear's head and hide were preserved intact so he could be given a portion of the feast. While dining on his own flesh, along with some dried fish, millet dumplings, and a beverage, the bear got to listen to speeches in his honor. With such a sendoff, he was expected to return to his family in the mountains with glowing reports about the humans below.

You wouldn't wish such hospitality on your worst enemy. But there is something remarkable here. The Ainu could have just gone bear hunting, butchered the poor beast, satisfied their hunger, and left it at that. But within their ritual, there's a clearly discernible respect for the bear and unease about killing him. They do all these things as if to try to have their bear and eat him too.

Divine Consent

Animals who want to be eaten are dubious creatures, but in a monotheistic view of the world, all permission has to come from on high anyway. The Hebrew bible says the ruler of the universe gave humans permission to eat animals. Case closed? Not, of course, if you live in a place where the Hebrew bible seems as foreign as the Blackfoot legends seem to us. And not if you regard the bible as a cherished part of the Western canon, but nothing more. *Caveat emptor* – I'm going to approach the Good Book with no special reverence, but simply as an artifact of a particular time and place.

God does give humans permission to eat animals, but the message of the bible is complex. We need to start at the beginning to see just how complex it really is. Yahweh creates the rest of the animals before human beings. They are created on the fifth and the sixth days, "and God saw that it was good" – animals seem to be good just for themselves, not for the resources they supply to people. At the end of the sixth day, Yahweh creates human beings differently from animals – "in his own image" (Genesis 1:27). The implication: we should not see ourselves in animals and animals in ourselves – at least not too much.

Humans are immediately given dominion or rule over the animals. "Fill the earth and subdue it. Rule over the fish of the sea and the birds of the air and over every living creature that moves on the ground." (Genesis 1:28) Does ruling include eating? Rule is many things – parents rule over children, kings over their subjects. Ruling and eating certainly *seem* like different things. And in the case of human beings and animals, the deity is explicit that ruling does *not* encompass eating. The issue is immediately clarified, right after the famous "dominion" passage: "I give you every green plant for food," God says to the first humans, "I give you every seed-bearing plant on the face of the whole earth and every tree that has fruit with seed in it. They will be yours for food" (Genesis 1:29). And then he says the same to animals, giving them "every green plant for food" (Genesis 1:30).

The authors of Genesis (plural, according to bible scholars) have it that these instructions were followed for a time. In the Garden of Eden humans and other animals live together peaceably. Because of the perfect climate, animal bones aren't needed as building material, fur isn't needed to make coats. The trees are laden with sustaining fruit. In the beginning it is roughly as Isaiah (11:6–7) foretells it will be in the end times:

> The wolf will live with the lamb,
> the leopard will lie down with the goat,
> the calf and the lion and the yearling together;
> The cow will feed with the bear ...
> their young will lie down together,
> and the lion will eat straw like the ox.

The Garden of Eden prefigures the peaceable kingdom, the harmonious world depicted in Edward Hicks' famous painting by that name (the first version made in 1820).

Paradise is ruined when Eve takes the serpent's advice and eats from the wrong tree; not one of the fruit-laden trees, but the tree of the knowledge of good and evil. Human beings degenerate, each generation becoming more lawless than the last. Yahweh decides to get rid of all living things in a giant flood. The whole project of creating humans and animals has turned out to be a big mistake. But he holds back: Noah's family and a pair from each species are allowed to survive on the ark until the waters subside.

Remarkably, in his very first speech to the survivors after they reach land, Yahweh says "Just as I gave you the green plants, I now give you everything" (Genesis 9:3). Whether animals may be killed for food is a matter with that much importance! The answer is that animals *can* be used for food, but it's a little more complex than that. Eat animals, yes, "But you must not eat meat that has its lifeblood in it" (Genesis 9:4), says the deity; "for the blood is the life" (Deuteronomy 12:23; see also Leviticus 17:11 and 14). What to do with the blood? Spill it out on the altar. Yes, the altar. For killing animals is not mundane work for butchers, but sacred work for priests.

Animals were *not* originally created just to be our food. After being designated edible, they retained a place in the deity's embrace. In fact, God establishes a covenant with humans *and* animals – "an everlasting covenant between God and all living creatures of every kind" (Genesis 9:15). Five times the covenant is declared, and each time animals are explicitly included. The deity sends human beings down a middle path: eat animals, use them, but (he seems to say) it's really not ideal. Animals "count" in the eyes of God, even as humans are given the prerogative to eat them.

The myths of the Blackfoot Indians, the Eskimos, and the Ainu all seem like symptoms of an underlying unease. They reveal a vision of animals not as mere things to be consumed and exploited, but as living beings, creatures that matter in a special way. The Hebrew bible reveals the same sensitivity, but engenders more puzzlement. There is a powerful god, the authors of Genesis tell us, one who created the universe and everything in it. He created animals that were good – good in themselves, and not just good as resources. But then ... what are *we* doing eating them for dinner, they must have wondered.

Answer: that's not what God originally intended. Things went downhill after a perfect beginning. It was either wipe us out or capitulate somewhat to our evil ways, and God chose the second option. Well, it was better than annihilation! And he didn't capitulate entirely: eat the flesh, he ordered, not the blood. Permission was granted, but not without qualification.

The message of Genesis is certainly an inconvenient one. Orthodox Jews today take the injunction not to eat the blood of an animal in all seriousness. Kosher meat preparation involves thoroughly draining an animal's blood and then salting the flesh to draw out every last trace. This is not a recipe for producing juicy steaks and it's only symbolically humane (for evidence that kosher practices today are cruel to animals, see the Humane Kosher website in the sources for this chapter). Surely the important thing is the way animals are treated while alive, a matter on which kosher rules say very little. Still, a true adherent of the bible will not be a blithe and indifferent animal exploiter.

The myth of animal consent is completely anxiety-relieving. The animals themselves consent to be eaten – there's nothing to worry about, no need for restrictions. In fact, that myth is coupled with the even more soothing idea that animals come back to life after death. Neither of these ideas is in the bible: animals don't consent to be killed; ideas about an afterlife in much later bible passages and especially Christian scripture apply to human beings only, never to animals. The bible's message about animals is a mixed one, bordering on contradictory, but it still gives us the green light. Permission from the ruler of the universe, like permission from animals themselves, absolves us of guilt. There are complexities and restrictions, but in the end the message is clear: killing animals for food isn't a crime.

Let's Make a Deal

The myth of consent has a modern version, free of whales who want to be eaten and gods who tell us what we may and may not do. Stephen Budiansky, a journalist who has written many books about animals, comes to the defense of consuming and otherwise using domesticated animals in his 1999 book *The Covenant of the Wild: Why Animals Chose Domestication.*

Domestication, he says, is a deal that's struck at the interface between town and country. The ancestors of dogs were wolves who hung around the camps of humans, helping themselves to our meat scraps and the warmth of our fires. These must have been the more docile and dependent members of the species, and with each subsequent generation, the even more docile and dependent were preferred and protected. Ultimately, a free and fair bargain was struck. Animals came to us for an easier life. We gave it to them, and in exchange we shortened the lives of some of them and used their bodies to meet our own needs. The comic book version of Budiansky's hypothesis would show (in Gary Larson style) a cow and a human being shaking hands, with the cow saying, "It's a deal. If I can graze in your pasture, you can eat me for dinner." So – not so different from the consenting buffalo, the generous whale, the happy bear – the cow actually consents to being eaten. Implicitly, of course.

The "covenant" has worked out to mutual advantage, says Budiansky. What's the evidence? We've been well-fed for thousands of years, and domesticated animals have thrived: there are estimated to be on the order of 1.5 billion cattle and buffalo on the face of the earth, 1.75 billion sheep and goats, 2 billion pigs, and 24 billion chickens.

The consenting whale and buffalo, the bear who's about to go home, all seem like creatures of the imagination. They seem like products of wishful thinking, tailor made to make people feel better about the violent things they have to do to stay alive. Budiansky's account is less fanciful, but I suspect no more plausible. The number of cows, pigs, and chickens in the world today hasn't been reached by natural means, with each mating being in any sense a vote for domesticated life and death. Reproduction in domesticated animals is largely under human control. Chickens don't multiply by choice, but as a result of business decisions, and often by artificial insemination. There are twice as many chickens today as there were ten years ago because executives estimated demand and manufactured supply. There are lots and lots of chickens for the same kinds of reasons that there are lots and lot of computers.

A true mutualism is another matter. Take, for example, the relationship between aphids and ants. The aphids secrete honeydew, a sugary substance they form by eating plants; the ants milk them by stimulating them with their antennae. (Actually, "milk" is a bit of a euphemism; this is really coprophagia, to put it delicately.) The ants get food from the aphids, and in return they protect the aphids from their predators, such as ladybugs. The metaphor of a covenant is poetic but apt.

But the number of chickens in the vicinity of humans can't be read that way. Chickens are powerless captives reproducing at a rapid rate because human breeders have production quotas to fill. Even if domesticated animals were proliferating naturally, and not as a result of business decisions, their numbers couldn't necessarily be counted as being to their advantage. The aphids are better off because of ants, and ants better off because of aphids. But our proliferating chicken stocks are crammed into their small cages for the duration of their short lives. Existence is not a good thing for the thousands of pigs packed tightly into factory farms. The covenant metaphor doesn't measure up to the modern realities.

Consider that Gary Larson-esque cartoon. No actual cow ever did strike such a bargain – "If you give me space in your pasture, I'll let you eat me." It's not even plausible that cows struck such a bargain implicitly. The cows of old wanted the pasture, period, and weren't capable of looking over the terms of a contract. But would they have, should they have, if it had been possible?

If there really were animal masters, archetypal cows that could strike bargains on behalf of all cows, and archetypal chickens who represented chickens, it's hard to say if they would. Certainly, we would not, not even if we were facing extinction. There are tiny indigenous tribes struggling to survive in inhospitable areas of the world and various bargains they could strike with richer nations to ensure their survival and proliferation. Human beings have no taste for each other's flesh, but a dwindling people could agree to be organ donors for people in affluent countries in exchange for being richly supported. To sweeten the deal, the donors could be guaranteed 50 years of life, before any donations were required. You can imagine a "covenant" of this sort leading to longer life for thousands of affluent westerners and a vast increase in population for the struggling tribe. The fact is, it would not be agreed to. The tribal leaders would consider the plan intolerably demeaning.

No chicken or cow has ever felt his position in life was demeaning. But the animal masters might wish to protect their brethren nevertheless, thinking one can be demeaned whether one knows it or not. They might. What's certain is that the animal masters would not accept the deal that's currently on offer. They wouldn't see the advantage of there being lots of chickens or pigs or cows, if each is trapped in a cage or squeezed into a stall; subjected to surgeries without anesthesia; transported to the slaughter house in a cramped, hot truck; and then killed young and possibly painfully. (For more on modern farming, see Chapter 7.)

Budiansky's bargaining cows and chickens are the pseudo-scientific shadows of the bear who returns to the mountains, the buffalo who gives his body to the people, the whale who cares more about humans than about herself and her own offspring. They're designed to relieve us of moral uncertainty. Even under the best of conditions, I don't think a farmer could look at his cow, on slaughtering day, and honestly tell himself the cow has agreed to be eaten. But today's industrial farmer must truly be guilty of self-deception if he thinks his relationship with his livestock is consensual.

The Blackfoot Indians, the Eskimos, the Ainu of Japan, and the ancient Israelites teach us to recognize our competing urges – the desire to have our bear and eat it too. For us these feelings tend to be buried, suppressed, and forgotten, so we would do well to pay attention. On the other hand, their salves don't work so well for us. We have difficulty believing that animals don't simply die when we slit their throats or strangle them. They surely don't consent to their deaths. Many Eskimos today still seem to sincerely believe that the whale makes a gift of herself to her killers, and it may seem disrespectful to say this is just not true, but we really don't pay respect to people by being uncritical of their ideas, as if they were hypersensitive children.

Whales don't have the mental equipment to think about humans and their needs, nor should we think they would put us before themselves if they did. If they really were such sophisticated thinkers and such altruists, there would be an overwhelmingly powerful reason not to accept their gift: whales would have to be seen as our fellows, not as our fodder. (Should the Eskimos stop hunting whales? We'll come back to this difficult issue in Chapter 9.)

We ought to shine the same critical light on cultures that are closer up and more populous. How plausible is the idea of a supreme being who takes an avid interest in our well-being, and gives people permission to eat animals? If there is a supreme being, maybe the bible is right, and he ordained on the sixth day that we shouldn't harm animals; he said "I give you the green plants for food" and never changed his mind about what we should eat. Or it may be that there's no supreme being at all, that a god who tells us what's good and bad is as mythical as a whale who consents to being eaten. In a divinely ordained world, it doesn't seem as if we'd even be tempted to eat the bodies of our animal cousins. They didn't *have* to be so tasty!

Our ancestors have to be honored for seeing the difference between eating fruit from a tree and snuffing the life out of another creature. Perhaps there is even some wisdom to be gleaned from their stories. For example, there may be a kernel of truth in the bible's notion of respectful exploitation. It might be right to listen to Eskimo talk about showing respect to animals. But what exactly does respect entail? Kosher meat-preparation rules go to great lengths to ensure that only muscle fiber and fat are consumed, and never blood. But does this do the animals any good? When a whaler gives a dead whale a "drink" by pouring a cup of water into its blowhole, is this really respectful in any important and substantial sense?

More basically, we are going to have to ask whether we should accept the "respectful exploitation" stance in the first place. On the face of it, respectful exploitation is an oxymoron. If we respect, we don't exploit. If we exploit, we don't respect. Or is the level of respect an animal is due something that varies depending on species, and that's compatible sometimes with using animals as food, fertilizer, farm machinery, fuel, and the rest?

The main point for now is that it *is* troubling to use animals to meet our needs, as all these people, so far apart in space and time, realized. Killing an animal is not like pulling a carrot out of the ground. When we kill, even to satisfy our most basic needs, we do something that should give us pause.

2

The Order of Things

Like Eskimo whalers and Ainu bear hunters, many philosophers have wondered about the use of animals as our resources, but they approach the matter in a different way. A philosopher's goal is to plumb the nature of things – to systematically explain what animals are, and what we are, such that we can (or can't) eat them, milk them, yoke them, and all the rest. If we didn't get the relief from perplexity we wanted from ancient and aboriginal peoples, maybe we'll get it here. Or at least, we'll consider ways of thinking we might want to avoid, and ways with more potential.

Perhaps the best tonic, if we could swallow it, is the idea that the very purpose of animals is to provide human beings with food and labor. You can't have too many qualms about using things in the way they are supposed to be used. But then, why are *we* the point of it all, and not some other single species?

Ecce Homo

In the *Politics*, written in the fourth century BCE, Aristotle observes that nature provides baby animals with food – developing chicks with the protein inside of an egg, mammals with their mothers' milk. By extension, he says, it makes sense to think that nature provides the older child and adult with food. So we ought to think plants are for the nutrition of animals, and animals for the nutrition of human beings. If we have qualms about eating animals and using them for our many purposes, we should recall Aristotle's reassuring words: "Now if nature makes nothing incomplete and nothing in vain, the inference must be that she has made all animals for the sake of man." Or rather, we should recall them *if* we can bring ourselves to believe them.

Who or what is this "she" ("Nature") who ordered things for the sake of human beings? It's not the Israelite's god, who was contemporaneously worshipped across the Mediterranean at the time of Aristotle. It's not one of the local Greek deities either. The personification of nature is merely metaphorical. Animals exist to feed human beings, thinks Aristotle, in just the way that the heart exists to pump blood. Seeing things that way doesn't require any particular theology or mythology. But can we really see things that way?

Aristotle actually knew that nature is not so neatly hierarchical. He was aware that there are carnivorous animals and he surely knew that people are omnivores. So if anything, animals exist to benefit people *and* other animals; and plants exist to benefit people *and* animals. You could even suppose that people exist for the sake of animals and plants. Aristotle must have known that human flesh is just as nutritious as any other flesh. Unlucky people have fed lions, sharks, and grizzly bears; corpses feed the worms under the ground; plants will grow more lushly where a corpse is buried.

Deep-seated ideas about the order of things lie behind Aristotle's simplifications. He sees human beings as being like a magnificent statue resting on a pedestal (i.e. animals), which rests on another pedestal (i.e. plants). The statue doesn't exist to give the two pedestals something to do; the pedestals exist for the sake of the statue. It's not only on the basis of a selective tally of who eats what that he places human beings on top. That's a place of honor, and we have it because there's something special about us: namely, that we can reason.

Reason must be in command, says Aristotle: the soul should rule the body, rational man should rule less rational woman, rational masters should rule irrational slaves. Likewise, humans should rule animals. When reason is in command, it's for the general good. "Animals are better off when they are ruled by man," Aristotle writes, "for then they are preserved." Why should the ox plow the field and the cow give us her milk? It's partly that the ox and the cow exist for our benefit, but partly because they're better off under our governance.

The two grounds for placing humans atop the double pedestal don't sit very well with each other. You can think we're above animals because they exist for our sake, to meet our needs *or* that we're above animals in the sense that living under our rational command is good for them. The herder who's been reading Aristotle would be wise to entertain the two ideas in succession, not at the same time. As long as he's tending his flock, he can think of his sheep as needing his supervision for their own good. They are like his children.

But on slaughtering day, when he has to slit their throats, he'd better give that up and remember that animals are just our food, like the egg white is for the developing chick to eat and milk is for baby mammals to drink.

It's an awkward change of attitude. In the world of children's books and movies, phase two is often problematic. Millions of us grew up with the story of Wilbur, the pig who was saved from becoming pork thanks to the clever schemes of Charlotte the friendly spider. Animals are rescued from becoming food in the popular movies *Babe, Madagascar*, and *Chicken Run*. But phase two is as natural as can be, as Aristotle sees it.

Aristotle could be the inspiration for quite a different way of looking at animals. The human species has its own natural way of life, its own inborn potential, he thinks: ours is to reason and to rule by reason. The naturalness of reason, for us, is a consideration that leads Aristotle to place reason at the center of human flourishing. But why not generalize? It would be Aristotle-*like* to say that every species has its own inborn potential, to acknowledge that lions flourish when they can hunt and birds when they can migrate. From there, it's only a few steps to the idea that lions and birds are better off thriving in the wild, instead of serving us in some way or other.

But Aristotle is primarily a champion of *reason*, not nature. Tame animals are better off than wild animals, he says, even though wild animals better express their true nature in the wild, not after they've been captured and pressed into human service. What we must deduce is that Aristotle attaches no absolute value to the development of natural potential. Since *our* natural potential is to make use of reason, we should develop it. But reason is what really counts. There's no good to be achieved simply by letting lions act like lions and birds act like birds. The potential for a more affirmative view of animals is visible under the surface of Aristotle's thinking, but he never developed it.

The Great Chain of Being

In the thirteenth century, Thomas Aquinas was the great synthesizer, ever trying to blend scripture with the sagacity of Aristotle, the one philosopher so authoritative as to be called simply "*the* philosopher." Here and there, he too addresses the status of animals. In an appealingly direct section of the *Summa Theologica* (Question 64, Article 1), Aquinas asks whether killing animals counts as murder.

Aquinas sees a perfect match between Aristotle's view that animals exist for our sake and Yahweh's speech granting Noah permission to eat meat after the flood (Chapter 1). But in fact, the ideas don't combine smoothly at all. Aristotle assimilates animals to the white of an egg and to mother's milk. They are meant for consumption. But this is not the thought in the earliest lines of Genesis. God creates the land animals, the birds, and the fish, and immediately "sees that it is good." If you wanted to believe God was merely stocking the pantry for the humans he would create on the sixth day, you'd run headlong into the fact that, as soon as he creates humans, he instructs them to be vegetarians. It's only later, as a merciful concession to human weakness, that animals are reclassified as edible. And even then, Yahweh establishes a covenant with animals, promising always to preserve them, and puts restrictions on how they are to be killed ("you shall not eat the blood, for the blood is the life").

The notion that animals exist for their own sake, and *not* merely as fodder for human consumption, fits well with the opening lines of Genesis but also with a tradition of thought that persisted for millennia. In his magisterial work *The Great Chain of Being*, Arthur Lovejoy traces the idea of plenitude from Plato's dialogue the *Timaeus*, through the neo-Platonists of the third century, the Jewish philosopher Maimonides and other Christian theologians in the middle ages, and on into the eighteenth century and beyond. Putting it with flair, Lovejoy sums up the principle of plentitude as the idea that "it takes all kinds to make a world."

Plenitude solves a problem that Aristotle's anthropocentrism stumbles over. If animals exist for our sake, then why are there 370,000 species of beetle (at last count)? Do we need every different fish in the sea and every different bird in the sky? What are the emperor penguins in Antarctica doing for us? What about the species in the darkest depths of the ocean? All the beetles and penguins and bottom-dwellers don't exist for us, on the plenitude view, but rather to make the world complete.

But why must the world be complete? The notion that it must grew out of a puzzle that first took shape in Plato but later found religious form in the hands of the medieval theologians. The puzzle is this: what possible reason could there be for a perfect and self-sufficient being, a supreme being, to create any world at all, and especially a world like ours, with all its messiness and grime? If he was perfect to begin with, he certainly couldn't have added anything to his perfection by creating a world, and especially not by creating a world with as many imperfections as this one.

Answer: God's perfect goodness includes fecundity. God must have had the idea of every possibility in his divine mind (that comes with being all-knowing). Then, because of his goodness, he had to overflow, granting existence to every possible life form, from angels down to all those different kinds of beetles (and plants and rocks and mud). Looking at reality this way, even the lowliest animal is an emanation of God's goodness. And that means, importantly, that all of nature is good, to one degree or another, every last ant and worm and beetle.

The plenitude school of thought rejects Aristotle's statue on two pedestals and replaces it with a very different image: the ladder of innumerable rungs that stretches from the most perfect thing down to the least perfect. We are somewhere in the middle, the medievals thought, more perfect than the rest of the animals, but less perfect than the many different kinds of spiritual beings that *must* exist, by plenitude logic.

Aristotle would have seen a stark contrast between humans and even our nearest neighbors, the apes, permitting us a thrilling sense of our own specialness. The plenitude school asks for a bit more humility, since it places humans above the rest of the animals, but only by *one* rung. There *ought* to be species that are very similar to us, on this view, and in fact eighteenth- and nineteenth-century plenitude thinkers were enthusiastic about the abilities of the great apes (and the deficiencies of certain human beings). In 1713, an English essayist wrote:

> Nor is the Disagreement between the basest Individuals of our species and the Ape or Monkey so great, but that, were the latter endow'd with the Faculty of Speech, they might perhaps as justly claim the Rank and Dignity of the human Race, as the savage *Hotentot,* or stupid native of Nova Zembia. The most perfect of this Order of Beings, the *Orang-Outang,* as he is called by the natives of *Angola,* that is the Wild man, or the Man of the Woods, has the Honour of Bearing the greatest Resemblance to Human Nature.

Somewhere along the way, the honor of being the only rational animal had started to seem like something that could be given up.

The plenitude conception of the order of things is not such a cleansing tonic as Aristotle's, when it comes to the conundrum of animal use. It reinforces some of our moral anxieties instead of purging them. From Aristotle's perspective, there's not much harm in using up one thing in the larder. Whales are dispensable if fossil fuels now take the place of blubber as an energy source and baleen is no longer needed to make corsets and umbrellas. If it is good that every kind of animal exists, because every kind is an extension of God's goodness, then the disappearance of whales must count as a great evil.

But as long as we conserve the existing species, are there any limits to the way we ought to treat animals? The thought that the lowliest mouse is an emanation of God's goodness would seem to warrant at least some small degree of concern for his welfare. But the concern will vary with the rung an animal occupies on the ladder of creation. The plenitude thinker – or at least one who troubles himself over the treatment of animals – should want more concern for whales than for mice, and the most concern for human beings (since angels seem to get along without our help). This is not an egalitarian conception, but it's not absolutely dismissive of the welfare of animals. In reality, though, the plenitude thinkers did not even go this far. They assumed, like Aristotle, that humans had carte blanche to make use of animals. Once again, an opening for animal-concern was ignored.

The Absent Soul

By comparison to the many-runged ladder, Aristotle's statue on a double pedestal is an image that reinforces human pride – our sense that we are in a completely different category, and the world is basically ours. But for all that we are above and "they" are below, Aristotle doesn't think humans and other animals are completely dissimilar. We are alike in having perceptions, feelings, and desires. For a vision of radical dissimilarity, the thinker to turn to is the seventeenth-century philosopher René Descartes, who famously argued that humans have souls and animals do not.

Aristotle is actually generous to animals, when it comes to souls. This isn't as remarkable as it first appears: a soul, for him, is not an immaterial thing temporarily housed in a body. It's a living thing's *power* to do specific jobs, to function in certain ways. Plants are ensouled, since they can accomplish such tricky tasks as converting food into fuel, and growing from infancy to maturity. Animals are doubly ensouled, since they do those things but also have powers of perception and desire and locomotion. An animal can see the water in a puddle, want to drink it, and then walk toward the puddle. Humans are triply ensouled, because they do all that, but also think and reason intelligently. They can think about the water in the puddle – safe or not safe? And what is the nature of water, to begin with? All humans, and none of the other animals, can *think*.

Aristotle's view is not inherently antiquated; it's one shared, in essence, by later psychologists of the nineteenth and twentieth centuries, who didn't use the word "soul" but thought similarly about the mind. One school of psychology looked at the mind as a set of faculties, something like the organs of the body. The faculties of reason, perception, memory, language, and so on, were thought of like the liver, the pancreas, the gallbladder, the spleen. Just as a person missing an organ would be missing the functions associated with it, so would a person missing one of the mental faculties due to injury or disease. Other faculties might in some cases be able to take over (like the liver can take over for the gallbladder), but the job wouldn't be done as well, or in the same way. Aristotle's idea, stated in these terms, is that animals are missing the faculty of reason. They have the faculties of perception, memory, and appetite, and thus can get around in the world without bumping into things, but their mental lives are fundamentally different from ours.

The soul that's missing from animals is just one of the three we possess, according to Aristotle. Descartes thought about souls quite differently. The brain, he thought, is merely the infrastructure that processes signals from the sense organs, and creates the possibility of seeing an image of (say) a red apple. Without the soul, there's no possibility of going on to think about the apple – big or small? worth eating or not? composed of indivisible atoms or not? But without the soul as receiver, there's also no perceived image. The soul underwrites not just thought and reason, but all of consciousness. Thus, when Descartes famously claimed that animals have no souls, he was saying something quite astonishing – that animals are completely devoid of thought *and* awareness. Though animals *seem* to navigate their way through the world in something like the way we do, a dog doesn't actually approach his bowl of food because of anything he smells, or any image he sees, or any sensation of hunger. All that transpires is a sequence of events in his sense organs, brain, and body. The dog is merely a machine, a furry robot.

If Aristotle pictured nature in multiple layers – humans (three souls), animals (two souls), plants (one soul), rocks (no soul) – Descartes has in mind an even starker division. Every natural thing falls into the same category, though mechanical complexity varies a lot. Human beings, because of their souls, are in a class by themselves.

How did Descartes arrive at such a dramatic dualism? The speechlessness of animals is the crux of the matter. Each person has immediate access to his own consciousness, and can deduce for himself that he doesn't just *have* a soul, but *is* a soul (possibly, and only temporarily, attached to a body). The belief that *others* are conscious is arrived at completely differently; it rests entirely on their speech, says Descartes. The sentences we hear coming out of the mouths of others *couldn't*, on his view, emerge just from bodies (with all the infinite variety of content that human language permits); speech is proof positive of other souls. But animals don't speak. We are thus lacking any reason to attribute souls to them. And so they must be just machines.

To Descartes, this is a conclusion that's attractive, not strange. "It seems reasonable, since art copies nature, and men can make various automata which move without thought, that nature should produce its own automata, much more splendid than artificial ones. These natural automata are the animals." Unlike Aristotle or anyone before him, Descartes makes animals *terra incognita*. There is no relating to an animal, because there is nothing that it's like to be an animal. The magic of consciousness is for humans alone.

Descartes's view is even better at allaying moral doubt than Aristotle's. The shepherd who's been reading Aristotle will at least think of the lambs' welfare up until slaughtering day, placing them under "rational rule" for mutual benefit. The herder who reads Descartes will not even do that. He can kick them, beat them, confine them in tiny stalls all to his heart's content, for on this view animals think nothing, want nothing, and feel nothing. "My opinion is not so much cruel to animals," Descartes writes, "as indulgent to men ... since it absolves them from the suspicion of crime when they eat or kill animals."

Descartes's views invited caricature and contempt even in his own time and he remains a villain in the eyes of animal rights advocates today. He's also sometimes accused of shocking behavior. Colin Spencer, the British food writer, writes, "Descartes, the father of modern philosophy, nailed his wife's pet dog by its four paws to a board and dissected the creature while it was alive." The claim meshes poorly with the fact that Descartes never married, but it's true there's no reason he shouldn't have nailed his wife's dog to a door, if he had had a wife, and she had had a dog. Descartes would have thought the barks and cries of the dog were no more signs of pain than the sputterings of a malfunctioning clock. Seventeenth-century experimenters at Port Royal, inspired by Descartes's views, did in fact conduct anatomical studies on live animals, ignoring their howls because animals were "just machines." Or so reported Nicholas Fontaine, an eyewitness to the goings on, in a memoir. We know Descartes did do anatomical studies on animals, but we don't know if any were alive at the time.

Let no one say Descartes was an animal lover, but there are a few things to be said on his behalf. He writes that his view "absolves men of the suspicion of crime," showing he thought there *would* be a suspicion of crime, if animals did feel pain. In fact, Descartes was evidently concerned with this moral issue and it played some role in his coming to believe that animals are mere machines. He wanted to absolve us, but he also wanted to absolve God, who would seem to have made a big mistake if he'd created a world in which animals are tasty, nourishing food, but in which they suffer as a result. As Descartes sees it, God did not create a world like that, because he did not create animals that suffer.

There is one idea in Aristotle that seems even more degrading to animals than the idea that they are mere machines – the notion that they are our larder, that they exist just to be eaten. Descartes contributed to the seventeenth-century scientific revolution that replaced long-influential Aristotelian ideas of purposes and natural tendencies in nature with mechanical notions of bodies in motion, interacting and forming compounds according to mathematical laws. A curious happenstance is that Descartes was a de facto vegetarian, preferring to eat vegetables from his garden for reasons of health (so says Tristram Stuart, in his history of Western vegetarianism, *The Bloodless Revolution*.) From Descartes's viewpoint, there is nothing especially peculiar about that choice. From Aristotle's viewpoint, by contrast, a vegetarian is an oddity. Like a baby who refuses to drink its mother's milk, vegetarians are perverse, a breach of the natural order.

The Tree of Life

The big pictures we've looked at so far once represented cutting-edge science. They are speculative and imaginative and contain no small measure of wishful thinking, but they all struggle to explain observed features of the natural world. These thinkers saw profound differences between our species and the rest and wanted to account for them. They also wanted to explain why there are so many different animal species, a fact that gradually came into view over time, as observations were pulled together from different parts of the globe, and the natural world was explored in ever more depth. The differences and the diversity are explained in three different ways by Aristotle, the plenitude thinkers, and Descartes, but none of them had the benefit of modern science. Darwin's theory of evolution was still far in the future.

The diversity of species was an especially puzzling fact before Darwin. The different species exist to supply our different needs, according to

Aristotle, but that doesn't do the observed diversity justice. There are too many species that go unused. The different species must exist to make the world complete, say the plenitude thinkers, but the great chain of being is unevenly spaced. In the region of beetles the rungs of the ladder are extremely close together; in the range of mammals, they're farther apart. There's really no explaining the patterns in terms of God's sheer fecundity. The different species are accidental combinations of matter in motion, says Descartes, but why so many accidents producing beetles, and so many fewer producing mammals?

The theory of evolution gives us the best explanation of diversity to date: it says the extraordinary diversity of species is due to the process of natural selection. There are so many kinds of beetles because there are so many different niches for them to occupy. A slightly new model of beetle develops because of a random genetic mutation. It does better than the old model in the niche it happens to occupy, producing more offspring. There are more mutations, and more, until the new niche is full of new-model beetles that can't reproduce anymore with the old ones. Over time, there are two species and then three, and on and on, until today there are 370,000 known species of beetles.

The theory of natural selection explains the diversity of species while leading us to expect underlying similarities due to common descent. And in fact the similarities are striking. Over 98 percent of our DNA is shared by the chimpanzee. Despite all the differences between different species, all vertebrates share important aspects of their body plan. We have arms and legs, eyes and mouths, we swallow, we copulate, we defecate. Even invertebrate insects and crustaceans are not utterly alien.

What must we think now about the sharp lines drawn by thinkers of the past? Were they illusory? Darwin did see evolution as having that likely upshot. His view was that the minds of animals are like the minds of humans, different in degree, but not in basic kind. He didn't just see the rudiments of human capacities in our nearest relatives, the great apes, but in all animals, even down to the lowly worm. In various species he saw signs of emotion, intelligence, self-expression, creativity, logic, and even morality.

Evolution doesn't require there to be high mental abilities in non-human animals. We do share common ancestors with birds, yet they can fly and we can't. It could also be that despite our sharing ancestors, we can reason, and birds can't. The effect of recognizing common descent is more subtle. Darwin offers the metaphor of the tree of life to explain the process of natural selection. The trunk (representing the earliest life forms) rises up into branches (representing later life forms) and the branches branch again, and those branch once more. At the top of the tree are "leaves" representing species that exist today. The image of the tree suggests continuity. If you recognize that all animal life is related, you don't *have* to believe the minds of human beings have much in common with the minds of animals, but it's very easy to believe it. How much similarity there really is remains to be seen, but the theory of evolution certainly paves the way to seeing it.

The story I've told so far makes Darwin out to be the hero who finally recognized the continuity between human and animal life. In fact, the notion of human–animal continuity has been with us all along, in a rather different form. Ancient Hinduism and all its later offshoots (Buddhism, and Jainism, for example) saw enough commonality between humans and animals that it was thought a particular animal could "come back" as a human being, and a human being could "come back" as an animal. Westerners tend to find reincarnation foreign and even ridiculous, but at the beginning of Western thought, the idea had its proponents in Pythagoras and Plato. Off the standard "intellectual history" track, Native Americans thought animal spirits were reborn into new animal bodies, though they didn't leap over the species line.

In Hindu schools of thought, the immaterial element that migrates from body to body is *atman* – breath, self, soul. *Atman* in a human being is identical to *atman* in an animal, so there is a kinship between animals and human beings. Buddhism inherited the notion of reincarnation, but denies there is a self, or *atman*, that migrates from one body to another; thus, a better word is "rebirth." An animal may have lived before as a human being and a human being may live in the future as an animal.

If dogs can be reborn as people and people as dogs, just how similar are they? Not necessarily just alike. Hinduism emphasizes that there are many things humans are capable of, but dogs aren't – like a spiritual life. For that reason, it's *bad* to be reborn as an animal, *good* if an animal is reborn in human form – a view on which Buddhism agrees. If *atman* can be continuous despite the huge difference between a dog and a human being, just what is the nature of the continuity? To what extent would *I* come back, if I were reborn as a dog? My efforts to figure that out have not been especially fruitful. Still, I think it's safe to say that there is a stronger sense that animals are our kin in cultures influenced by Eastern religions. As an indirect but striking piece of evidence, consider the fact that some Hindu gods have animal bodies. A favorite Hindu god is the elephant-headed Ganesh, son of the entirely human Shiva and Parvati. This is especially striking in light of the fact that Ganesh is god of Wisdom, Intelligence, Intellect.

In the Tramell Crow Asian Art museum in Dallas, there are figurines of the Buddha composed of ivory, and elaborately carved representations of Hindu legends also carved into ivory. Of course, ivory was a popular material for religious art in the West for many centuries as well. Such a lovely material; it looks so much like polished stone that it's easy to forget ivory comes from tusks, and tusks are parts of elephants. You don't separate elephants from their tusks unless they're dead. And ivory hunters don't courteously wait around for elephants to live out their long lives. They shoot them with spears or guns or create trap ditches for them to fall into. You'd think ivory Buddhas and ivory Ganeshes might not exist, considering that Buddhists and Hindus think elephants could have once been human, and that we could be reborn as elephants, and that Ganesh is the elephant-headed god. But they do.

Buddhist monks aspire to a vegetarian diet, but don't strictly speaking have to adhere to one – and most don't. Many Hindus don't adopt vegetarian diets, but they can still hope to do so during a later incarnation. Just how similar are we to animals, from these Eastern perspectives? I leave the question unanswered. Some greater continuity is contemplated, but it's not quite clear what it amounts to or what it means in practical terms. The custom of exploiting animals is alive and well in every part of the world, even in places where animals are seen as (in some sense) kin. Like other fast-developing countries, India has seen a sharp rise in consumption of animal products in the last 20 years and the expectation is that this will continue for decades to come.

The Kind that Counts

All of the thinkers of this chapter struggle with the difference between humankind and animalkind. We must know what a human being *is* and what an animal *is* to know our own place in the world, and to understand how we should treat other creatures.

The connection between kinds and appropriate treatment is written into the English language. "Kindness" and "kinds" share a common origin, the old English *cynd*, also the root of "kin." To be kind, if we take etymology as our guide, is to treat someone as kin, as "my kind." An enlightened extension of the idea is that not just family members matter, but all members of my kind – my tribe, my nation, or even my species. And an even more enlightened idea allows that members of other species could be my kind at least to some degree, and in a morally relevant sense.

Today's debate about animals is particularly influenced by two views of the kind that counts, morally speaking. In the eighteenth century, the great philosopher Immanuel Kant insisted that all obligations to others are founded on respect for their dignity. Where there is dignity, there are powerful duties to those who have it: we must not treat another person purely as a means to an end, and we must also take steps to further the ends of our fellows. But human dignity is founded entirely on morality. If the local squirrel is amoral, he does no wrong when he steals the seeds out of our birdfeeder, but he lacks dignity, and we have no obligations to him. In the sense that matters for morality, he is a member of an utterly different kind.

This is hardly a view that will appeal to animal advocates, but Kant personally seems to have been rather tender-hearted. He is repelled by the thought of a dog being shot by his "master," once he's no longer of any use. And he recounts with admiration the way the renowned German philosopher Gottfried Leibniz would gently remove a worm from a branch for observation, and then carefully put it back. "The more we come in contact with animals and observe their behavior," he writes, "the more we love them, for we see how great is their care for their young. It is then difficult for us to be cruel in thought even to a wolf."

Possibly moved by his own fondness for animals, Kant came up with a way to make sense of deference to animals, even assuming we have duties to humans, and humans alone. He proposed that we will do better by other people if we practice by being kind to animals; similarly, cruelty to animals causes cruelty to human beings. Causation is hard to prove, but there does seem to be a rough correlation between the way people treat animals and the way they treat other people. If that's so, it's possible to follow Kant and say there are no ethical duties to animals whatever, but still say there are "indirect duties" to humans that involve animals. So no, you should not beat your dog, but that's not because you owe him anything; it's because you have a duty to the person you might wind up later mistreating as a result. The appearance that we have duties to animals is just an appearance. The reality is that all duties are to other human beings.

The Utilitarian school of thought, founded in the eighteenth century as well, looks at the fundamental nature of morality completely differently.

We are obligated to others, Jeremy Bentham claimed, so long as they can feel pleasure and pain. The prime directive, morally speaking, is the "greatest happiness principle": we must maximize the balance of pleasure over pain for all. Any action that elevates total happiness to the highest possible level is right. Any action that does otherwise is wrong. For Utilitarians, the local squirrel belongs to the kind that counts as long as he has feelings of pain and pleasure. For them, but not so much for Kantians, the geography of animal sensation is critically important.

Bentham decried the mistreatment of animals and traced it to sheer prejudice, in this famous passage, written in 1789, when the morality of slavery was being debated in England and France:

> The day may come, when the rest of the animal creation may acquire those rights which never could have been withholden from them but by the hand of tyranny. The French have already discovered that the blackness of the skin is no reason why a human being should be abandoned without redress to the caprice of a tormentor. It may come one day to be recognized, that the number of the legs, the villosity of the skin, or the termination of the os sacrum, are reasons equally insufficient for abandoning a sensitive being to the same fate. What else is it that should trace the insuperable line? Is it the faculty of reason, or, perhaps, the faculty of discourse? But a full-grown horse or dog is beyond comparison a more rational, as well as a more conversable animal, than an infant of a day, or a week, or even a month, old. But suppose the case were otherwise, what would it avail? the question is not, Can they reason? nor, Can they talk? but, Can they suffer?

Animals find some of their staunchest advocates today in ethicists who approach moral questions in Utilitarian terms.

Could it be that animals have no moral significance, for lack of moral capacity and therefore dignity? Or that they are members of exactly our kind, so long as they can suffer? We will find, in later chapters, that none of the thinkers of this chapter gets things exactly right, but some have lessons to teach us.

Animalkind. Humankind. We are taught that there's a big difference, and venerable Western philosophers have said as much. The assumption lies behind great swaths of life – what we eat, what we wear, what recreational activities we engage in, how we test drugs and do medical research. Are there morally important differences between humans and animals? Before we pursue that question in more depth (starting in Chapter 5), we need to look more closely at animals themselves.

Venerable philosophers tell us animals have no experiences and feelings at all, or that, if they do, they are completely devoid of reason. Is there anything to these crude, traditional contrasts? If they are too crude, is there really no deep difference between animals and human beings? Or is the difference just more subtle?

Part II

The Nature of the Beast

The Western tradition draws sharp lines between *homo sapiens* and all other species. It's even the view of some philosophers that only we are conscious. Today it's more common to deny higher thought in animals than to deny sheer experience, but even this tendency is on the wane.

3

Animal Consciousness

To think about whether animals belong to the kind that counts, morally speaking, we need to think about what kind of thing they *are*. It doesn't seem to matter whether they have tails and we don't, or that they are quadrupeds or fly or live under water, while we walk two-leggedly on land. It's not important whether a creature is warm-blooded or cold-blooded, covered in fur or feathers or scales. The bodily differences aren't the sort of difference that could put humans and the rest of the animals in different moral categories. The critical thing is our minds. If animal minds are vastly different, that could certainly matter.

The greatest difference possible is the difference made by consciousness. If we have it and animals don't, then we are most assuredly in totally separate moral categories. And so that's our first question. Are animals conscious?

Right now I am *tasting* my coffee, *seeing* my computer screen, *feeling* a little too warm, and getting slightly *hungry* for breakfast. Is my cat – right now sitting next to the computer screen, staring at my face, and purring – also having an assortment of experiences? Does my cat *see* images of my face, *feel* the table under his paws, maybe also *feel* a bit warm? Obviously, my experience doesn't match my cat's element for element, but is there at least the similarity that I am having conscious experiences, and he is too? Is there awareness in my cat's head, like in mine?

The Question

Once engaged by the consciousness question, we are liable to become hopelessly confused if we don't carefully define our terms. "Consciousness" is a word that seems to create particular trouble. In a chapter of his very engaging book *Minding Animals*, the animal ethologist Marc Bekoff shows no patience for skeptics. He writes, "To deny animals' emotions is to deny a large part of who these beings are." In another chapter, he writes, "If 'being conscious' means only that one is aware of one's surroundings, then many animals are obviously conscious." But three pages later, he writes (speaking for himself and a collaborator, Colin Allen): "While Colin and I do not rule out the possibility that humans are the only individuals who are conscious, we believe that it is too soon to make such a judgment."

Consciousness in animals is "obvious" on some pages, and possibly nonexistent on others. Presumably what's happening is that the word is changing meanings. When Bekoff is most skeptical, he's equating consciousness with *self*-consciousness or with a cluster of higher abilities sometimes called "extended" consciousness.

The same equivocation can be seen in the fine PBS video *Animal Minds* – an overview of modern animal psychology, with chapters on the work of many of today's leading researchers. After a long sequence that leaves little doubt that animals have thought, feeling, and awareness, the narrator asks, ponderously "But are animals conscious? Do they have a concept of self or death?" All of a sudden, consciousness has become something so sophisticated that even human beings wouldn't have it until some late stage of childhood, and adults wouldn't have it in the haze of just awakening or experiencing extreme pain or confusion.

This chapter is mainly about the simplest question – whether animals feel, see, hear, smell, whether there's anything experiential inside of them. We can ask follow-up questions about the sort of awareness found in animals – does it include pain? Does it include self-awareness? Does it include a sense of the future? Those questions (and others) could be pivotal, for purposes of coming to grips with the moral status of animals. But our first task is to consider where animals fall: with rocks, cars, trees, all presumably not aware at all? Or with you and me, definitely aware?

Who would take it seriously that my cat, as he sits by my computer screen staring at me, might be no more aware of the world than … my computer? Is this a position anyone actually defends, nearly four centuries after Descartes said that animals were nature's automata? In a word, Yes.

One modern Cartesian is Oxford science and religion professor Peter Harrison, who is motivated by a difficult theological issue, the problem of evil. A problem for theists is that God's existence is hard to reconcile with all the awful things that go on in the world. If God is all-powerful, he could prevent murders, genocides, infant diseases, natural disasters, and all the other causes of great suffering. And if he is all good, then he would surely want to. Animal suffering is particularly hard to square with the existence of a loving God. Why does God allow it to exist? Harrison has a simple answer. He doesn't. There *is* no animal pain, he argues. So there's nothing that needs to be squared with (or can't be squared with) the existence of God.

Journalist Stephen Budiansky and philosopher Peter Carruthers aren't trying to get God off the hook; they're trying to get us off the hook. What better way to undermine the case for animal rights and human obligations than to show that animals aren't even conscious? If animals feel literally nothing, then the animal rights movement ought to disappear, or at least take a completely different course. If they don't feel anything, at most we should care about animals in the way we care about trees or flowers or impressive artifacts. The animal rights movement should calm down and proceed like the horticultural society. With empathy out of the picture, the shape and depth of the concern would to be much altered.

Some of today's skeptics about animal consciousness are in it for the money. Money? Today's industrial farmers are increasing their profits by squeezing animals into the smallest amount of space possible, denying them the most basic creature comforts, ignoring their instincts and their natural diets. When they are challenged, a favorite ploy of farmers, meat packers, and their advocates is the ignorance defense. How, they wonder, can we be sure? How do we know hogs mind being trapped in a stall every minute of their short lives? How do we know they mind being castrated without anesthesia, or having their throats slit before effective stunning (as happens a percentage of the time)? How do we know that they feel anything at all? Curiously enough, it pays to find these questions deep and unanswerable.

And some doubters just doubt. With a sufficiently philosophical cast of mind, you can have doubts about animal consciousness without being driven to it by any particular agenda, especially when it comes to "lower-order" animals. Just about anyone is susceptible to uncertainty about the mental life – if any – of a worm, a lobster, or a mosquito.

So much for the question of animal awareness and why it's asked. On what grounds do "the deniers" deny that animals are conscious?

Mind and Brain

The case against animal consciousness tends to start with the deniers simply trying to make room for doubt. We are asked to appreciate the difference between a brain process that keeps us on track, and a conscious experience. A favorite example of the consciousness deniers is distracted driving (Budiansky and Carruthers both discuss it). You know the feeling: you suddenly realize you've been lost in thought for the last 20 minutes, and you're 20 miles down the road. You've maintained a safe distance behind the cars ahead of you, avoided driving off the road, kept your foot on the gas pedal, but none of it (apparently) with any conscious thought. All the crucial brain processes have transpired, but, the deniers want us to agree, there's been no accompanying experience. If you find that plausible in your own case – they continue – then it's at least conceivable that in animals appropriate brain processes go on *all the time* without their enjoying any conscious awareness.

Of course, the deniers aren't saying that animals are distracted, like distracted drivers. If animals were distracted, it would mean that they *were* paying conscious attention to *something*. So they would have conscious experiences after all. It's silly to think that a bull being castrated might not consciously feel pain because his mind is on something else. What could be that diverting? Still, the example of distracted driving gets us thinking about an important possibility. The distracted driver's brain is doing everything it needs to do. Effective brain processes could just conceivably take place in animals without the accompaniment of conscious feeling.

In fact, unconscious mentation is not just a possibility, but a constant reality. Things happen in our brains that we "personally" know nothing about all the time. The Freudian unconscious is especially dark and intriguing, but the cognitive unconscious plays a more fundamental role. In the nanosecond between seeing this sentence and understanding it, you figure out the meaning, but the way you do it is hidden from you. A penny on a counter leaves an elliptical image on your retina, but somehow you see it as round. The moon low on the horizon looks larger than the moon high in the sky; your cognitive unconscious makes you see it that way. (Not only is the process opaque to you personally, but nobody really knows how it works; umpteen books and articles have been written about the moon illusion.) All these examples show that the brain can accomplish much without any accompanying conscious awareness.

The non-conscious parts of *our* minds demonstrate at least the bare possibility that an animal's mind could be like that through and through, that *everything* in my cat's mind could go on without accompanying experience. If that's the case, then my cat experienced literally nothing as he sat by my computer screen staring at my face. He walked behind the screen and stared out the window for a while without experiencing a thing – no cool table under his paws, no images of a squirrel outside the window, nothing like hunger or thirst or warmth. He negotiated the leap off the table onto the floor without the slightest awareness, and then the journey to parts of the house unknown, without consciously seeing the way ahead of him.

All of this is not totally impossible. But the deniers think it's more than a remote possibility. They think it's reasonable to believe that cats and other animals have brains that function without conscious awareness. There's something about animals, as opposed to people – something to arouse that suspicion. But what?

The suspicious thing about animals is not what's inside their heads. On the level of gross anatomy, the brains of mammals are similar to each other. In every case there is a neocortex, the folded outermost layer of the brain, even if it's most extensive (and most folded) in humans. The brains of all mammals include a frontal lobe, where many higher functions seem to be housed, judging from studies of human patients with frontal lobe abnormalities. With these similarities and many more, there's no immediate, brain-related bar to imputing consciousness to mammals. In fact, comparing brains ought to make us more inclined to grant animals consciousness than disinclined.

But not completely sure. The reason we can't be sure is because we don't understand the neural basis for consciousness. We know *we* are conscious, and we know a certain amount about our brains, but we don't know which features of our brains support consciousness. So says the neuropsychologist Michael Gazzaniga in his book *Human: The Science Behind What Makes Us Unique*. He does his best to draw sharp lines between human beings and other animals, but he admits that we just don't know what parts of the human brain are crucial for consciousness, so don't know what to look for in animal brains to determine whether or not animals are conscious.

The *similarities* between human brains and the brains of other mammals suggest consciousness without proving it. But between our brains and non-mammal brains, there are more differences. Non-mammals don't have anything exactly comparable to the neocortex. Could the *differences* between our brains and non-mammal brains show that birds, fish, reptiles, etc., are probably *not* conscious? That doesn't follow. For one, the specific neural structure that supports consciousness, whatever it is, could be common to otherwise different brains. Gazzaniga speculates that "long-range connection loops" could possibly be relevant, but observes they exist in birds as well as in primates and human beings. Then again, there could be entirely heterogeneous structures that produce consciousness. "We have a problem when we compare anatomy," he writes. " It is not the same thing as comparing function. There may be more than one way to skin a cat" – forgive the expression – "that is, there may be neural solutions or routes to consciousness other than those in the human brain, which could result in different types of consciousness."

Different anatomy-same function is something we see in the animal kingdom many times over. Animals accomplish temperature regulation with hair, feathers, sweat, shivering, hibernation, "anti-freeze" in the blood of cold-blooded animals, migration, intelligence (building fires, making blankets), and much else. Structurally, these are all drastically different from each other, but they get the same job done. It's possible that brains very far apart in important structural and chemical respects share the power to "make" consciousness.

Considering our present ignorance about the neural basis of consciousness, and the possibility of different substrates for consciousness in different species, it makes sense to focus more on what consciousness *does* for an individual, instead of on its neural substrate. While consciousness might (I only say "might" because this is a hard question in the philosophy of mind) require one specific neural condition, or any of ten, or any of myriad conditions, we're probably better off trying to decide which animals are conscious by looking for more indirect clues. Like doctors diagnosing diseases before the advent of microbiology, we might just have to go on symptoms, instead of focusing on the underlying phenomenon in the brain.

The deniers' case against animal consciousness is actually based on their understanding of what consciousness does, not on doubts about animal brains. So what – on their view – does consciousness do?

What It Does

Imagine driving to work and consciously seeing the blossoming pink trees alongside the road. Peter Carruthers says to be a *conscious* experience, seeing the flowers has to be able to give rise spontaneously to subsequent thoughts – about the flowers, and beyond that, to thoughts about the thoughts about the flowers, and so on. This account of consciousness helps us decide whether animals are conscious without literally getting into their heads. Presumably your dog is not going to have later thoughts about the flowers, or thoughts about the thoughts about the flowers. The same goes for seeing a cat by the side of the road, which might make your dog jump up and bark and wag her tail wildly. Of course, her eyes took in information, and there were subsequent events in your dog's brain, which caused the frantic behavior, but Carruthers' claim is that your dog couldn't have *consciously* seen the cat, since we're pretty sure that seeing the cat didn't have the requisite ripple effect.

Peter Harrison makes a similar point about the way conscious experience holds the potential for later thoughts and experiences. Suppose you are given drugs during surgery that both paralyze you and stop you from remembering anything, but you're not given any regular anesthesia. The surgery takes place and you don't flinch a bit as the surgeon slices into you. You wake up with no memory of the operation. Did you feel pain when the surgeon cut into your body? (Remember, there was no anesthesia.) Some people will say No because of the missing subsequent memories, and that's Harrison's intuition. Whatever state you were in during surgery, it didn't lead to further thoughts – like the thought that this was the most excruciating thing you ever endured. The amnesia drug blocked that from being a possible outcome. And so there was no pain during the surgery.

Are Carruthers and Harrison really serious when they say that animals feel no pain? Harrison tempers his conclusion with a warning against abusing animals, but Carruthers takes the point to its logical conclusion. He writes,

> Much time and money is presently spent on alleviating the pains of brutes, which ought properly to be directed toward human beings, and many now are campaigning to reduce the efficiency of modern farming methods because of the pain to the animals involved. If the arguments presented here have been sound, such activities are not only morally unsupportable but morally objectionable.

When it comes to animals it really is "anything goes."

Carruthers' book has a charming dedication to his child, "whose animal days are almost done." Yes, very small children in some ways have minds like animals. Small children don't appear to think back on earlier mental states any more than animals do. But I am pretty sure – in fact, certain – that young children do feel pain. The knife hurts, whether there's any later thinking about the hurt or not. We play down the impact of childhood circumcision (should we?), possibly because the misery is not drawn out – there's no emotional suffering due to anticipatory dread or subsequent brooding. But we surely shouldn't think the infant feels nothing.

If small children have conscious mental states, then Carruthers' account of consciousness is much too cerebral. To be conscious of those flowers by the road, he thinks I must be able to continue being conscious of them later on, and even be conscious of being conscious of them. These are states of mind we associate more with reflection and introspection than with plain vanilla consciousness. Carruthers means to be offering an account of basic consciousness, but it turns out he really isn't.

Basic consciousness is a relative of paying attention. A woodpecker is tapping away as you work, and gradually you become aware of the sound; the tapping becomes the object of your attention. Whatever is going on, it's nothing especially intellectual or reflective; it's not a matter of slowing down, looking back, scrutinizing. Some metaphors used to explain attention are highlighting and enhancement. You highlight text by giving it an overlay of a bright color, not by making it reverberate over time. Whatever this might mean in neural terms, attention is not a high-flown intellectual aptitude. Thus, you wouldn't be tempted to say that only humans are capable of paying attention.

Right now I'm paying attention to my computer screen, but I'm conscious of a larger visual field, the feeling of my toes, the sound of my cat scratching in the litter box, etc. So attention and simple consciousness aren't the same thing. If simple consciousness is also due to highlighting or enhancement, there must be two kinds of highlighting or enhancement. The enhancement underlying attention produces a sort of dominance of one bit of consciousness over others. That dominance makes us capable of processing information we're paying attention to in ways we otherwise could not. The other sort of enhancement, that underlying consciousness, produces … what? What is it that our conscious mental states *do* that differentiates them from unconscious mental states?

Carruthers and Harrison are right to ask this question, and by answering it we ought to be able to make some headway on whether animals are conscious. They just don't seem to have given us a plausible answer. In effect, they've wound up theorizing about something else, not the very simple and basic phenomenon of conscious awareness.

Global Availability

It would be helpful if we could use the Vulcan mind-meld technique (as Star Trek fans will agree). We could simply "get inside" the minds of animals and find out what's going on in there. Do they experience the world, or is there really nothing going on, nothing but mechanical processes chugging away in the dark? Since we can't find out directly, we are forced to make complex inferences about the presence or absence of consciousness, drawing on the most plausible premises we can find.

Consider again the contrast between conscious and unconscious mental states. Something goes on in your brain unconsciously, so you see the moon as large when it's close to the horizon. At the end of that process, whatever it is, you consciously stare at the moon, marveling at its size. What does being conscious *do* for the outcome of that hidden process, consciously seeing the moon as large?

In his influential book *The Conscious Mind*, David Chalmers suggests that consciousness goes hand in hand with what he calls "global availability." Consciously seeing the moon as large is distinctive because it's available to the rest of your mind. As a result of that general availability, there are many "moves" you could make next. After seeing a huge-looking moon, I've often pointed to the sky and told my children to look at the moon. Or I've discussed the moon illusion with my husband. Or I've told myself to have another look at a book on the moon illusion I read long ago. Conscious awareness puts you in a position like a hiker with many trails to go down.

With global availability comes a mental life with a more open, flexible character. A thought or experience at one moment leads in many possible directions. Without it, mental processes march along inexorably in one direction. An *unconscious* information-processing task is accomplished reliably and efficiently, but with just one possible outcome. Since I can't "get into" the unconscious thought process that produces the moon illusion, I also can't change it. I'm helpless to see the moon on the horizon as being anything but big.

You can see how each type of brain state would have evolved, conferring fitness on individuals for different reasons. Brains that have conscious (globally available) states are capable of coping flexibly in complex environments. But unconsciousness (local availability) is useful too, considering how it helps an individual cope reliably with well-defined problems or in simple environments. Since I don't know how I wind up seeing the moon as huge, I can't interrupt the process, reflecting on some particular step, or telling someone about the step, or trying to do things differently. Things get done more reliably when they're done unconsciously, which is not to say they always get done correctly – the moon illusion is an *illusion*. Based on the way it looks, anyone would think the moon was closer or bigger when it's on the horizon, and the truth is that it is not.

If conscious awareness goes hand in hand with global availability, that should be very helpful for purposes of figuring out which animals are conscious. We can discern globally active mental states in animals, based on behavior, much more easily than we can discern whether there's any "feel" or "glow" of consciousness inside their heads. If the "glow" is the underlying phenomenon we're really interested in, global availability is a symptom that's much more readily detected by the outside viewer.

But first things first. Thinking about consciousness in terms of global availability has to give us pause about some of the deniers' favorite examples involving human beings. As you drive distractedly, maybe you *are* actually conscious of the car in front of you. The sight of that truck, with the Coca Cola logo on the back door, quite possibly *is* ready for global active duty. You *could* say something about it, or make a plan based on it, or do something about it, if you were prompted. The visual experience is just never used, and as the saying goes, "use it or lose it." The person undergoing surgery without anesthesia may also be conscious, and his pain experience ready for global active duty. The experience is just never given a chance to do all the things it *could* do (like cause him to scream and writhe) because of the paralytics and amnesia drugs. It's poised to do all sorts of things, but then prevented.

Now we're ready for the critical question: which species have mental states with the character of global availability, and should thus be presumed to be conscious? It depends what ethologists and comparative psychologists tell us about the mental lives of chimpanzees, dolphins, dogs, fish, birds, and all the way down to insects. We will gather more evidence about the minds of animals in Chapter 5, but the bottom line is that animals do not, as a group, have minds lacking the critical characteristic.

Think of your dog hearing a slamming door. She no doubt hears the sound (as loud or soft, coming from this direction or that) as a result of unconscious auditory processing, like we do, but at that point there's a possibility of uptake involving a variety of separate faculties. She can run, she can stop and look, she can bark. We have good reason to think her perception of the sound is globally available, and therefore presumably conscious.

In fact, if the notion of global availability is used as a guide, we have to conclude that innumerable species are endowed with consciousness. A squirrel discovering a jar of seeds on my patio can peer at them, stick his head inside the jar, or make desperate little sounds. A penguin faced with an incubating egg that has broken can signal to a mate, tap the egg with her beak, or make sounds. It's simply not true that an animal's mental life always moves inexorably from this to that, in the way that our minds do when we are at our most automatic.

If consciousness correlates with global availability, it goes along with a sort of sophistication, but this is not the sophistication of being able to ruminate about earlier experiences or being able to have thoughts about thoughts. It's not a sort of sophistication we immediately associate only with that special animal that is us. Consciousness turns out to be something that emerges from a sort of mental flexibility. That it should emerge in many species, and not just in ours, is not surprising. It's rare in the biological world for a feature to exist in one species and in no others. Rather, we find the same features recurring here, there and everywhere, across the animal kingdom. Whether it's flying, respiration, vision, the immune system, or sexual reproduction, nature returns again and again to the same solutions. It would actually be astonishing if consciousness *were* truly unique to our species, if none of our relatives had this most basic of powers.

With all this reasoning as a basis, can we now say that animals have conscious awareness, without a doubt? We cannot even attribute consciousness to each other "without a doubt," so that would be too much to hope for. Suffice it to say that we can attribute consciousness to animals of many species "without a reasonable doubt." The deniers' attempt to plant reasonable doubt does not succeed, since it presupposes a spurious conception of basic consciousness.

The Grey Area

In everyday life, we don't laboriously figure out what to attribute consciousness to; cognitive scientists say our minds are outfitted with a special-purpose mind–attribution module that makes quick decisions for us. We get a positive reading when we point our mentality-detector at the familiar mammals that live among us – like the cat who was standing by my computer screen when I started this chapter. Is there a reason to think that there's a line between "higher" and "lower" animals below which our mind-module starts generating a "mind illusion," an error like the moon illusion? This seems possible, but at what point does the detector start to misfire?

Certainly birds are well above the line, at least as a genus. All the sorts of reasons that support attributing awareness to my cat would also support attributing it to Irene Pepperberg's African grey parrot Alex. Her interesting and entertaining book *Alex and Me* would convince anyone but the hardened skeptic. Alex (who died recently, after 30 years in Pepperberg's lab) had a mental life, as evidenced by his behavioral repertory, with the rich and flexible character that's the hallmark of consciousness awareness.

Taking just one bit of an animal's repertory as evidence can be misleading. Geese respond to an egg that's rolled out of their nests in exactly the same way every time. Visual registration of an egg can lead to one thing, for this bird, and one thing only. So, no global availability in evidence there, but that's not the only thing a goose ever does. We'd have to look at the full range of goose behaviors to arrive at a fair assessment. A toad always sticks his tongue out when his visual cortex registers fly-like input, and that's the only response he's capable of. Again, no global availability in evidence. Robotic behaviors are some clue to lack of consciousness, but have to be put in context with all an animal's behaviors.

Some animals seem to display robotic behavior and nothing else. A tick jumps onto a host's body as an automatic response to warmth, and then sucks the blood of the host in response to chemical inputs; the meal then induces egg-laying and the tick's death. It all works like clockwork, with no variation. And that's the tick's whole life. Conscious or not conscious? The trouble is that with an animal this simple, the whole distinction between local and global availability seems to break down. The tick's brain does have states responsive to the environment and responsible for behavior. These states do permeate her mind, small mind though it may be. Her perception of host blood is as globally available as it could be *for her*. But you could just as easily say her brain is nothing but a simple mental module, in which processes are local and automatic. Unfortunately, at this point local availability and global availability converge. Thus, the concepts give us no leverage. There must be some fact of the matter – either the tick feels something as she gorges herself, or she doesn't. Short of having the Vulcan mind-meld technique to give us the inside view of a tick's mind, how should we decide what to think?

The fact is, we don't have much to go on. There is certainly a vast difference between human brains, which clearly do possess conscious awareness, and tick brains. Unfortunately, that doesn't firmly close the book on the issue. As Gazzaniga says, we don't know what the neural correlate of consciousness is in humans, and there's no reason to think it must be the same thing in every animal. Brain-wise, the tick is not completely out of the running.

This exploration has to end on a note of puzzlement, but there's no need to be discouraged. We have strong evidence of the correlation between consciousness and global availability in the minds we know best – our own. It would be strange if the correlation were peculiar to our species, and not pervasive in our animal cousins. It would be even stranger if consciousness had evolved in the human animal and no others. If there are physical preconditions for consciousness, there's no good reason to think they are met in us, and in none of our animal relatives. So a vast number of animal species, including mammals, birds, fish, and reptiles, can reasonably be assumed to possess conscious awareness.

When we come to the simplest animals, all of our inferences do start to flake out. The line starts to blur between global and local processing. The physical make-up of these creatures is different enough that it certainly *could* make the difference between supporting consciousness and not supporting consciousness. In fact, our mind–attribution modules respond indecisively in the presence of animals that look and behave very differently than we do. We don't have a clear-cut reaction, and we seem to have little ability to reason our way into more certainty. But the problem is not pervasive. Being unsure about the tick doesn't mean I must be unsure about my cat. There's a grey area covering many species, but that grey area doesn't make everything grey. It would be disingenuous to suggest that worries about ticks *really* give us serious reason to wonder about consciousness all across the animal kingdom.

What It's Like

Most of us crave not just an answer to the question whether animals have conscious experiences or not (yes, surely many do), but a deeper familiarity with what their experiences are like. We really want that Vulcan mind meld; we want to get inside the minds of animals. I would like to know what it feels like to live life under water, or to be aloft in the sky for many days, part of a flock migrating to some distant land. I wonder what it's like to be a salmon on the way upriver, with hormones surging and a body literally changing form in the course of the journey back to its birthplace, where it will spawn and then die. I would like to know what was going through my cat's mind as he stared at my face.

It's not surprising that we can't imagine these things, since one of the primary mechanisms of empathy is imitation. When you see expressions of pain on another human face, you understand in part because some of your own neurons – those involved in the emotional, not the sensory, experience of pain – start firing. Any emotional state you can mirror is one you can understand better and more easily. If you can't experience an emotion at all, you may not be able to attribute it to others. For example, brain lesions that stop people from feeling disgust render them unable to attribute disgust to others. People born without the capacity for pain have deficits when it comes to recognizing pain in others. Without being able to feel just what another feels, we become more detached and skeptical, more liable to misinterpret, or not to understand at all.

One part of animal consciousness is particularly important from a moral point of view. We especially need to know whether animals experience pain and pleasure. For a certain brand of Utilitarianism, that's all we need to know about animals, to determine whether they're "the kind that counts" – as I said in Chapter 2. That remains to be seen, but it's certainly one thing we need to know. On any understanding of morality and animals, their having (or lacking) the capacity to feel pain and pleasure will make a difference to the way we ought to treat them.

We know that animals across the spectrum, including mammals, birds, fish, and reptiles, have nociceptors – injury-sensitive neurons that travel from many sites on the outside and inside of the body to the brain. In all animals, there is sensitivity to heat and various other insults. Do animals feel their cuts and burns? That's the most basic question, but one we intuitively think we can answer; more urgently, we want answers on the fine points. At its worst, does a dog's pain have all the depth and scope of human pain? Do all animals feel pain, including fish, birds, lobsters, insects …?

Temple Grandin has a unique perspective on these questions. An animal science researcher and educator at Colorado State University, she was put in charge of improving the design of slaughterhouses that sell to fast food restaurants starting in the 1990s; because they buy a huge percentage of meat in this country, they have come under pressure from animal activists to demand more humane animal care standards from their suppliers. Grandin's role makes her the paid agent of businesses that want to look more humane at minimal expense, and so she might reasonably be suspected of having a financial incentive to underestimate animal pain. But those suspicions actually make her *more* believable, not less, since she does attribute ample pain experience to animals.

Grandin also might have an edge when it comes to her capacity for empathy. Throughout the bestseller *Animals in Translation* she makes the case that she understands animals better than most because of her own experience with autism. On her view, she thinks in pictures, and so do animals; she is highly prone to fear and anxiety, and so are animals. She writes with great credibility, combining the results of empathy and observation with relevant animal research. Plus, she does what it takes to increase her understanding of an animal's point of view. After spaying, female dogs are not normally sent home with pain relievers, for the reason that they can't be told to rest quietly, and need the discomfort of unmedicated recuperation to keep still. After Grandin went through a hysterectomy herself, the nurses told her she was using much less IV pain relief than most patients. When no one was looking she got on all fours by the floor by her bed and asked herself if she'd be tempted to jump up, if she were a dog. I suspect Grandin sees into animal minds better than most of us do because of a natural aptitude, thorough research, *and* because she makes a bigger effort.

So what does Grandin say about animal pain? One thing she says is that behavioral evidence has to be sifted carefully. It pays for prey animals like sheep and antelopes not to attract the attention of predators. Absence of pain behavior, in them, isn't good evidence of absence of pain. But predator animals and animals protected from predators by domestication are likely to express pain more openly. There are a couple of behaviors that are reliable signs of pain, Grandin claims, in any species. There's no reason to be wary of thinking that a freshly debeaked chicken must be in pain, since she's pecking less. There's no problem with thinking that horses are in pain if they put less weight on a leg. If you put together the notion that an animal is conscious, plus its having nociceptors sensitive to injury, plus the behavior of pain-guarding after the injury, there's little room left for skepticism. Grandin argues that all those types of evidence are available to show that fish and reptiles feel pain too.

And then there's more. Researchers have tested out the presence of pain in various species by determining whether animals consume analgesics after injury. In one study, rats were injected with bacteria that gave them temporary arthritis. Afterwards, they were given a choice between sugar water and a solution containing pain-relievers. They chose the pain-relievers … but not forever. When the effect on their joints wore off, they went back to preferring sugar water. In fish, there are naturally occurring endorphins that surge when nociceptors are firing, just as there are in human beings, suggesting that nature provides them with built-in pain relief.

But wait. Mammals have a neocortex, while birds and fish do not. The frontal lobe in a human is much bigger than it is in any other animal, and the neocortex in a human is more extensive than in any other mammal. Does all that make any difference? Grandin discourages us from thinking than the absence of a neocortex proves the absence of pain. "The fact that a fish doesn't have a neocortex doesn't have to mean that a fish isn't conscious of pain, because different species can use different brain structures and systems to handle the same functions." The sheer size of brain structures is generally unreliable too. As we're going to find out in the next chapter, birds are much smarter than you'd expect them to be, considering their small brains.

Still, is there no difference in pain experience resulting from the fact that humans have bigger frontal lobes and a thicker neocortex? Grandin makes a cautious, nuanced concession that there is some difference. There's a difference between feeling pain and caring that you are feeling pain. She speculates that the caring goes on in the frontal lobes. That seems to be shown by leucotomy patients from the 1950s, who were treated for intractable pain by having their frontal lobes severed from the rest of their brains. They reported still feeling pain, but seemed to care about it less. They still asked for pain relievers like aspirin, but not for the strongest pain relievers. If severing the frontal lobe reduces caring about pain, then does an individual with a smaller frontal lobe to begin with care less about pain? The reasoning is not air-tight, but that's what Grandin speculates. Or rather, she compromises:

> I think injured animals are probably somewhere in between a leucotomy patient and a normal human being. They do feel pain, sometimes intense pain, because their frontal lobes haven't been surgically separated from the rest of their brains. But they probably aren't as upset about pain as a human being would be in the same situation, because their frontal lobes aren't as big or all-powerful as a human's.

This speculation makes particular sense to her because relative pain insensitivity is one of the hallmarks of autism, and she sees commonalities between animal minds and autistic minds. But don't blow her point out of proportion.

If a body insult is severe enough, the raw physical pain involved will be intense no matter how much "caring" is involved or not. Think, for example, about the use of laughing gas for kids at the dentist. That reduces caring about a quick shot of Novocain, but they're still given the shot; just reducing caring doesn't suffice to make unmedicated tooth drilling bearable.

If animals care less about pain than humans, Grandin says, fear is another story. Fear is centered in older parts of the brain and does not require connections to the frontal lobe. Think about your own experience with dogs and cats, and possibly you'll be convinced. My cat becomes frantic when he's forced into his carrier, stuck in the car, and taken to the vet. All the signs of fear are there – the wild attempt to escape, then (once caught) trembling, urinating, defecating, crouching in a corner. On the other hand, when he gets to the vet's office, he's vastly more indifferent to shots than small children are. Grandin suggests that some of our concern about animal pain is a projection of our own priorities. Fear is a kind of suffering, and deserves greater attention. In Grandin's work redesigning slaughterhouses, she's worked on eliminating pain, but she's particularly worked on reducing fear.

In the next chapter, we will continue trying to get a grip on animal minds. Assuming many animals are conscious, what's going on inside their minds? Do animals think? What do they think about? Without being able to employ the Vulcan mind meld, we'll have to continue making inferences and conjectures. Certainty isn't to be expected, but with careful attention to recent research, we can take steps toward understanding what it's like to be an animal.

4

Dumb Brutes?

Today's defenders of human uniqueness most often point to one thing that separates humankind from the rest of the animals: not consciousness, but reason. Reason is the jewel in the human crown, but it's not easy to say what that jewel amounts to. To reason is many things: to ponder, think things through, understand, deduce, intuit, reflect, investigate, figure it out, deliberate, decide, and plan. Reason is also associated with a certain sort of control over ourselves. Reason gives us autonomy and freedom. It gives us the power to put on the brakes, slow down, and maybe turn in a new direction.

Reason is classically contrasted with instinct. Instincts dictate that baby mammals seek their mothers' nipples, caribou rut in the springtime, and salmon migrate to their birthplace to spawn and then die. Reason is also classically contrasted with emotion. An irrational person is thought to be buffeted about on waves of emotion. Without reason, a fit of rage makes a man yell and strike out; grief overwhelms him and reduces him to tears; passion sends him rushing headlong into the wrong person's arms. Without reason, you can't pull yourself together.

If animals lack reason, but have emotions, then they're not quite robotic. Then again, attributing to animals the full range of emotions seems to traditionalists implausible: how could an animal feel nostalgia or remorse or ennui? For many, even emotions of grief and love are "too good" for animals. So on the liberal view that allows animals emotions, they are still quite beastly and inhuman.

The conventional wisdom, if it can be gauged, is a mixture: it makes animals out to be mostly instinct-governed, and lacking the fine-tuned conscious intelligence and self-control that are characteristic of people, but also emotional within a narrow range. Animals know not what they do, but they feel, at least crudely, while they do it.

In response to this portrait of animals as governed by instinct and crude emotion, the impulse of animal champions, from Darwin in the nineteenth century to contemporary scientists like Jane Goodall and popular writers like Jeffrey Moussaieff Masson today, is to point to some clever achievement in animals, some moment of apparent cogitation or deliberation to oppose the idea that animals are purely instinctive. Or some instance of fine-tuned emotion to oppose the idea that an animal's emotional range is extremely limited. The animal champion wants to elevate animals by arguing that they are much more human than first meets the eye.

As we'll see, evidence does show that animals are smarter and more emotional than conventional wisdom and Western thought allow, but it's going to pay to take up another topic first. Human beings are really much more "animal" than first meets the eye. Our first job is to see *ourselves* more accurately.

Human, All Too Human

"Instinct" is a word that calls to mind beastly behavior – copulating dogs and fiercely protective mother bears. We don't often think about our own instincts, and some of our instincts have faded because of cultural influences. Anyone can figure out how to give a baby a bottle, but many women (mammals, all) have trouble getting used to breastfeeding, and there are even lactation teachers in large hospitals. But instinct is not merely a force that helps out with the basics. Any capacity that comes to a considerable degree pre-loaded in the standard human brain is an instinctive capacity.

Our brains don't deploy the lofty resources of reason to accomplish every task. This ought to be readily admitted considering the fact that our brains' first responsibility is to regulate what goes on in our bodies. It's the brain that regulates temperature, hormone levels, rhythms of sleep and awakeness. These regulatory jobs are taken care of so far behind the scenes that it would be unnatural to think of our *selves* as being involved at all. Keeping track of your body temperature is something your brain does, not you, just as extracting nutrients from food is something your intestine does, not you. Your brain automatically deals with many of the problems interior to your body, and so it wouldn't be surprising at all if it dealt with the external world automatically as well, at least in certain respects.

When you hear a noise, how do you determine what direction it's coming from? Unless you've studied auditory processing, you probably have no idea. It turns out that when you hear a high frequency sound your brain uses the difference in volume at your two ears to determine which direction the sound is coming from. When you hear a low frequency sound, your brain uses the interval between the moments when it reaches each ear. In these two different ways, your brain makes use of the fact that you have two auditory receivers – two ears – separated in space. It's awfully smart of your brain to do it this way, and it is *your* brain, but you don't get any credit for the cleverness. You don't make these calculations.

Our basic sensory awareness is automatic, but so are many more sophisticated functions. Try looking at the object nearest your right hand and *not* categorizing it as a stapler, a cup of coffee, or whatever it might be. Basic categorization is a task your brain performs automatically. If I'd rather not think of the stapler as a stapler, too bad; I really have no choice in the matter.

Even so celebrated a capacity as the ability to speak is in important respects instinctive, as Steven Pinker argues forcefully in *The Language Instinct*. Of course, you do have to receive inputs from the world to become an English speaker, or an Italian speaker, but the evidence for a huge innate component is overwhelming: a first language is acquired without formal instruction, just about equally well regardless of a child's intelligence, with great ease during the standard learning period (ages 0–3) but with great effort later on. Once you've learned a language, no effort is involved in speaking and understanding it. Next time someone is talking to you, try *not* to understand; processing language inputs is automatic and effortless, to the point of being unavoidable. We could no sooner *not* do it than a salmon can resist swimming upstream when it's time to spawn.

Alright, perhaps when we're just hearing a sound, seeing what's in front of us, and understanding what someone is saying, the underlying mental processes are automatic and innate (i.e. instinctive). But surely the thoughts we have over the course of the day are up to us! Well, sort of. We are less in control of ourselves than we think. The cognitive psychologist John Bargh had volunteers unscramble sets of five words to make sentences and then observed how they interacted with the experimenters afterwards. When the words involved rudeness ("brazen," "aggressively"), the volunteers behaved more rudely. If they involved the elderly, the volunteers walked more slowly. If they involved professors, people did better later at the quiz game Trivial Pursuits. Psychologist Jonathan Haidt goes so far as to say that "everything you do on the way [to an airport] will be automatic: breathing, blinking, shifting in your seat, daydreaming, keeping enough distance between you and the car in front of you, even scowling and cursing slower drivers."

As psychologists advance into more areas of human experience, the number of spheres that seem instinct-driven is increasing. Marc Hauser argues in *Moral Minds* that moral thinking takes place in a special innate faculty that runs without the assistance of explicit reasoning. Jonathan Haidt has another version of the innateness hypothesis that also breaks the connection between morality and reason. Even religious impulses are starting to seem, to some psychologists, more automatic and biologically driven, instead of being conscious and entirely up to us. All of these developments are controversial and there's no telling now what the consensus will be in another 25 years. Nevertheless, it's starting to seem as if we don't the least bit denigrate animals if we say they are instinct-dominated or that they are frequently "on automatic pilot." If both are true, that doesn't stop them from having extremely impressive and sophisticated capacities.

It also doesn't stop them from being a lot like us. How much they are like us really depends on just what their instincts are – whether they include the instincts we find most distinctively human. Do animals only have instincts to make nests, build spider webs, and the like, or do they come closer to us, having instincts for language, for example, or even morality, or (most surprisingly) something like religion?

That's one line of questions, but there's also the traditional question. We are not all instinct all of the time. We do, after all, have our godlike moments. We *do* truly think and deliberate. Sometimes it's not just your *brain* that solves a problem, but *you*. You're trying to accomplish some task – getting all the bricks from the front yard to the back yard; figuring out how many bags of mulch will cover the garden; pouring fertilizer back into a narrow-necked bottle. You think about such problems and (aha!) you discover the solution. We give *you*, not just your brain, the credit for that sort of achievement.

Do non-human animals figure things out, like we do? Do they make discoveries? Do they even really *think* at all? These are key questions for psychologists who want to understand how similar animal minds are to human minds. We need to tackle them, but we also need to compare human and animal instincts. Do innate mental faculties in humans have their analogs in animals, or are humans not only more rational, but endowed with a completely exceptional set of instincts?

Thinking

Awareness and thinking are subtly different. Awareness can be as primitive as having one's whole mind occupied with pain. In the middle of the night you start to wake up with the growing awareness of a headache. As the pain plagues you, it wouldn't necessarily be right to say that you're thinking. You're simply suffering. As you wake up more and consider where you've left the bottle of Tylenol, and whether it's worth getting out from under the warm covers, you've begun to think. We often think in a deliberate, goal-oriented way; we think our way toward the solution of some problem. But there are other sorts of thinking, involving less control or direction. We can wonder, or muse, or just attend to some situation or issue. But thinking involves something other than mere awareness. (Can you think unconsciously? Perhaps you can, but as we look at animal thinking, we'll keep the focus on conscious thinking.)

Can animals think? As legions of tough-minded scientists have insisted, we do need to be on our guard against anthropomorphism – the tendency to uncritically project human qualities onto animals. As children we are exposed to countless books and movies that make animals out to be humans that just look different on the outside. Popular books about animals sometimes uncritically favor the most generous interpretation of their behavior. They underestimate the difficulty of establishing what's going on inside animal minds.

But Frans de Waal, a leading primatologist, points out that "anthropodenial" is another force that shapes the way we look at animals. Some of us cannot bear to think that animals share much of anything with us, despite the evolutionary and physiological evidence that they must. Uncritical anthropomorphism will lead us into error if the truth is that animals are very different from us. But anthropodenial is also dangerous, since it's quite possible that animals are in some ways similar.

All too often eagerness or reluctance is evident in animal researchers and writers. The eager writer is happy to slay claims of human uniqueness with amazing animal stories taken at face value. The reluctant author is always raising the bar. If animals seem to get too close to having a "human" ability, the ability is redefined as something a little more sophisticated; and then, if an example demonstrates that animals do after all have *that* ability, more conceptual work is done to raise the bar. The best animal authors are prepared to admit whatever they find in the animal world – ingenuity, stupidity, similarity to humans or dissimilarity. As in the story of Goldilocks and the three bears, the attitude we ought to have toward animals is neither too generous nor too stingy, but "just right."

There are some philosophers who object to the notion of animals as thinkers for conceptual, not empirical, reasons. No animal feat will cause them to see animals as capable of thought, because they think there's a deep-seated incoherence to the very idea. This view is floated (but not entirely affirmed) by the philosopher Stephen Stich. Putting it in a very small nutshell, the idea is that there always has to be a content sentence that can be used to characterize a thought – or there's no thought. We run into trouble filling in the content sentences if we attribute thoughts (and all other contentful mental states, like hopes and desires), to animals. Suppose my cat comes to the kitchen, looks toward his water bowl, and then starts meowing piteously. Should we say he thinks that the bowl is empty, or that there's no water in the bowl? For that to be the right description, we have to suppose he possesses concepts like *emptiness* and *water*, and perhaps he does not. After all, to grasp *emptiness*, there are other concepts to be grasped, like *fullness*. To grasp *emptiness* in one situation, there seems to be a require-ment that you can grasp it in many others. If it's a *water*-thought we're tempted to impute to the cat, does he really have the relevant associated concepts, like the concept of *matter*, or *transparency*, or *liquidity*?

These worries should give us pause next time we are tempted to assign crisp contents to animal thoughts, using English sentences. Maybe the use of our sentences to characterize *their* thoughts does lead us into some trou-ble. But we have that problem when we're trying to describe the thoughts of distant people too. What were Paleolithic hunters thinking when they looked at their water-collection urns and thought they were empty or water-less? Did *they* have our concepts of *matter* or *transparency* or *liquid-ity*? I have no idea, but it would be absurd to think, because of the trouble we have describing their thoughts, that they simply didn't have any.

So there's no in principle objection to granting thought to animals, but when is their thoughtfulness in evidence? Oddly, it's sometimes when they seem least impressive. Even if key tasks in the life of an animal are instinct-governed – like the way a bird builds a nest, or rolls wayward eggs back into a nest, or responds to mates, or feeds her chicks – the minute-to-minute course of her life seems impossible to attribute entirely to instinct. To take this worm or that worm, to turn right or turn left? These moment-to-moment unimpressive behaviors, oddly enough, strongly suggest *some* sort of thought is standard fare for animals.

Perhaps you have a dog or a cat who wanders around your house. If you watch your pet, you will probably surmise that he has decision-making moments throughout the day. Your cat hears a noise. You see him perk up and look this way and then that. He stands up for a moment, preparing to jump off the couch, but then relaxes, loses the alert look, and lies back down. What was happening in that 10-second interval but "thinking"? Not human thinking, of course, not thinking we should imagine as being just like ours, but still thinking.

One night my cat climbed up a tree near the side of our house and then jumped on the roof. The tree trunk was skinny, while the roof was broad, so going in that direction was easy. Reversing his course was more difficult. He walked to the edge of the roof and looked at the tree, face alert, then looked at the ground far below, and back to the tree. He walked a few feet away and looked toward the ground again, then walked back to the tree. He was surely making up his mind. You couldn't call it anything else *unless* you were fixated on the idea that reason, cognition, thought – everything "higher" – is reserved for human beings.

Sure my cat spends some of his day thinking. The real question, the question that will absorb a person without an ax to grind either on behalf of human uniqueness or on behalf of animal excellence, concerns the *way* animals think. Is their range of thought severely restricted? Is their way of thinking unintelligent? Is animal thinking at all like our thinking?

Wolfgang Kohler famously looked for "insight" in chimpanzees. The chimpanzees were given an unfamiliar problem to solve – how to capture bananas that were hanging from a high wire overhead. Without many repetitions, and so without mere "trial and error," they solved the problem: they stacked up crates, climbed on top of them carrying a stick, and whacked at the bananas. It's just about impossible not to suppose that the animals ran through the steps of this process – stack, climb, whack – before climbing the crates. They figured out what to do before doing it.

It should not be thought, either, that chimpanzees are an exception because they're so genetically similar to humans. Instances of insight have been observed in animals from many different species and genera. Crows given novel problems can figure out how to solve them. For example, they have no instincts when it comes to pulling fishing line out of water to eat the bait, but Bernd Heinrich has shown that they can devise a method to do it efficiently.

Animal architects – animals that build enduring structures – provide many examples of apparent intelligence. Beavers construct dams that maintain a pond with a constant water level and construct lodges – conical piles of sticks they live under to stay safe from predators. No two dams or lodges are exactly the same, but the strongest evidence of intelligence is the way the beavers deal with damage. They don't do a mindless patch job, but make things work properly again. In their book on animal architects, James Gould and Carol Gould offer an anecdote about a family of beavers that had been observed for many years. The dam was damaged by local children, and a good Samaritan tried to help the beavers by repairing it with large stones. Water flowed a bit between them, but they slowed the draining of the pond. When the oldest beaver discovered the patch, he or she improved upon it by collecting vegetation and plugging the holes on the downstream side, not the side beavers normally work on.

Even an orb spider builds a web in a way that's not rote, but custom-designed for a particular environment. We all know a snowflake always has six branches, but what's the standard number of radii in a spider web? Trick question! There isn't one. Some situations need more radii than other. "Each web is a custom production," as the Goulds say. When a web is damaged, spiders don't just start over, and follow the recipe all over again. Researchers have tried snipping webs to see how spiders respond – and they repair them with finesse. (As I've said, thinking and awareness are two different things. If there's thinking here, is it conscious thinking?)

It seems groundless to assume that thinking is an exclusively human capacity. A more reasonable hypothesis is that there is something in the general category of cogitation in each species – chimpanzee-like for chimpanzees, crow-like for crows, spider-like for spiders. There is really no chance of substantiating the age-old notion of animals as instinct-driven beasts and humans as demi-gods. There is too much that's beastly on the human side, and too much thoughtfulness on the animal side.

Still, if animals do think and figure things out and make discoveries, the whole focus of their mental life could be quite different. A line may still separate people and animals based on what people, and only people, think *about*. Well, what *do* we think about?

Self and Other

For one, we think about ourselves a lot, and also about other people. An animal, some psychologists have said, is stuck in a world of mindless objects.

Although an animal *has* a mind, animals never *think* of themselves as themselves, and never think about the inner mental worlds of others. Now, in one sense this can't be. Animals take special care of their own bodies. They run away from predators, eat when hungry, nurse their own wounds. They are self-involved, self-interested, and maybe even selfish. They also clearly act *as if* aware of the mental states of others, coordinating their behavior with the behavior of conspecifics, predators and prey, or with us. The naysayers' hypothesis is a subtle one about the way they think: yes, they are self-involved, but they never think of themselves *as* themselves. They coordinate with others by responding to outward signs, not by representing other individuals' mental states.

Having a sense of self is many things, and many of them are complex and sophisticated. We have the sense of one body as our own, in contrast with anyone else's. That's one thing, but we sometimes mean much more by calling someone self-aware, or saying a person has a sense of self, or self-understanding. A grasp of oneself can have a mundane sort of value: many a problem can be solved by knowing one's own nature and strategically planning around that knowledge. Case in point: one thing I know about myself is that I tend to feel miserable in a dentist's chair. Another thing I know is that it relaxes me and occupies my mind to read. So a while back I resolved I would henceforth read while having my teeth cleaned, even at the cost of looking ridiculous. Ever since, I've been much less miserable going to the dentist. At the deeper end of the spectrum, self-awareness is something profound, something we work toward over a lifetime.

In some respects, "sense of self" certainly seems distinctively human, but it's perfectly conceivable that animals have some elements of it too. Why shouldn't an animal see her face as *her* face, or her paw as *her* paw? The problem is how to test for that perception, considering that our own moments of self-awareness typically go on in the privacy of our own minds. How can you tell, from the outside, that someone is self-aware?

The natural concern for testability has generated a decades-long focus on one specific ability – the ability to recognize oneself in a mirror or mirror-like screen. We take this for granted, but it's interesting to recall a moment of hyper-conscious self-recognition. You've probably had the experience of looking into the window of an electronics store and seeing a TV screen displaying images of wide-eyed, pointing shoppers. It didn't interest you much until you suddenly realized that a video-camera was aimed at you and you were looking at an image of yourself. With a sudden jolt you realized

"That's me!" Nobody can observe that thought but you yourself, but the thought triggers certain kinds of behaviors. You look more closely. You point. You make faces. You remove a crumb from your cheek if there happens to be one. The question then is whether animals behave that way in front of mirrors and mirror-like screens as well. If so, it's logical to think they also have the power to think "that's me."

Charles Darwin himself got the idea to put mirrors in front of animals in 1872. He put orangutans to the test at a zoo, but they failed the test. Instead of examining themselves, they searched behind the mirror for the "other" animal and quickly moved away. Mirror testing of animals took off again in the 1970s when comparative psychologist Gordon Gallup started to study chimpanzees. He discovered that many chimpanzees do pass the mirror test (but for some reason many do better in their middle years than when very young or very old). Gallup made use of a very specific behavioral test. He let the chimps play with mirrors to get used to the phenomenon of reflection, and then surreptitiously affixed red dots to their faces. If they looked into the mirror and then touched the dots on their faces, he construed that as a positive result. Obviously, the test has had to be modified for different species, but the score is now roughly this: in addition to chimpanzees, some dolphins have passed the test, one gorilla, as well as some tamarind monkeys, some elephants, and an orangutan. Most kinds of monkeys do not pass the test, nor do baboons. Of course, most species simply haven't been tested.

The mirror test seems to be irresistible to comparative psychologists, at the same time that some doubt how much it really tells us. For example, Marc Hauser discusses it for many pages in *Wild Minds*, surveying a great deal of data, but says half way through the survey, "I don't think the mirror test provides any leverage with respect to self-awareness." Why not? Hauser points out that there are human beings with a form of the neurologic condition called "prosopagnosia" who cannot recognize their own faces in mirrors, yet do have self-awareness (by their own reports). Mirror self-recognition and self-awareness *can* exist independent of each other. You might also start doubting that the test must be passed by animals who have self-awareness when you think about how fair the test really is. We are a highly visual species, with a high degree of interest in appearances, and much-experienced with mirrors. But some animals aren't any of these things. Furthermore, as Hauser points out, seeing oneself in the mirror is initially like staring straight into the eyes of another individual (someone who looks just like you). Humans habitually make eye contact, as do chimpanzees, but monkeys and many other species don't. In many monkey species, staring is a hostile behavior, so the monkey in the mirror is experienced as threatening. And then, as comparative psychologists Leslie Rogers and Gisela Kaplan point out, there are animals that may have their "that's me" moments via a different sense modality. For dogs, recognizing the smell of their own urine may be a moment of self-awareness.

Some students of animal psychology insist quite reasonably that an individual doesn't have to pass the mirror self-recognition test to be self-aware. Others just as reasonably wonder how much the mirror self-recognition test really proves, even when it's passed. Just to have a "me" concept, so that you can grasp one body as yours, is not to have a whole lot of self-awareness. It is no proof of the many levels of self-awareness that human beings can achieve.

There's evidence of animals having an awareness of other minds, yet all of it is controversial. Chimpanzees clamber for position in their close-knit societies. The alpha male tries to stop other males from mating with females; the others don't simply submit, like beta males do in wolf packs, but connive their way into dalliances. The lower-status males sneak around behind the backs of the dominant male. But sneaking around seems to imply knowing what the dominant male prefers and what he can see. This sometimes even involves being aware of two other minds at the same time. In his thoughtful and entertaining book *The Philosopher and the Wolf*, Mark Rowlands describes a situation in which a male simultaneously displays his erect penis to an interested female on one side of him and holds his hand up to hide it from a competing male on the other side. He is evidently aware of what each of his fellows can and can't see, from their perspectives.

It's very difficult to come up with deflationary interpretations of this kind of evidence. You can say that the tumescent male is displaying his penis to the female's *eyes* and hiding it from the male's *eyes*, without understanding the seeing behind the eyes. But it makes no sense that the animal should do this if he doesn't understand the mental states of the female (desire) and the male (antipathy). Or are we to think that desire, to the chimpanzee, is nothing but red genitals, and antipathy is nothing but a certain constellation of aggressive behaviors and facial expressions? Though there's something to be said for hard-headedness, persisting with these reinterpretations does seem like a symptom of the begrudging attitude that Frans de Waal calls "anthropodenial."

Locked in the Present?

In *Stumbling on Happiness*, Harvard psychologist Daniel Gilbert offers another theory about what makes humans unique: humans and only humans think about the future. It's surely true that people are *very* focused on the future (and the past). But are animals really entirely oriented to the here and now? Is that a stereotype, just another attempt to erect a sharp boundary, or the truth?

The image of animals as locked in the present has an initial appeal. The animals we are most familiar with, our cats and dogs, seem to go about their days completely oblivious of yesterday and tomorrow. But many animals are more oriented to the past and future. Birds build nests for future laying. Some species migrate thousands of miles to breed. Many animals bury food in preparation for the winter. Later on they seem to look backward at the moment they hid the food, in order to retrieve it. With so much past- and future-oriented *behavior*, it's certainly worth looking closely at the question whether animals have past- and future-focused *thoughts*.

In the hit movie *March of the Penguins,* emperor penguins are shown walking 60 miles to breeding grounds in the interior of Antarctica to breed. There they mate and the females lay eggs, which the males will protect for several bitterly cold months. While the males are on egg-duty, the females go back to the sea to load up on fish. While they are gone, the eggs hatch and the chicks await a first meal regurgitated from Mom's stomach. Back again the females march to the interior. Then it's the males' turn to head for the sea. The ideologue looks at all of this and feels completely certain that the mental life of the penguin is a void. The penguin must surely trudge along without thinking, without images in his or her mind of things to come, without any goal whatsoever. There are no thoughts along the way about the meal to come, and no memories of the mate or egg or the youngster who was left behind.

Certainly, it would be easy to impute too much mentality to the penguins. There's a "free-floating rationale" for their behavior (to use a phrase of Daniel Dennett's) – a set of reasons that aren't in any sense represented in penguins' minds. Nobody believes penguins thought it through and decided it would be better to mate inland because the ice is more reliable there. They never worked out the turn-taking approach to childcare and feeding. Evolution selected these behaviors because they promoted survival. A more intellectual creature might have arrived at these strategies at the end of a lot of thought and debate, but we're quite sure it didn't go that way for the penguin.

Still, it doesn't seem absurd to suppose that *some* looking back and looking forward – mental time travel, as psychologists call it – is involved. Careful definition is needed here, because the issue is not about whether animals have memory. Of course they do. There must be information in memory for the penguins to be able to pick up the route back to the sea, and for the mothers to rejoin their mates and offspring. But memory is one thing and time travel another. What psychologists mean by *time travel* is recalling the past, what we do when we look back on an event an hour ago, or a day ago, or last year. I can recall an event last night more or less as a brief video – though one that's gappy and jumbled. I don't just remember *that* we all sat around reading *Harry Potter*, I remember *doing* it. Episodic memory, memory of an episode, is different from semantic memory – storage of facts. It's episodic memory that's the issue here.

Episodic memory is central to some of our most human experiences – reminiscing, writing a memoir, talking to a therapist about your childhood, giving testimony at a trial, writing a report about "what I did last summer." This is all pretty fancy stuff. To reminisce, you have to have a sense of yourself as an ongoing being with a past that proceeds up to and merges with the present. A sense of self and notions of time are involved. But all episodic memory needn't be as fancy as that. The plainest variety of episodic memory is a flashback. You are taking a walk and, unbidden, a scene from yesterday comes back to you. Flashbacks are replays of earlier neuronal events, and there's some reason to think that animals have them too. We know that dogs do dream, and we know that the parts of the brain that are active during dreams are the same parts involved in daytime activity. So the common assumption that a dog might be dreaming of playing Frisbee as she twitches in her sleep makes sense. The same thing has been observed in rats. The parts of the brain that are active while a rat runs a maze are reactivated during the rat's later REM sleep.

It's a feature of human intelligence that we recognize the value of episodic memory and intentionally use it to solve problems. At will, we can choose to focus on different parts of a remembered scene, extracting now this and now that information. We deliberately use the strategy and teach others to do so as well. "Sit down and try to remember the last time you used the scissors," I tell my children, when they wander around the house looking for them. If animals have episodic memory, it doesn't follow that they deploy it in the deliberate fashion we do. Still, they might have it.

Nicola Clayton at Cambridge University has extensively studied the Western Scrub Jay, a bird common in the western United States, and a master at caching and retrieving food. The question she has tried to answer is whether the jays only retain a memory of the location of cached food, or they actually remember the incident of hiding the food (episodic memory). She determined that they do remember hiding food by exploiting a subtle difference. As it happens, jays like to eat fresh larvae, peanuts, and old larvae, in that order. In one trial, jays hid fresh larvae and peanuts, and then returned after a few hours. In a second trial, they hid the food and then returned after a few days, when the fresh larvae had become old. When they returned after the briefer interval, they mostly dug at the larva sites, but when they returned after the longer interval, they dug at the peanut sites. (Before they searched, the food was removed from the caches so smell wouldn't be a factor.) The birds in some sense must have expected old larvae at the older sites (yuck!) and fresh larvae at the newer sites (yum!). That suggests "episode-like" memory, says Clayton: they must remember the moment of hiding the food, with some memories seeming older (dimmer?) and some more recent (more vivid?).

Alas, Clayton's results are subject to multiple interpretations. As other psychologists have pointed out, jays could file what-where-when factoids as they go about storing their food. So when they encounter an old cache, recognizing it as a specific "where" could trigger a particular "what" and "when." If the birds have semantic memories like this, it's impressive that they store temporal information (in what form is it stored?). But that's not the same thing as having a capacity for video-like replay of past events – episodic memory. It will take considerable ingenuity to design experiments that tease these two possibilities apart.

If there's anything harder than knowing whether animals ever think about the past, it's knowing whether they think about the future. We have our own experience with animals to guide us, but it can only take us so far. When your dog reacts with glee when you pick up her leash, surely she's anticipating going for a walk. She may have some going-for-a-walk images in her mind. If my cat darts around the house avoiding being put in his carrier, he's surely anticipating an unpleasant trip to the vet. But an anticipatory state is one thing, and thinking about the future is another. That means not just having certain images in your mind, but having them in your mind *as* future: thinking of next weekend's big date *as* an event that will take place next weekend.

Our pets are probably the animals least likely to give us the impression of being oriented to the future. We do everything for them so that they don't have to prepare for the future. Animals that work hard for their own future survival give us our strongest clues that animals might not be so trapped in the present after all.

Caching food for the winter is an example of present behavior with a future payoff. Animal architects provide a plethora of other examples. Beavers spend a great deal of their time sawing down trees and using them to build lodges that protect them in the winter. Male bower birds endlessly work on building and decorating little edifices they use for no other purpose but to impress potential mates. Spiders labor away on webs that will trap their meals.

These activities seem to be largely instinctive, but that doesn't mean they can't also involve thoughts about the future. Our own mating behavior is partly instinctive, but a person can certainly look forward to instinctively desirable future events – like the big date next weekend. And in any case, future-oriented animal behaviors are not *rigidly* instinctive. As noted before, a dam isn't built in exactly the same way every time, but in response to local conditions. Animals can respond appropriately when things don't go normally. "It's just instinct" is the thought that seems to come along and dislodge every intimation that an animal does have thoughts about the future. But we shouldn't give in to that (dare I say?) instinctive reaction.

But is there empirical proof, yet, that animals think about the future? It helps to focus on an artificial experimental setting, so that an impressive behavior simply can't be categorized as "merely" instinctive. A group of researchers at the Max Planck Institute in Leipzig tested for foresight in five bonobos and five orangutans (see Gazzaniga, in the Sources). An apparatus contained a food reward, but could only be opened with the appropriate tool. After the primates had been given the chance to experiment and discover the right tool, they were taken to another room for up to 14 hours before being brought back to the apparatus. But first the tools were cleared away, apart from any the animals collected to take with them. The subjects must have been able to foresee opening the food box, considering that they took the appropriate tool, and no other tool, 70 percent of the time.

Experiments like this create the impression that thinking about the future is a kind of circus trick that animals can only be cornered into under the most contrived conditions, but we should bear in mind that the contrivance is *for us:* we need it in order to acquire observable proof of future-directed thoughts in animals. If there are such thoughts, they go on all the time, when we're not looking, and without being cleanly separable from instincts.

What we are able to coax out of animals in artificial settings is only the tip of the iceberg.

Human Morality

We long for clear, sharp differences. Surely it must be possible to identify a fundamental mental capacity that belongs to all humans but no animals. A favorite candidate has been morality. We have it, but animals don't. True? A barrier to figuring that out is that there are many competing theories about our own moral psychology. Thus, to be like us, morally, could require many different things. Morality in us could be a kind of explicit, conscious reasoning, or it could be a set of emotional responses; it could even be mostly a set of instinctive reactions. It could be some combination of the three.

The morality that's associated with moral *philosophy* is an arcane and abstract thing, not so suitable for animal minds. Immanuel Kant thought humans have morality implanted in their innate reason in the form of a basic moral law. The "categorical imperative" requires that we ask what principle we're acting under (if only implicitly), and whether the principle could be adopted by all, or we'd want it to be. If you're about to grab the biggest piece of the pie, you (possibly) stop yourself, because not everyone can follow the principle of "me first," nor would you want them to. The classic pie-sharing principle, "one divides, the other chooses," passes the Kantian test. Utilitarianism puts forth the greatest happiness principle – "so act that you produce the greatest happiness for the greatest number." Another view is that there are many rules that have to be simultaneously respected to discern what's right in specific situations, rules that require keeping promises, promoting happiness, not harming others, and so on.

On all of these views, morality is something rarefied, and not likely to be within the reach of animals. A dog may sometimes, by accident, do the right thing, as defined by one moral theory or another, but will not satisfy the demands of morality consistently, and certainly won't grasp the principles themselves. If a rarefied morality captures the truth about morality and has some connection with the real workings of human psychology, it's certainly not the whole story. Abstract moral thinking didn't spring forth fully-formed at any point in history. There were precursors, patterns of thought and feeling that paved the way. It doesn't seem possible either that any person today, no matter how intelligent and morally astute, is constantly driven just by an ultimate morality, even on the best of days. We might occasionally think through a decision along the lines of Kant's categorical imperative, and sometimes use the greatest happiness principle (showing ourselves to be impure Kantian–Utilitarian hybrids). Maybe we deploy lots of different moral principles in different situations (so we're ultra-impure "polybrids"). But an ultimate morality or mixture of moralities is for the moments when we are at our most reflective. Most of the time when we react to people and situations with labels like "good," "bad," "permissible," and "impermissible," something more basic is going on.

Reciprocation is one of these more basic proto-moral propensities. Since you gave me a gift worth about $20, next time it's your birthday I'd better give you a gift that's worth about $20. It would be impermissible to just give you a card. But on the other hand – you were mean to me, so don't complain if I'm mean to you. Giving to get is deep-seated, but surely our paragons of morality get a lot less than they give, so how can that be the underlying pattern? In *The Origins of Virtue*, Matt Ridley explains that really good people do actually get a subtle return for their efforts. Ridley homes in on the way ethical goodness enhances a person's reputation. As the philanthropist starts to be highly trusted and admired, he or she may wind up being richly rewarded. PR firms know what they're doing when they link companies to noble causes. Likewise, celebrities aren't being completely saintly when they talk about global warming and the AIDS crisis in Africa. But let's be careful. Giving to get and reciprocation shouldn't be thought of as entirely displacing principled morality. Rather, they're more like a springboard. It's because we have an instinct for reciprocation that we're occasionally able to reach the heights of much more abstract moral thinking.

To add more complexity to the picture, there are emotions and attitudes to the emotions of others that are central for human morality. Some say these emotions are the very core of morality (and abstract principles be damned), but at least they seem to pave the way to an ultimate morality. Sick children in your own house move you to sympathy, which spurs immediate action. They wouldn't trigger sympathy except for the fact that you can imagine what they're feeling: you have empathy. Other people's children trigger the same feelings, and then so do children in TV charity appeals. Based on a few perceived equivalences between children close-up and far away, a person can become motivated to help children in distant places.

Strong and immediate feelings place us on a trail that leads to concern that's gradually less visceral and more universal.

Animal Morality?

Frans de Waal has spent many years studying reciprocity in captive groups of chimpanzees. What he's discovered is that chimpanzees are acutely sensitive to slights and favors. A nice grooming session will lead to more food sharing later on in the day. Will the groomed animal just be in a sharing mood, letting anyone in on his supply of fruit? No, the groomed animal will share specifically with the groomer (inviting once again the question about time travel – is that dependent on episodic or semantic memory?). A violent attack is remembered and later on the attacker may find himself attacked. Chimpanzees know how to reciprocate.

De Waal has also observed something like a sense of fairness in capuchin monkeys. Animals were given food in exchange for tokens while watching a neighbor also receive food for tokens. When a neighbor received a more desirable food in return for the same sort of token, there were complaints. And they were louder in this situation than when the more desirable food was simply visible, but not given to the neighbor.

None of this is ultimate morality. Chimpanzees don't put their maxims (what maxims?) to the test of the categorical imperative, or calculate what will produce the greatest happiness for the great number. There's no evidence they even have the concepts of "morally right" and "morally wrong." It's debatable just how extensive and refined their sense of fairness is. There does seem to be enough here, though, to stop us from drawing a clear, sharp line between human beings and the rest of the animals on moral grounds.

Proto-moral emotions also break the species barrier. After learning to press a lever to get food, rats will stop pressing if they see that their behavior causes electric shock to another rat. Soon they go back to pressing, rather than go hungry, but rhesus monkeys are even more responsive. In one study, a monkey abstained from pulling a food chain that shocked a companion for five days, and another for twelve. (The human experimenters didn't empathize enough to spare the rats and monkeys electric shocks. Does that suggest moral impairment on *their* part?)

Chimpanzees go a step further than monkeys. A chimpanzee will put an arm around a companion who's just been outdone in battle. Adding to the impression that the consoler feels empathy, there's the fact that the more serious the aggression perpetrated against the victim, the sooner the consoler will come to his aid. Chimpanzees console, but even more strikingly, they rescue. At zoos chimpanzees are sometimes kept on islands surrounded by water, and individuals will rush into the water to save hapless companions from drowning. De Waal points out that "empathy is not an all-or-nothing phenomenon: it covers a wide range of emotional linkage patterns, from the very simple and automatic to the highly sophisticated." Granted, what the animals are feeling may be fairly primitive, but it seems like sheer anthropodenial to call it anything but empathy.

The better we understand human morality, as opposed to moral philosophy, the more we understand moralizing as rooted in our basic instincts, attitudes, and emotions. Seeing morality that way also reveals elements of morality in non-human animals. Humans, it turns out, are not super-principled gods, and neither are animals sheer brutes.

What Else?

Is it language animals lack? But animals very clearly do communicate, with different songs, squawks, growls, dances, and gestures having distinct and specific meanings. Communication is accomplished in humans and some animals by means of a vocabulary and grammar. Granted, the language faculty in a human being is vastly more intricate, but the difference is not best captured by a clear, sharp line. Is it art that they lack? But maybe there is artistry in the way Bower birds fashion their displays, and perhaps in the vocal performances of other birds.

Descartes claimed that animals are nature's automata – they're like robots. The more we learn about the mental life and emotions of animals, the more this seems scandalously distorted. Animals do seem to have emotions and thoughts, unlike robots. Could you make a case, though, that they are similar to robots in having no freedom? Free will, in the least problematic sense of the phrase, is having your own behavior under the control of your own thoughts. That means an absence of external constraints; you're not free if you've been bound and gagged. Being free also means not being controlled by a hypnotist, or by mind-altering drugs. Furthermore, freedom involves having the "me" part of your brain determine some of your behavior, not the impersonal, "un-me" regions that control your body temperature, the way you hear sounds, whether you're awake or asleep, etc. And then, there's more freedom the more that, in a battle between your thoughts and your emotions, the thoughts at least sometimes win.

Animals are not always in chains; they're seldom at the mercy of drugs, let alone hypnotists. So: no difference from us. But, the determined animal demoter might say: in an animal, the "me" and "un-me" parts of the brain are not so distinct. The way we wake up without choosing to – a case of unfreedom – is the way animals do everything. In an animal, all mental events just happen, while in people there are different levels of personal control. Furthermore, battles between thought and feeling are always won by feeling in animals, and sometimes won by thought in us.

The last point is emphasized by Marc Hauser, who describes the following research. Pairs of chimpanzees were presented with food choices, with one being the selector and the other the receiver. The selector had to point to one bowl of food – which would then go to the receiver. The experimenters made this challenging by putting different amounts of food in the two bowls. Since the selectors could be presumed to want the greater quantity, it was striking that they consistently pointed to the greater quantity – thus ceding it to the receiver. Hauser interprets this as showing that the urge for more food short-circuited the animal's ability to think about how to get it. Feeling won out over thought.

Again, a few embers of difference look like they're being fanned up into a raging fire. Let's return to that utterly ordinary moment when my cat vacillated between coming off the roof by jumping or by walking down the tree. There does seem to be "someone" in charge of the cat's behavior – the cat himself – and not just the impersonal workings of his brain. How can I tell? I can't be sure, but I presume so based on the cat's attentive eyes, his glances toward the tree and back to the ground and back – all signs that he's *deciding*, instead of running on automatic pilot. It doesn't seem worlds away from what it's like when we make similar ordinary decisions. And as for thought taking precedence: a mouse on the ground would not induce my cat to throw himself off the roof. It's true that he has poor impulse control where someone else's agenda is concerned – he can't resist getting on the kitchen counters. But he is not incapable of what we would see as self-control in ourselves.

What to make of the experiments Hauser describes? It seems peculiar to draw sweeping conclusions from this highly artificial set-up. Pointing is a behavior drawn from our human gestural repertoire. Granted, the research animals, considering they had been subjects of many experiments, probably had a great deal of past experience with pointing, but the meaning of the gesture had been changed in this study. Normally the rule is that you point to what you do want, not to what you don't want. In any case, more naturalistic descriptions of chimpanzees in their natural environments reveal that they are fully capable of inhibiting strong urges. Sex with a desirable mate often has to be postponed or hidden from others, as Frans de Waal amply illustrates in *Chimpanzee Politics*. We have abundant evidence that chimpanzees do not give in immediately to every temptation.

But then again, who could deny that human beings have a *degree* of freedom that's orders of magnitude beyond what any animal has? Humans change course more often and more drastically. We choose among whole ways of life, or even invent our own. Huge changes, driven by judgments about ethics and value, are not just possible, but common. Animals are free after their own fashion, but they don't have the power to make this sort of wholesale reevaluation. The narrower range of their thoughts may explain why they look, to us thought-aholics, like nothing but automatons. But that is not, all things considered, a fair description.

The line-drawers have traditionally homed in on the "self" that is at the core of a human being, that self's capacity for rational reflection and self-determination, and the powers of that self to probe past and future and be concerned about right and wrong. By contrast, animals have been seen as robotic; at the farthest extreme, they've been thought to be not even conscious, "feeling" beings, as the consciousness-deniers of Chapter 3 assert. If not quite that robotic, they've been viewed as totally instinct-governed. If not quite that limited, it's still been thought that they are terribly restricted in what they can think *about* and what they can feel.

Many ethologists and comparative psychologists today are questioning just how limited animals really are. We are learning that there may be some self-awareness and awareness of other minds in some species, and something akin to morality. Even some of our most treasured emotions – sympathy, empathy, righteous indignation – are not entirely missing in the animal world. As we learn more about animals *and* ourselves, we are confronted with more continuity than the line-drawers like to contemplate. It's not just that animals have more "human" abilities, but that *we* are more "animal." Our minds work mechanically in many respects; we are more instinct-governed and less deliberate and "free" in our thought and behavior than we realize.

Even our most treasured abilities – like our capacity for morality – are not such pure products of reason as we'd like to think.

Darwin's bold theory that human beings evolved from non-human animals made it seem likely that there are similarities between any two species, but especially between species not vastly separated in geological time. Open-minded study of animal and human minds reveals this is true. Morally, we must contend with the likeness between ourselves and other animals. But we also must contend with differences – as much as they are matters of degree, not basic kind. There is self-awareness in animals but there is more in human beings, and it takes many more forms. There are precursors of morality in animals, but full-blown morality in human beings (at least on our best days).

Since there are other animals that at least approach our abilities, must we allow the strongest competitors into our moral community, in every conceivable sense? Or, since we are clear winners in important categories, are non-human animals left out in the cold, forever second class, or third class, or no class at all?

What I'll be defending in the chapters to come is a "middle way" that steers between these two extremes. We do owe serious consideration to animals, but not exactly what we owe to each other.

Part III
All Due Respect

What moral stance should we take toward members of other species? It's illuminating to first look at dramatic situations that pit human lives against animal lives. When must we save animals? May we ever kill them for our benefit?

5

The Lives of Animals

The scientific study of animals can tell us a lot about factual differences, but that's just the start. To decide how we ought to treat animals, we must figure out what difference the differences make. Animal lives are not entirely like ours, but how does that affect questions of value and morality? Do animal lives have less value? And if so, what is the upshot in real-life situations?

A fundamental sort of moral quandary arises in a rescue situation. A firefighter comes to a burning building and knows the baby's in one room, a grandparent is in another, a world-famous scientist is in the basement, and the dog is in the bathroom. What to do? These scenarios are so artificial that they seem to tell us nothing of any real significance. But rescue situations do come up, and it will pay to think about them before anything else.

The need to weigh human lives against animal lives came up in a real and vivid way after Hurricane Katrina forced the evacuation of New Orleans in September 2005. After the city flooded, thousands of poor, old, infirm, or just unlucky residents were stranded for many days. Boats rescued people marooned on the tops of their houses. Helicopters slowly evacuated people out of hospitals. Finally, buses came to the overcrowded convention center, where thousands had languished for five days without adequate food, water, and sanitation. The rescuers faced a repeated dilemma: what to do about animals? On the news the rest of the country started seeing heartrending scenes of families being separated from their pets. There wasn't room for everyone on the buses and a "people only" policy had been observed.

In the years since Katrina, animal welfare organizations like the Humane Society have worked hard on disaster preparation. Changes to US law have been made. But how far should we go? Should animal lives be given the same priority as human lives?

Pride and Prejudice

No philosopher has had more influence on the modern animal defense movement than Peter Singer, author of the 1975 manifesto *Animal Liberation*, and now a professor of bioethics at Princeton University. The book is required reading for anyone who wants to be well versed on the subject of ethics and animals. As shocking as Singer's descriptions of factory farms and animal labs certainly are, perhaps even more memorable is his diagnosis of a malignancy he calls "speciesism," using a word originally coined by British psychologist Richard Ryder. If the word reminds you of "racism" and "sexism," it should. We no longer think it's acceptable to assume blacks are unintelligent and lazy, or women are weak and emotional. Singer asks us to recognize and reject similar prejudices about animals. They are "just animals," we think, reflexively. So of course they don't get a seat on the bus. We don't have to save them from death and suffering if it's inconvenient. In fact, we can go much further, and even inflict harm on animals for our benefit.

Speciesism is the engine behind much of the downgrading of animals we've seen in the first two parts of this book, according to Singer. The notion that animals lack consciousness or lack reason, that they consent to their deaths or are given to us as food by a supreme being … all of these ideas are mere "ideological camouflage." What lies behind the veneer of insight is a gut-level bias in our own favor and against other species.

It's easiest to see species bias in operation if we look first at biases for and against particular species. We dote on dogs, some of us even buying them clothes and Christmas presents, but pigs are dirty, rats are repulsive. Spiders are interesting, but cockroaches are alarming. We even have different attitudes toward the same animal at different life stages. Caterpillars are a little unpleasant, while butterflies are lovely. Collectively we think of animals as vastly beneath us. "Animal" is even used as a term of abuse, and "human" (as well as "humane" and "humanitarian") as a compliment. Often we articulate our pride in ourselves, as humans, by marking some contrast with animals. There is even a faint suggestion that we are not animals at all, so deep is our desire to be special.

Singer is surely right that prejudice against other species and pride in ourselves operate in something like the way that sexism and racism do, causing us to see things askew and make unfair and hurtful judgments. We should do our best to rid ourselves of prejudice, whether it relates to race, gender, species, or any other charged characteristic. Pride in our own group can be enjoyed without the denigration of other groups. But if we succeed in eliminating bias, where will that leave us? What sorts of conclusions should we countenance as being bias-free?

When it comes to race and gender, we are pretty certain of the answer. People who see great differences of intelligence between blacks and whites are very likely to be racists. Those who think women are too emotional for political office are very likely to be sexists. We have been thinking about issues of race and gender long enough that we have at least a rough notion – though controversial around the edges – what it's like to be bias free. If we are without prejudice, we will not see vast differences separating men and women, blacks and whites.

But if we are without prejudice against animals, surely we *will* still see vast differences. Species differences are much greater than race and gender differences. Granted, they are exaggerated by a tradition that puts animals on the other side of some profound divide – casting them as devoid of consciousness, or reason, or emotion, or anything resembling morality. Still, even if the differences are not so stark, they are real. There is far more reason in people than in crows, even if crows are impressive. Morality is much more highly developed in people than in dogs. If we declared males or whites superior in these ways, we'd be sexists or racists. But if we notice deep differences between different species, we are simply being realistic.

Cured of speciesist bias, we will still see great differences between our species and other species. But will we see differences that add up to differences of value, generating profoundly different sets of obligations to animals versus other people? If we cleanse ourselves of speciesist bias, will we become complete, through-and-through egalitarians?

People and Chickens

The Nobel Prize-winning Jewish author Isaac Bashevis Singer once compared the way we use animals for food to the nightmare of the Nazi death camps. In a short story called "The Letter Writer," a character speaks to a deceased mouse:

> What do they know – all these scholars, all these philosophers, all the leaders of the world – about such as you? They have convinced themselves that man,

the worst transgressor of all the species, is the crown of creation. All other creatures were created merely to provide him with food, pelts, to be tormented, exterminated. In relation to them, all people are Nazis; for the animals it is an eternal Treblinka.

The analogy became visual in a traveling exhibition called "The Holocaust on Your Plate," created by People for the Ethical Treatment of Animals (PETA), in 2003. On one side of each image were skeletal prisoners packed into railway cars or concentration camp bunks; on the other side were animals in factory farms or on the way to the slaughter house. One image showed emaciated men peering out of a four-story concentration camp bunk on one side, and caged chickens stacked on shelves on the other. The message, of course, is that one situation is comparable to the other. But is that correct? Are the six million deaths of Jews during the Holocaust really comparable to the six million deaths of chickens that take place every six hours in the United States?

Another Nobel Prize-winner, the South African writer J. M. Coetzee, embraced the analogy in a 1999 work of fiction called *The Lives of Animals*, or at least his main character did. In the story, a fatigued, despairing novelist gives a series of lectures about animals, at one point saying that we don't want to know about the modern industrial animal farm, much as ordinary Germans didn't want to know what was going on in the concentration camps that dotted Germany. Coetzee presented these fictional lectures as a set of lectures of his own at Princeton, where Peter Singer was an invited commentator. Singer's reply also took fictional form, with his stand-in being one thinly disguised "Peter," who talks about the lives of animals with his daughter Naomi.

The first chapter of *Animal Liberation* is named after a slogan adopted by the upstart pigs in George Orwell's *Animal Farm:* "All Animals are Equal." Singer resurrects the slogan not to ridicule it, but to embrace it; all animals *are* equal, in a very important and central sense, he argues. Because he takes that position, it's a surprise how he responds to Coetzee. His avatar doesn't side with Coetzee's avatar, but says a person's life *is* worth more than a chicken's. In the story, Naomi does what daughters tend to do; she accuses her father of being inconsistent. But Peter insists his position is not at all biased, but based on the nature of value. "The value that is lost when something is emptied depends on what was there when it was full, and there is more to human existence than there is to bat [or chicken] existence." Emptying a bottle of soymilk is one thing, he says, and emptying a bottle of

Kahlua is another. What's spilled in the case of a normal human being is more precious stuff – our bottles are full of self-awareness, planning for the future, meaningful relations with others, and abstract thought. What's spilled in the case of an animal is a life without these assets or at least with each one to a much smaller degree.

That doesn't stop people and chickens from being equal – says Singer – in a very important sense that we'll come to later. It also doesn't stop the occasional person from having a life no more valuable than the occasional chicken's life. The worth of a life is only decidable case by case, he says, not based on species membership. A member of *homo sapiens* without the standard human capacities, he admits, *would* have a life with less intrinsic worth. A miraculously super-capable animal would have a life with extra worth, maybe even matching the worth of the typical human's life. But no, the tragedy of the Holocaust doesn't take place every six hours in chicken processing plants.

Should we go along with the notion that animal lives typically do have less value? If we're going to either affirm or reject the lesser value of animal lives, we'd better proceed with caution. What gives value to a life in the first place?

Weighing Lives

Singer speaks of bottles and the type of good they're filled with, but what's this a metaphor for? In places where he deals carefully with the nature of life-value, he says that intrinsic worth is generated by the satisfaction of desires (or preferences or wants or interests – I'm ignoring niceties that may distinguish these terms). The satisfaction of a very strong desire counts for a lot; the satisfaction of a weak desire for less. A life has more value the more it's replete with satisfied desire. Further sculpting of the theory may be in order. The intrinsic value of a life seems to turn more on self-regarding desires than on other desires: more on an individual getting the things she wants for herself than on just anything turning out as she prefers. Maybe it's not good to satisfy desires that are developed due to false information or bad logic. But the core idea about what makes for value is still very simple. An individual's life has more value the more that it is full of desire-satisfaction.

Looking at things this way, at least some of our capacities are indirectly relevant to the value of our lives. Because we can think about the future, we can have desires for the future. We have desires for the next hour, for tonight, for tomorrow, for 10 years from now and 25 years from now. The horizon of an animal's life is much closer. There may be some future to it, but not a lot. Looking at them very generously, and using the language of "desire," it's at least conceivable that emperor penguins (see Chapter 4) do desire a mate, a successful trip to the sea, and the like, but it's very hard to believe their desires are anywhere near as detailed as a teenager's when she's dreaming of the future.

In other ways as well, our cognitive superiority results in a profusion of desires. We are aware of a lot more of the world, so have a chance to want much more; we can want things to be a certain way on the other side of the world (I can want this book to sell well in Australia), and a dog can't think about the other side of the world. We are also aware of ourselves in a different way; so we can want to be better people, or to be more compassionate, or more forgiving.

With our huge repertory of desires, we have the potential to live lives that are stuffed with satisfaction, and thus very, very valuable, on the desire-centered view. Of course, we also have the potential to live extremely bad lives, if all those desires go unfulfilled. With a smaller set of desires, generally there are fewer satisfied desires in the normal course of an animal's life, but also fewer unsatisfied desires. Animal lives don't stand any chance of being as good as the best human lives … or as bad as the worst ones. But the best human lives are worth more than the best animal lives.

Now that's all reasonably crisp and clear, but let's step back. The desire-centered account of the worth of lives has an appeal, but would we really want to rely on it? You might have some ground-level doubts about the good of desire satisfaction. Is it really good to get the life you want, no matter what kind of life you want? If you don't want much, are you automatically worse off than someone who wants a lot, and gets it?

There are other ways we could look at the value of a life. Does a life go well simply because desires are fulfilled, or because a person exercised her best capacities, achieving happiness, self-expression, autonomy, some level of intellectual development, and the like? The fulfillment of good potential seems relevant to assessing a life, both where human lives are concerned and where animal lives are concerned. It's not entirely clear what birds desire, but their lives seem to go better when they can make use of their natural potentials. A caged bird is a sad sight, even if the bird has stopped desiring anything, or never had a clear-cut set of desires to begin with. Factory farmed animals could be drugged into desiring nothing, but it still seems like it's bad for a veal calf to be tethered to a narrow stall for life, and thus prevented from exercising his most basic capacities.

The desire-fulfillment theory is questionable because it focuses exclusively on desire, but also for another reason. The theory fuses together two things we might want to keep separate. When we think about an individual – say, a particular five-year-old child living in a specific place at a specific time – we might wonder about the basic, "built-in" value of her life. But then we might also think about how the child has fared so far and will fare in the future. Over her entire lifespan, how much good will there be in her life? Of course this depends a lot on the circumstances the child has been in and will be in, in the future. To attach value to a life on that basis is to make predictions about how things will go for the child. Built-in value is not so sensitive to circumstance. It's a matter of a life's potential, not the way it's actually going to play out.

Focusing on value "over a lifetime" instead of on "built-in" value can make it difficult to think about questions of life and death. Bill Gates has made extraordinary efforts to solve problems in the most destitute parts of the world. Suppose he is considering investing in a region afflicted with extreme poverty. The program he envisions will prevent children dying from easily treatable diseases, and might also include investments in schools and infrastructure. Alternatively, he could invest in a region that's much better off, but still troubled. Perhaps there's the same problem with easily treatable childhood diseases, but there is already considerable prosperity. Gates, let us imagine, is still a hard-headed investor because of his experience at the helm of Microsoft. Every day, there are thousands of unnecessary deaths that could easily be prevented, if resources are made available. He knows he can't save every life. So he's got to prioritize. Just like he wouldn't "save" divisions of the business that are worth less, he wouldn't want to save lives that are worth less – if such there be. Now, if he relies on the "over a lifetime" understanding of life-value, what's he going to think? Perhaps he will just be perplexed. The future of the lives in the destitute region isn't at all certain; not only is the future hard to predict, but the future in this region depends partly on whether he makes his investment in schools and infrastructure. But perhaps he'll conclude that those lives *are* worth less, because even if he does make his investment, the future will still be relatively bleak in this region, and lives will go less well than elsewhere.

I would rather see Gates make a decision based on the basic value of lives, the built-in value that doesn't depend on circumstances or how things will go in the future. This is consonant with a very deep-rooted belief that *we* are not our circumstances. The child is one thing, the environment she's placed within – which no doubt has a huge impact on the actual unfolding of her life – is another. By keeping the focus on the built-in value of each person's life, the potential, we stop ourselves from writing off a child based on shaky assumptions about the future. Moreover, we make room for hope. Yes, things look bleak in the more destitute region, but there's at least a chance that wise development will make a difference.

Now, at the very extremes the focus on built-in value might steer us wrong. There are lives that play out in situations that are utterly bleak, where the future is completely clear. Relative to such a place, hope might be naïve and might lead to the squandering of resources. Suppose there's a "factory" chicken farm – not really a farm at all, but a huge building lined with caged chickens – threatened by flooding, and the owner wants government resources to be spent on transporting the animals to a second chicken facility, where they'll be placed right back in the same circumstances. He tries to convince the authorities to take quick action by talking about the great built-in value of chickens. They really are quite amazingly intelligent, sociable creatures, he points out. Well, indeed they are. But their built-in capacities are never going to get a chance to be exercised in the confines of a "factory" chicken farm. They have a fixed and clear future, and it's not a good one. The value of the lives saved, in this rigidly controlled, predictably bleak situation, may as well be equated with the value they're going to have over time. But this is certainly the exception. Generally, it makes better sense to estimate a life's worth in terms of its potential. Nothing more is known with certainty, and to pretend we know more could mean denying the disadvantaged a fair chance at a good future.

If a life goes well or badly based (at least partly) on the way capacities are exercised, then what is built-in value, more precisely? It's natural to think of it in terms of capacities themselves. The more valuable of two lives is the one that *could* amount to more, over a lifetime, if both individuals had a chance to "be all that you can be." If capacities are what give value to a life, then to compare animal and human lives, we must compare animal and human capacities. Differences in capacities matter directly, and not just indirectly, as they do on the desire-fulfillment view of the value of lives. But now we have to confront a difficult question. Are human capacities superior to animal capacities?

Animal Lives

Human beings do have more orientation to the future and past, though some animals have some (as the last chapter suggested). People have a deeper and more multi-faceted sense of self, though some animals have some sense of self. People have the wherewithal to think in moral terms, even if rudimentary morality is present in some animals (as we've seen). We could go on and on. There's more creativity and culture in humans, though not a complete absence in animals. Animals have some level of autonomy, but people have more. There may be some aesthetic ability in animals, but there's more in people. All of these differences in capacity have a bearing on the worth of different lives, but not just these. Just as relevant are the running abilities of a cheetah, the migratory abilities of a whale, the loyalty of a wolf. All valuable abilities add to the value of lives.

We get the result that human lives are especially valuable *if* we attach special value to the capacities that humans have in particular abundance. But should we? The possibility of residual bias is brought out nicely in the children's movie *The Ant Bully*. A young boy is magically miniaturized and joins a colony of ants. After sharing their exploits and demonstrating ant-like virtuosity, he's finally accorded the highest praise: the queen ant proclaims he's achieved the greatest possible success – he's become an honorary ant! The important value-boosting capacities from an ant's perspective would not be the capacities we value most.

What are we doing when we attach particular value to self-consciousness, rationality, art, and the rest of the capacities at which we excel? Are we indulging in the distinctly human form of speciesism or are we being just plain reasonable? We can study the lives of animals with an open mind. We can try to be less arrogant and proud. But then we must make judgments, because real-world choices depend on doing so. The judgment most of us arrive at is that there is something special about our capacities and thus about us. The worry about latent speciesism ought to make us more humble, more open to new evidence, more tentative. But we have to move on with our understanding of the way things are, imperfect though it may be.

The Great Chain of Being picture of nature (Chapter 2) sees animals as ranging in perfection from the very lowly to the most exalted. Each species is a link in the chain, or a rung on the ladder, some exact distance from human beings, who are perched half-way between the other animals and celestial beings. Leaving the celestial half out of it, what are we to make of this image of an exact order? It's elegant, but surely we should expect the truth to be far less precise. There are many capacities to which we assign positive value, but we don't always have a definite idea of their relative values. If we're trying to rank bower birds, crows, and wolves, it depends what's more valuable, artistic ability (which favors the bower bird) or sheer intelligence (which favors the crow) or sociability (which favors the wolf). We're not going to be able to put these three species on separate rungs of a ladder, in any particular order, and neither is the situation quite as crisp as a straightforward tie. We just don't know how to assign them a place on the ladder, relative to each other.

We can make some comparisons with confidence, but life-value judgments are crude, and higher rankings emerge gradually, out of an accumulation of pluses, not all at once, based on some pivotal merit. We don't exalt typical members of a particular species on grounds simply that they have reason, or morality, or self-awareness. The various merits all affect our judgment in a non-formulaic manner. As you read books about a species, like Bernd Heinrich's books about crows, the realization that crows have many amazing capacities gradually elevates them, with no clear point where their lives start seeming worth more.

If we're biased in placing ourselves on a higher rung than other animals, it's a bias we can't avoid, but there's a related bias that we can and should avoid. That's the bias that says there's something special about other animals the more they are genetically and evolutionarily close to us. Thus, it's traditionally been assumed, primates are just below humans, and more precious than other species. All mammals are superior in ability to all birds, and so on. This is a kind of anthropocentrism that has been increasingly refuted by animal research in the last 20 years. Birds have been steadily rising in our estimation because of their surprising intelligence and even linguistic abilities. Marine mammals have many of the capacities of primates. Elephants are special animals with particularly complex social relations, prodigious memories, strong family bonds, powers of communication, and possibly even a sense of time and death. We may be at the top of the ladder, but the rest of the order is not an order that maps neatly onto biological distance from us. Animals with especially valuable lives don't necessarily look like us or share our genes or share the same recent ancestors.

It's not easy to weigh lives and make comparisons, and not possible to make comparisons with great precision, but make them we must. And now let's begin to see what they do for us.

After Katrina, the thoughts of policy-makers were probably simply the traditional ones. As much as we love our pets, animals are just animals. Humans are in an entirely different category. There's just no *real* question about who gets a seat, the person or the dog. The policy-makers were, of course, steeped in our culture's deep-rooted speciesism. But you can still construct a sound rationale for the policy if you replace speciesist prejudice with the considered judgments I've tried to make. A jeweler running out of his burning shop would run out with the gold and leave behind the silver. If animals really do have less-good lives, it means the people-first policy adopted was a sensible one.

At least, this was the best approach available in a bad situation. After the 2005 debacle, the Humane Society and the US government worked assiduously to avoid that situation ever repeating itself. Congress passed PETS, the Federal Pets Evacuation and Transportation Standards Act. Now provisions for pets would have to be included in disaster planning. In 2008, as Hurricane Ike was bearing down on the Gulf Coast, those plans were implemented. A massive evacuation brought thousands of people *and* their pets to facilities in neighboring states. My local news channel in Dallas showed images of pets being carefully tagged and kept in spacious cages that were ready for the purpose. Owners had no reason to stay behind with their pets this time – as some did in 2005. Granted, this hurricane turned out to be much milder than Katrina, but lessons had been learned, and if it had been worse, it looks like rescuers would have had far fewer occasions to insist (sadly, but correctly) that people had to be rescued first.

What follows from the general idea that human lives have special value? That we can do anything whatever to animals, that they exist to serve our purposes? Great Chain of Being thinkers sometimes did draw that lesson from humanity's place above the other animals. But what's the logic of that inference? They thought there was a supreme being resting on the top rung of the ladder, just as distant from us as we are from the lowest animals. They hardly thought God had unlimited rights to exploit and torment us – maybe with an overwhelming hurricane? – simply because of our inferiority. The belief in our prerogative to exploit animals has such instinctive appeal and tenacity that we can think we've supported it when we've done nothing of the kind. We must see, step-by-step, what privileges we are entitled to because of our special capacities (the rest of this chapter and Chapter 6). Just as much, we will need to see what prerogatives we are *not* entitled to (Chapters 7 and 8).

A Painful Question

If human lives really do have more value, does that make any difference when we are dealing with problems that don't have life-and-death import? During the Katrina debacle, medical units were eventually set up in New Orleans. Many people had suffered non-life-threatening injuries and there were not enough emergency workers to attend to them all. No doubt, there were pets as well in need of medical attention. Whose problems come first?

Now Singer's striking claim that all animals are equal becomes central. What does it mean, if *not* that animal lives have as much value as human lives? It means – he says, in the first chapter of *Animal Liberation* – that the exact same interests ought to receive the same response, whatever the species (or gender, or race, or whatever) of the interest owner. "To each according to his or her interests," as you might say. Emergency workers had a moral obligation to respond in just the same way to the same interest in pain alleviation, whether the pain's owner was male or female, black or white, human or not human. (Or, to be more precise, they had that obligation if there were no further interests at stake, whether interests of the victims, their friends and family, or any other affected or concerned party.)

Not as radical as the idea that all lives have equal value, this is still a radically egalitarian demand. It would force us to act very differently in all sorts of situations, as Singer is at pains to show throughout *Animal Liberation*. Yet, though Singer's egalitarianism is radical, it's also, in a way, modest, sane, and logical. How *could* there be a basis for responding in different ways to exactly the same pain?

It's not easy to see how, but perhaps not impossible. There are a couple of conceivable lines of defense for assigning higher priority to some pains than others. First, there is the thought that there are relationship factors that legitimately enter into our patterns of response. Up to a point, I *can* respond to equal pains differently if one belongs to my child, the other to yours. Likewise, someone might insist that their conspecifics are entitled to more of their consideration than members of other species. Reasonable?

The problem is that the analogy between family members and conspecifics is strained. I don't know about you, but an unfamiliar conspecific competing with me for scarce resources seems nothing like a family member. It's not even clear to what extent preference for family members is legitimate to begin with. Helping my child before other children seems fine, but nepotism is not fine. It's not so clear either how preferring conspecifics is different from preferring members of your own race (racism) or gender (sexism).

A second sort of thought is that pains actually *can* matter more and less depending on their possessors, that a normal human being's pain matters more than a dog's or a squirrel's. Of course, that wouldn't be because dogs and squirrels are furry and have tails. It's not because of our upright posture.

Rather, we must consider the possibility that differences in "whole life value" trickle down and make human problems matter more than animal problems.

In fact, there does seem to be a connection between how much a pain matters and the value of the sufferer's life. For one, pain isn't bad just because of what it feels like. It's also bad because it drains the value out of hours or days of our lives. Rather than experience an hour of intense pain, in most cases most of us would rather be in a dreamless sleep, in essence losing that hour of our life. In effect, pain causes you to lose a little Kahlua from your "bottle." Since there is less value to be lost in an animal's life, pain (like death) takes less from them.

If my headache is stopping me from writing a stunning piece of music, and a squirrel's headache is keeping him from racing up and down a tree pointlessly, it does seem as if my headache matters more. You could press the principle of equal consideration for equal interests into the service of explaining the difference; maybe headache relief would fulfill multiple interests for me, and a single interest for the squirrel. But what we're discovering is that the principle is (at best) emptier than it seems. Many apparent cases of equal interests are really nothing of the sort.

But maybe the principle really has to be rejected altogether. Take a case in which the very same pain sensation costs a human being and an animal the same thing. My headache stops me from pleasantly sitting around doing nothing. A squirrel's equally severe headache stops him from pleasantly sitting around doing nothing. So we have exactly the same interest in relief. Does it matter that my interest is satisfied exactly as much as it does if the squirrel's interest is satisfied?

It may seem so, but think of a limit case, a really primitive creature that suffers pain. Suppose there are tiny "pangfish" swimming around in a lake by the millions. I know it's not very realistic, but imagine they have headaches just like ours, and no other mental life. (How do we know about their headaches? Don't worry about that. We just do.) Occasionally people help out by tossing painkillers into the lake, and then the fish just float around in a semi-conscious haze. I'll grant that it would be better if the pangfish didn't have their headaches. The well-wishers really are doing them a kindness. But if I'm forced to adopt priorities, wouldn't it be alright if I placed their headaches lower on my list of things to deal with than comparable human headaches?

Well, would it? The case forces us to ask the most basic question of ethics. Why should I ever do anything for anyone? Why should I consider the problems of another creature *my* problems? Do I *have* to care about the pangfish?

The Utilitarian moral tradition that Singer belongs to provides an extremely simple answer. It's the problems themselves that compel a response. Pain is intrinsically bad, and I have a duty to reduce it. Pleasure is intrinsically good, and I should increase it. Or, on more complex variations on the Utilitarian theme – an unfulfilled desire is bad, a fulfilled desire is good. If you think this way about why I should be worried about anyone's problems, then you will think the pangfish really do warrant a considerate response. They've got pain, pain is bad, and I should reduce it as much as I can.

But there is another very natural way to think about obligations. The alternative is to think there are really two steps to grasping an obligation. First, you recognize another individual as having a pull on you. In the most traditional moral thinking, the pull is due to a social role or relationship. The other individual is your mother, your child, your priest, your president, your commander, your tribesman. Or perhaps the other individual has done something for you in the past. A more enlightened outlook may take account of roles, relationships, and past deeds, but also looks beyond them and finds at least some grounds of obligation in individuals themselves; all human beings thus have a pull on us. We owe them consideration because of some special power or merit that's universal (or nearly so). We must care about other human beings because they are rational or moral, for example, or the thought might be that we owe things to others because we have an implicit agreement to help each other, or at least not hinder each other. In any event, recognizing another individual as generally being owed consideration is step one. After that, the question is what the individual's problem is – do they need headache relief, or food, or fresh air, or education, or what? How you will respond depends on the level of consideration you adopt in step one and on your assessment of the problem – is it serious, trivial, central, peripheral? There are two steps here, not one.

On this way of thinking, the pangfish are owed some level of consideration, anywhere from none to a great deal, depending on the first step. And the thing is, the proper level seems to be much closer to none. The fish are so primitive that there is really nothing about them that could make you feel that you owed them anything. That doesn't mean their pains aren't bad and don't matter. It does mean we can't be expected to feel much of the regard and respect that would have to precede the sense that we ought to do something for them. The pains of the pangfish pull on us a little like dents on an old car. Dents aren't good, but it takes caring about the car as a whole to do anything to get involved in repairs.

Now, what does it take for an individual, as a whole, to elicit a moral response? One possibility is that there's a trigger property. You've got "moral traction" if you have it, and not if you don't. So consideration is a yes/no affair: an individual is owed full consideration or no consideration. A case in point: recall from Chapter 2 that Immanuel Kant thought we must have respect for individuals who can grasp ultimate moral principles – in fact, he thought they were owed "infinite" respect – and none for individuals who can't; therefore, there are very strict duties to the morally savvy, and no duties at all to the morally ignorant.

Respect makes plenty of sense as a necessary antecedent of moral consideration. But what elicits it? In fact many things, and some of them are to be found in animals. Intelligence, autonomy, creativity, nurturing, skill, resilience, and innumerable other assets elicit respect, and so (in a low-level, imperceptible way) does consciousness itself. The sheer fact that a real mouse is a conscious entity, unlike a wind-up toy mouse, is impressive.

The pangfish, then, count a little, but even if we are as open-minded as we can be, there's not a lot about them that elicits respect: at most, their sheer capacity for consciousness. Granted the general sense that we ought to increase happiness and decrease pain has some clout, and does make the behavior of well-wishers not irrational. But I really don't have the same basis for tending to their problems that I would have if a child had a headache, or even the squirrel in my backyard. The squirrel is actually a pretty clever fellow, the way he's able to collect nuts, hide them for the winter, and find them again. If the cleverness is largely hard-wired, it's still clever. And his conscious life seems obviously much more complex than that of the pangfish. But in the child there are vastly more things to respect. And so we will reasonably respond in different ways to the different creatures.

David DeGrazia's term for the nuanced view I am defending is "the sliding scale model." On this view (which he ascribes to no one), "Animals deserve consideration in proportion to their cognitive, emotional, and social complexity." He admits it's a view that appeals to intuition and common sense, but writes "We cannot responsibly accept it without an explicit, compelling justification for giving less-than-equal consideration to animals ..." The presumption is that unequal consideration makes no sense, he says, so a reason must be found to support it. I offer the points above as reasons.

I admit that it can sound harsh and elitist to say that differences in whole lives justify differences in amounts of consideration. People who genuinely admire and feel concern for all animals of all kinds are naturally reluctant to make comparisons. Animal psychologists Leslie Rogers and Gisela Kaplan wisely say we should "guard against, or at least be very cautious about, the temptation of creating a scale of lesser or greater value of one species over another," but I believe the second alternative will suffice. We should be very cautious. But once we recognize a rough, sketchy scale, we do have to recognize it makes a general difference to the way we regard members of different species, both when lives are at stake and when other circumstances force us to set priorities.

People and People

Escaping the forces of prejudice as much as we possibly can, there are still grounds for seeing animals and people as not quite equal, or so I have argued. This inequality doesn't immediately open the floodgates to all the ways we have exploited animals in the past. Why emphasize it though? Don't most people already, out of sheer bias, have low enough regard for animals? Why work so hard to demonstrate differences?

For one, measured inequality – the sliding scale – is not at all the same as the extreme inequality that's been thought to separate humans from other animals. It's not the same as what speciesists have always believed in anyway. It raises the status of animals to see them in the nuanced way I am suggesting. But it's also important *not* to elevate animals to a status we can't seriously regard them as possessing. When animal advocacy and egalitarianism are too tightly coupled, those who reject the latter may also reject the former. So, ironically enough, it's out of a concern for animals (as well as sheer truth) that I'm going to persevere here and defend the idea that all animals are *not* equal. It needs defense against an objection that will occur to anyone who's spent even a little time with the animal ethics literature.

Throughout that literature, "marginal cases" are forever being used to leverage better treatment for animals. Marginal cases are intellectually impaired children or adults. Genetically, they are people, but in every other respect they are like (we are to suppose) non-human animals. Their thoughts and feelings, and their general capacities, are comparable to those of a member of another species. One "marginal case" (the term is not winsome) might have roughly the capacities of a normal chimpanzee.

The marginal cases maneuver could easily be used against the conclusions reached in this chapter. Here's how this would go: "If animals are not our equals, because of their comparatively limited capacities, then normal people and 'marginal cases' are not equals either, because of the compara-tively limited capacities of the latter. They too should have been left off the first buses out of New Orleans, and given lower priority at triage centers. But that's absurd. So animals are not actually unequal to us because of their limited capacities. And there's no justification for giving either their lives or their pains lower priority."

In a practical sense, the marginal cases maneuver is unfortunate. In a deeply speciesist culture, comparing people with disabilities to animals comes across as an insult to the disabled. It might even have an unintended effect: lowering the status of the disabled instead of raising the status of animals. We are not, after all, securely past the day when people with dis-abilities *were* regarded with scorn or pity, and treated as second class. There's also something objectionable here from an animal-friendly perspective. Animals are not just humans with reduced capacities. They have their own capacities, their own spectrum of aptitudes and behaviors. No, an impaired human being is not very much like a normal chimpanzee.

But never mind all these problems. Clearly, the animal advocates are assuming that people with disabilities are *not* second class: they are assum-ing they *are* the equals of everyone else, despite their reduced abilities. And we're not supposed to take the comparison between animals and humans as an exact one. Looking just at the gist of the argument, and ignoring the infelicities, does it succeed in proving that all animals are equal after all?

Most of us have an instinct to say there's a difference: it's appalling to leave people with disabilities off the buses or make them wait for medical treatment, but OK to do the same to animals. If we see it that way only under the influence of speciesist bias, then we should get a grip and force ourselves to see things anew. But if there's a reasonable basis for seeing the situations differently, then that's another matter. Which is it? What's going on when we think one way about animals, and another way about humans with (sort of) animal-like abilities?

Sometimes we give preference to "marginal" humans because they are our relatives. After Katrina many of the infirm and impaired had family members who certainly had a reason to push for their best interests. But then, what's the reason for everyone else to accommodate the urgings of kin? And what of the elderly or disabled who had no family members to advocate for them? It doesn't seem that family ties are the whole answer to our question. They sometime exist and may make a legitimate difference, but they don't fully explain why "marginal" cases are generally entitled to better treatment than animals.

Our special concern for the incapacitated can certainly be dissociated from malign speciesist thinking. In fact, the thoughts we have about people with impairments make good sense. The infirm elderly have lost powers they once had, we think. The disabled may have lost powers, or may have never had them; they've had worse luck than others. A normal chimpanzee, by contrast, has lost nothing and is not unlucky. When people are impaired – less capable than before, or than they "should" have been – we don't simply think of them as *sui generis*, simply as the kind of thing they've come to be. That would be to ignore their trajectories through life and their missed chances; it would be to ignore the way their lives extend through time and tell a story. It makes sense to be extra distressed by the combination of the original misfortune and the prospect of a person being left behind.

Our extra sympathy is no doubt bound up with a bundle of what-ifs. What if I'm in that position some day? What if it were my child? What if it were my parent? The extra sympathy we feel is connected to our own sense of vulnerability, or even a desire to lay the groundwork for our own future protection. All the more reason to be extra-protective. These thoughts may be somewhat egocentric, but they're not flat out selfish or directly related to feelings of species-based superiority.

Our feelings of extra concern for the elderly and incapacitated are understandable and possibly benign, but let's not leave it at that. There's more than all-of-the-above involved when we affirm that all human beings are equal. Human equality is one of the profoundest tenets of civilized societies, enshrined in the famous words of the Declaration of Independence: "We hold these truths to be self-evident, that all men are created equal, that they are endowed by their Creator with certain unalienable Rights, that among these are Life, Liberty and the pursuit of Happiness." Though this is holy writ and very beautiful, "created equal" does not qualify as a clear and reasoned explanation why humans are equals only of each other. Can we coherently explain why equality extends to the species boundary and not beyond?

Choosing Equality

Affirming human equality is deeply important, but before we give that any more thought, let's notice that we don't actually *always* affirm human equality. Comparative judgments about the value of whole lives do lurk in the background of some of our ordinary, unobjectionable decision-making. So the pattern of thought that applies legitimately to animals isn't totally inapplicable when we are thinking about human beings.

Two acquaintances are both trying to raise funds to pay for expensive, experimental medical procedures. In an ideal world, both people would get their treatments. But if a choice must be made, must we ignore everything else we know about the two people? It seems not: an individual's life, taken as a whole, is one permissible consideration – one of many – at least in some situations. Quite reasonably, we want to contribute to "a good cause," and some people's lives seem more like a good cause, and some less.

That doesn't mean we have license to be insensitive or arbitrary. We can't be indifferent to John's acute problem, but care about Jane's no more acute problem, because Jane is a slightly better pianist. But overall differences between the lives of two people are not ruled out as morally irrelevant when we decide how much to care about some problem they have in common. If you think back on a time when you helped, or didn't help, you probably won't discover anything extremely simple – that you care more about the sufferings of creative people, or that morally admirable people are always the ones who elicit your greatest concern, or that smart people matter more to you, or industrious people matter more. But you may very well discover that all these factors add together in indeterminate ways, giving some people more pull on your compassion than others.

Responding to whole people first, and then to their problems "accordingly," is a matter of course in private settings, but there are limits. We don't want firefighters or paramedics to arrive at the scene of a fire and make more or less effort depending on the worthiness of victims. We want doctors, judges, paramedics, teachers, and others to treat us as if all our lives were the same, even if they aren't. None of us really thinks our assets are so glaring, and so obvious to all, that we'd be safe in a world where on-the-spot assessments were made by the people who are pivotal to our basic welfare. So professional codes are drawn up that guarantee the same treatment for all. Throughout our lives, we all enjoy the security that results from this sort of enforced equality. Whatever distributional problems result – e.g. the saint gets too little, the sinner gets too much – everyone consents to the system.

Of course, equality is the assumption in many other areas of social life, determining who gets voting rights, job opportunities, a public education, health coverage, and innumerable other "social goods." Presumably in all these cases, we have good, essentially self-interested reasons to choose equality, but let's stick to the sort of case at hand. Must we choose equality between humans and animals too, feigning blindness to interspecies differences? If we choose equality for ourselves, must we choose it for all members of all species? A practical problem is that this would increase the population of creatures needing services. It's not only pets that needed treatment after Katrina, but farm animals and wild creatures too. There were drowning rats, trapped squirrels, injured birds. Obviously, there wasn't the time, money, or personnel to provide equal treatment to all. It would have been literally impossible.

Feigning blindness to species differences is also problematic because animals can't agree to do it. Ordinary and extraordinary people (so to speak) agree that professionals should be blind to the differences; the extraordinary, in essence, give up their rightful place at the head of the line and a better way of life results for all, one less marred by fear, insecurity, and invidious comparison. But apes don't give up their right to be favored over mice and it wouldn't make sense for us to make ourselves their proxies and give it up for them. When people do favor apes over mice, the impact isn't what it is in the human case: the result is *not* a generalized fear of winding up in the less favored position. Such fears are beyond the powers of animals to feel.

We choose to see each other as equals in many settings for the benefits that pretense has for all who are prepared to buy into it. (See Chapter 6 for more on equality, and why we choose it.) But it is not the truth of the matter, and not something we must abide by in every setting. There's nothing that says we must make that choice across the board, giving equal status to literally every sentient creature, or even all creatures great and small.

––––––––––––––

It's one thing to purge ourselves of bias against animals – by all means, we should. Our responses to animals should have a basis in reason and evidence, not in human pride and speciesist prejudice. But freed of bias, we have many ways of approaching animals open to us. Radical egalitarianism is not the only approach, and not the most plausible.

Members of different species have lives with different amounts of value, and this matters; it matters when lives have to be saved, but also when it's not a matter of life or death. Pain interferes with life as usual, so it's got to vary how crucial it is to alleviate pain. Furthermore, our initial response is to the whole individual; that's what establishes respect and some level of obligation, great or small. With that response in place, we will decide whose suffering to alleviate, whose happiness to increase, whose potential to fulfill, whose liberty to protect. Or perhaps we'll ignore that initial response, as we do by agreement in some of our dealings within our own human society. But in general, the value of an individual's life has moral significance. The sliding scale model is not just intuitive, but reasonable.

As soon as we reject equality and recognize differences, our speciesist instincts are likely to come flooding back. We're eager to think the differences are huge, and such as to justify the status quo. "Aha, animals are not our equals, so we can do practically anything to them for our own benefit!" But that is not at all the conclusion we should draw. *All* that we've seen so far is that we *can* save humans before animals in a disaster, and respond to human suffering before equal animal suffering. But that's a small piece of the whole pie. What we most often confront is not the question how we must help animals, but how we may use them to serve our purposes. Carefully, cautiously, step-by-step, we'll explore that question.

Enough now about evacuation and triage. Let's think about what's for dinner.

6

Caveman Ethics

Every day we take for granted a vast number of ways of exploiting animals for our own benefit. We yoke them and use their labor, we take away their incubating eggs and the milk meant for their young, we shear the coats they grow for their own warmth, and we kill them to supply ourselves with food, leather, and innumerable other goods and benefits. We even kill them just for the sport of it. All these things are so familiar it's hard to even get a purchase on the problem. So let us avoid the excessively familiar and confront a very simple question: what rationale could people have given when they first started to use animals to meet their needs, way back at the proverbial dawn of time?

The permissibility of killing for survival seems like a given. But when we give the matter closer attention, it's surprisingly hard to say anything coherent about it. I can't kill you for survival, and you can't kill me. So why are animals fair game? These questions seem almost silly, but if we don't understand the ethics of killing to stay alive, then we can't expect to understand the ethics of the things we do on a daily basis, for less urgent reasons. Did all of this exploitation of animals *ever* make sense, and if it did, did it ever *stop* making sense? Our survey will take us far and wide, and hopefully roaming into unfamiliar territory will give us a fresh perspective on our current problems.

The "Ur" Problem

Consider, if you will, Mr. Caveman, a Paleolithic hunter-gatherer, who's about to hurl a spear into the side of an aurochs – the massive six-foot tall "ur ox" that's the ancestor of today's cattle. Nearby, his mate and children are watching, and counting on him to save them from starvation. He'll throw the spear because it's natural, and he's hungry, and it's what he's supposed to do for his family. If by some miracle he asks whether it's right, what's the answer?

It's tempting to say that it must be right because of all of the above: it's natural, and he's hungry, and it's what he's supposed to do for his family. But it's easy to think of cases where all of those things are true, and desperate actions are understandable but still not right. In a crowded refugee camp in the contemporary world, some people will cut in line, steal from each other, sneak extra portions – all no doubt natural, and due to hunger, and expected – but strictly speaking not pure as the driven snow, not innocent. You could say, "It's OK because the aurochs is just an animal," but we've decided to keep speciesism under close watch, and that rationalization is much too dismissive to be warranted.

Considering how basic killing-to-survive is, it's strange that it isn't more often discussed. For example, it's never discussed by Tom Regan in his important 1983 book *The Case for Animal Rights*. Animals have rights just like people do, he thinks; in particular, they have a right to be treated with respect owing to the sheer fact that they are sentient beings with lives and interests of their own. So the violent and degrading things we shouldn't do to people are also things we shouldn't do to animals. Animal agriculture, experimentation, and sport hunting should all come to an end. Is there an exception for hungry Mr. Caveman?

There are some exceptions. If you're an Eskimo being attacked by a polar bear, yes you can kill her in self-defense. (And then why not eat the corpse, especially if you're at risk of starvation?) But in the "ur" scenario, self-defense isn't the issue. Most of the animals that humans contemplate killing for food are not threats to them. They're herbivores, like the aurochs. Or they're too small to be threatening, like birds, rabbits, and the like. Or even if they're carnivores, they pose no imminent danger.

A "prevention" situation is also morally exceptional, Regan says. For example, four men and a dog are on a boat that's sinking. If just one is thrown overboard, the rest will survive. If none, then no one survives. Regan assumes someone's got to go, and it ought to be the dog, since, though the dog does have rights, his life is not destined to be as rich. Regan is one of the many animal advocates today who admit that animal lives do have less value (though when animals have unusual talents and humans unusual deficits, there can be exceptions). The differences are not black and white, as we saw in the last chapter, but if the dog survives, he's not going to have deep friendships, read poetry, struggle much with morality, or discover the laws of nature. So the dog has the least to lose. That's crucial to Regan's thinking, and so is the fact that the dog isn't being lifted out of a safe situation and used to solve someone else's problems. The problems the four men are facing are his problems as well.

Does this help sort out Mr. Caveman's problem? Unfortunately, No. Just as the "ur" scenario doesn't involve self-defense, it's also not a prevention situation. There Mr. Caveman stands, poised to hurl his spear into the aurochs. If he does nothing, the animal will be fine. She's got plenty of vegetation to fill her stomach. There's no denying that Mr. Caveman is about to lift her out of a safe situation and use her to solve problems that are his own. Bottom line: survival hunting *isn't* in a special category and, as far as Regan is concerned, Mr. Caveman should put down his spear.

Utilitarian ethics tell Mr. Caveman to do whatever makes for the greatest balance of pleasure over pain (or on some versions, fulfilled interests over unfulfilled interests), when all sentient creatures are taken into account. If killing the massive aurochs takes away 10 units of animal happiness but produces 50 units of human happiness, the caveman has the green light. Total happiness in the world has been increased. This reasoning makes Mr. Caveman's survival hinge on some pretty shaky assumptions. If he's lucky enough to be a very happy caveman surrounded by miserable animals, the math may work out in his favor. But perhaps times are lean and the next ice-age looms; life is not happy at all for him, but happier for the better-adapted animals in his midst. Now he may not be entitled to do any hunting.

Is Utilitarianism the right moral approach, to begin with? The literature on this question is vast but it doesn't take long to generate some doubts. A Utilitarian takes every unit of pleasure or pain in all seriousness, but not so much the individuals who have the pleasure or pain. This could lead to behavior that's respectful to no one. Everyone in the clan wants a red feather from the Scarlet Wonderbird. They're pretty adornments. Sadly for the Wonderbird, she's densely feathered, so by killing just one of her, 100 people get that little bit of pleasure for a long, long time. The happiness-math justifies the killing, but concern for individuals doesn't. It's not good for the bird to be killed, and it's no more than trivially good for any individual to get the feather. Respect and concern don't mandate Wonderbird hunting, while Utilitarianism seems to.

Respect

What we want in an ethical caveman is a well-tuned attitude of respect, and action that expresses it. The question is whether respecting animals as much as they deserve to be respected would stop him from killing the aurochs. There's no question that it's disrespectful to end an animal's life, then dismember her and turn her into stew. That's clear. So – end of story? And end of Mr. Caveman?

Imagine the caveman reveling in respect for animals, and unable to bring himself to spear the aurochs … or a rabbit, or a squirrel, or a bird. He stands idly by, admiring the wildlife while he and his kin gradually grow colder and weaker for lack of nourishment, warm clothing, and shelter. There seems to be something wrong with this fellow. It's not just that he must be lacking the normal human instincts and emotions; he seems to not see things right.

I suspect what the idle caveman doesn't see is that he and his fellows have a right to be treated with respect too. Granted, just letting someone expire or letting yourself expire is not a case of *using* someone. The caveman won't be manufacturing anything out of his family, actually imbibing or wearing them. But using isn't the only way of disrespecting. Standing by idly while someone fades away, or letting yourself fade away, can involve disrespect as well.

There's something else the caveman ought to see. Two individuals can both have a right to be treated with respect, but one can have more respect due to him than the other. One can simply be more deserving of respect. Having the same right makes them out to be equals. But if there's a big difference in the respect they deserve, inequality lurks under the surface. This is not radical inequality – one gets infinite respect and the other none. We are looking again at the possibility of a sliding scale model (to use David DeGrazia's term once more – see Chapter 5), with respect being proportioned to capacities. There may be more for the caveman to respect in himself (and fellow humans) than in the aurochs.

If respect is so fundamental, we'd better be clear what it is and isn't. It isn't reverence, another attitude that's been stressed in the literature about animals. The great humanitarian Albert Schweitzer defended vegetarianism on the basis of an ethics of "reverence for life." Reverence is tied up with awe, wonder, and maybe even worship. For the caveman to revere the aurochs in front of him is practically to treat her like a god (or goddess). Is there something about all animals that makes reverence an apt response to them? You can just about see revering the magnificent aurochs, but it seems too much to think we must revere every field mouse, every squirrel, or even every human being. Schweitzer talks about revering worms, gently moving them to the side of a road after it rains; he talks about keeping the lights off at night, so moths don't get too close and overheat; he talks about revering the clovers in a field … and goes on to make icicles (living things?) seem sublime. These are the responses of a saint or a poet to the natural world, not the responses everyone is obliged to have.

Respect is something else. In the hands of Immanuel Kant, respect is what we feel toward persons because of their dignity, which is founded on their grasp of "the moral law." That, and nothing else, gives human beings intrinsic worth, indeed "infinite worth." The philosopher Kwame Anthony Appiah makes an interesting observation about Kantian respect in his recent book *Experiments in Ethics*. Though it's something to be accorded equally to every human being, its roots are in hierarchical arrangements. The verbiage in Kant calls to mind the attitude a subject would have to a monarch, a slave would have to the master, a plebeian would have to a patrician, or a child would have to a parent. Respect has invisible ties to attitudes of inferiors to their superiors, though Kant democratizes it, making it what every rational human being is entitled to.

In point of fact, there are many other things besides morality that elicit respect. We respect people for their musical talent, their emotional sensitivity, their ingenuity, their cooking. Really, all things we admire elicit feelings of respect. Respect changes over time as we learn more about an individual. It's not black and white, and not governed by one specific trait. Respect is what we feel when we see the value in things, esteem them, take them seriously. It contrasts with denigrating or ignoring. Since it does key off of all valuable traits, we have it for animals, but we have it to different degrees. An animal that's highly intelligent and sociable, that possesses rudimentary morality and complex social emotions, will garner more respect than a more primitive, less intelligent animal.

Like Kant, Tom Regan thinks of respect as a response to a single characteristic. For Kant, the characteristic is grasp of "the moral law." For Regan, it's something far more crude: the characteristic of being a "subject of a life." We respect the sheer fact that a creature has its own life, a well-being of its own. The characteristic is present in huge numbers of members of the animal kingdom. Where it *is* present, it's present no more in one individual than in another. Regan does admit differences between animals, and even differences in life value, but denies that the basic right to be treated with respect varies with these differences. The same basic respect should be accorded to mice and men.

It's true that being a subject of a life is a pivotal characteristic. Given that an animal has it, we must ask ourselves what it is like to be that animal – what feelings an animal has, what matters to the animal. But some individuals have "more of a life" than others. Though it's fair to say every creature with a life has a right to be treated with respect, they are not all owed exactly the same *amount* of respect.

Once we feel respect, we are in a position to treat an individual respectfully. We think the individual's well-being matters. We become sensitive to what really matters in her life. That might be relationships or freedom or opportunities for knowledge or creativity, or just simple happiness and freedom from pain. It could really be anything. But we begin by appreciating the whole of the individual and then work "inward," considering how we ought to respond to her various problems and interests.

The respectful caveman faces a dilemma. The aurochs has a right to be treated with respect, and not being speared matters to her a great deal. He and his family have a right to be treated with respect, and eating matters to them a great deal. It's not possible for him to give everyone, the aurochs, himself, and his family, all possible respect. Schweitzer plainly avoids confronting this. The ethics of *reverence* for life abjures comparisons. Every life gets infinite respect – at least verbally. But in practice, no. The clover does have to be cut, if *necessary* to feed the cow. The lab animal does have to be sacrificed, if *necessary* to carry out a significant and well-designed life-saving experiment. But what determines when *this* individual's death is necessary for *that* individual's life? In every one of Schweitzer's examples, the answer is clear but unstated. It's the lesser being's death that's occasionally, tragically, necessary for the higher being's life. And this seems essentially right.

There's a comparative judgment that we must sometimes make in these situations, but not a calculation along Utilitarian lines. Killing the Scarlet Wonderbird is not necessary just because it would give 100 people a kick to have a red feather. In a modern setting, a baby seal's death is not necessary just because it would give an affluent mother in Paris great pleasure to buy her toddler a soft and warm fur hat. The feather doesn't matter to the feather-lovers and the fur hat doesn't seriously matter to the mother or her toddler. What's driving a thoughtful judgment that A's death is necessary for B's life is a more subtle assessment of what respectfulness entails in that situation. It's a judgment sensitive to all sorts of factors, among them the nature of creatures A and B.

In the case of the caveman and the aurochs, the judgment will let him (finally!) throw his spear. Even if he's wracked by ambivalence because he does find much to respect in the aurochs, he does the right thing. If he kills the animal, he's still given everything all due respect.

Carnivores and Cannibals

This account of Mr. Caveman's rationale for killing is going to have many ramifications in the rest of this book, so we'd better be clear about it and give it further thought. I'm saying the caveman can justify killing the aurochs even though it's disrespectful. The justification turns on two thoughts: (1) Respect for himself and human others propels him to do the deed. After all (we are assuming), he and the others would die if they didn't eat. And wanting to avoid death isn't a "mere desire" but a desire connected to esteem for himself and others. And (2) while respect for the aurochs tends to stop him from carrying out the killing, he justifiably has less respect for the aurochs. Thus, all things considered, respect militates for the killing, not against it.

This is the way I would propose we think about other dilemmas concerning animals. We ought to decide whether respect militates for a course of action or against it. This will involve asking the same sorts of questions. When a course of action seems disrespectful on its face – we are about to kill, harm, hurt, restrict, or use an animal – we ought to ask (1) whether we have self-respecting goals in doing so. Is it a "mere desire" that's motivating us, or do we have a more serious and compelling goal connected to self-respect and respect for others? And then we should ask (2) what level of respect must we have for the potential victim? Respect will sometimes side with us and sometimes with the animals we have designs on.

Though just a rough outline for thinking things through, and nothing like a crisp algorithm, this will rule some things out as well as rule some things in. Yes to Mr. Caveman, no to the Parisian mother and the Wonderbird hunters. But further thought is needed. The rationale I'm offering to the caveman may seem like "too much," from one perspective, but like "too little" from another.

You might say that (1) and (2) are "too much" to expect by way of justification – such strong claims can't be needed to justify what the caveman does. That's what you may think if you look at the caveman and aurochs as just another predator and prey, as basically two animals. If we imagine animal carnivores trying to justify their killings, they will often be unable to invoke anything comparable to (2). So why should the caveman have to?

Take a miraculously reflective lion who's about to pounce on a gazelle. He gets as far as (1) but stumbles on (2). I'm sure a determined lion looking to seem righteous could dream up a reason why his life actually is more valuable. He's a hunter, and that's impressive. The grazing gazelle is a docile lightweight, in his eyes. But in our eyes, it's another matter. The value of a gazelle's life just doesn't seem much different from the value of a lion's. If you take the proposed rationale seriously for all carnivores, the morally scrupulous lion is going to have to rush around trying to fill up on worms.

Of course you might just not take it seriously. There aren't really any miraculously reflective lions. But that doesn't seem like enough of an answer. If (1) and (2) are really a good guide to right and wrong *for us*, it seems as if it ought to be possible to plant them in the breast of anyone – adult, child, beast, angel, demon – and get good results. Whether these plantings are fanciful or not seems beside the point.

Then again, (1) plus (2) might seem like too little justification for killing, if you change the cast of characters from caveman and aurochs to two people. Under better-eats-worse logic, the least perfect specimens of humanity will be eaten by the most perfect in times of famine. When people need organ transplants, the much less capable will get rounded up and sent into surgery. If two people are lost in the wild, struggling to stay alive, a huge asymmetry between their character and talents will permit the better to devour the worse. None of this seems the least bit right.

With objections coming in from all sides like this, there's a temptation to abandon ship. We can arrive at all the right verdicts, intuitively speaking, if we just accept a dramatic distinction between humans and animals. We are related as sacred to profane. Humans are virtually inviolable, almost never expendable just to satisfy the needs of another. Animals are bits of the natural world, almost always expendable to satisfy the needs of another (human or animal). If you'll draw that line, then the caveman really doesn't need to work overtime to justify killing the aurochs. As Aristotle says, animals exist to feed us. They are in another class altogether. Humans, on the other hand, are utterly misunderstood if construed as food.

How reassuring to look at the world that way, and for everything to fall into place so easily! As a teacher of mine used to say (in response to strained philosophical theses), "Believe it if you can." I can't believe it, so I must try to understand what (if anything) justifies the caveman *without* simply writing off the aurochs as a hunk of meat. Let's see if we can stick with the justification I've outlined, and see if we can respond to the problems of the carnivore and the cannibal.

According to the rationale I've given the caveman, humans can kill cattle to save their lives, without moral error; the cattle have lesser lives. Whales can kill krill. Cats can maybe kill mice. But the lion who dines on the gazelle and the grizzly bear who dines on lost hikers are unwitting transgressors. I propose we just bite the bullet: yes, it's wrong, but of course it's also natural. It should come as no surprise that the natural order is not a moral order. Some things that are normal can't be given an ethicist's seal of moral approval. It doesn't mean we should intervene. We can teach our children not to bully (maybe bullying is natural). We can teach soldiers not to rape and plunder after vanquishing the enemy (it's always been done, and maybe it's natural). Naturalists can intervene here and there and prevent the misdeeds of amoral wildlife. But we shouldn't mount some massive campaign to keep predation within moral limits.

Remaking the whole natural world to meet our standards seems to suppress another sort of respect we ought to have, besides respect for individual animals. That fantastically complex world of living things has evolved and thrived on earth for a couple of billion years. Anybody who studies biology and gets up close to the natural world is inevitably filled with awe. We've intruded on it with industry, clear-cutting, carbon-emissions, unsustainable levels of hunting and grazing, all of which are flagrant negatives. But moralizing and micromanaging are intrusive too. The imperative to leave nature alone, to thrive by its own logic, is much more resounding than the imperative to fix things everywhere, to give the lion a makeover so that he measures up to our standards. Random acts of kindness – protecting the baby whale being chased by a team of orcas, defending the birds in the backyard – are merciful and satisfying, but turning ourselves into overbearing masters of the natural world is another matter.

So much for carnivores. If it takes thoughts like (2) to make their killings permissible, they are not always in the right, but there is wisdom in offering them forbearance. But now let's consider cannibals. If we agree that (1) plus (2) suffice to make a killing permissible, we might have cornered ourselves into too much forbearance!

The Social Contract

First, consider what you would think about a cannibalistic scenario set in the pre-historic world. The caveman is having a really hard time of it – berries are few, animals are scarce. So he and his tribe-mates conduct raids on the neighboring Dummy Tribe. Suppose that these folks really are dummies, and not just perceived as such by their biased neighbors. They hate to do it, but out of respect for themselves, Mr. Caveman and his friends go people-hunting, thinking that their neighbors are entitled to less respect than themselves. Not pretty, but is that actually deplorable? Should they let themselves go extinct?

But now think of the hungry "superiors" as eating inferior members of their own tribe, or fast forward to the modern world (just to forestall a tendency to be tolerant of people who are far away, long ago, and exotic). It doesn't seem like a good idea to round up people with very low IQs to feed them to the smarter members of the community, in times of famine. And yet, the justification I'm handing to Mr. Caveman seems to let us do so. Is something amiss?

The answer, I think, is that placing predator and prey into a single community does add new dimensions to the problem. So in the human case, there really are considerations beyond (1) and (2). That doesn't mean Mr. Caveman ought to have more complicated thoughts about killing the aurochs.

The issue of equality (see Chapter 5) is germane again here. Recall the question there was whether the old and incapacitated could have been left off the first buses leaving New Orleans. Once again, in a cannibalistic scenario we would surely feel a special sympathy for the losses or ill-luck of our fellows. Furthermore, the public servants who might have to carry out such a scheme would be expected to ignore differences, by general consent. We might also want to appeal to the very basic idea of a social contract that people who live together in a single community implicitly make with each other, for mutual benefit.

The benefit of a no-cannibalism agreement is clear. In *The Road*, Cormac McCarthy's vision of a post-apocalyptic world, nothing living remains but a few human survivors who scavenge through burnt out houses for scraps of food. The most vulnerable – the old and young – are hunted by bands of survivors. A man and his child journey through this bleak landscape, going years between interactions with other human beings. Though they are determined to still be "good guys," as the child puts it, other people cannot be counted on. All lose out on the benefits of community and cooperation. They are living in the state of nature, as the social contract tradition puts it, and paying a terrible price, even if cannibalism keeps the strongest alive a little longer.

Possibly it's too late for the survivors in that bleak world, who have little to gain by cooperating, but the social contract tradition imagines that all of us once lived in a state of nature, and did have reason to agree to a kind of laying down of arms that includes not killing, not stealing, not restricting basic liberties, not eating each other or using each other as organ banks. There are many rules of behavior we would agree to in a kind of founding constitutional convention.

Now, children and the incapacitated don't have the attributes of reason and self-interest, so can't be thought of as parties to this sort of an agreement. It's up to the normal adult framers to determine their status. But knowing that this decision could affect their own relatives and children and even possibly themselves, it makes sense for the framers to be generous, giving them full rights. Under the social contract we've implicitly agreed to, the stronger cannot eat the weaker, however much they may differ in the capacities that give value to our lives and create grounds for respect.

Would it make sense for the contractors to give animals full rights? If their motive for contracting with others is self-interest, then surely not. It's simply not in their interests to include animals, making it impossible to justify killing them even for purposes of survival.

If the social contract component of morality were the whole story, then animals would be completely out in the cold. We'd have carte blanche to treat them in any which way. But even many social contract theorists see it as only part of the story. There is more to morality than the limits we'd place on ourselves in a self-interested agreement with those we find threatening. There is also the simple right to be treated with respect that things have just in their very nature. Apart from any conventions and agreements, we'd be wrong to see a person as a mere thing, using bulldozers for crowd control, for example, or being indifferent to the suffering of others. When we are dealing with other people, we can often give more than one reason why we must do what we must do. I'll help a lost child because the child is scared and needs help; her well-being immediately and directly matters to me. I'll also do so because I've got an implicit contract with other parents, agreed to out of sheer self-interest, to look out for each other's children. If we just have one of these layers when we are deciding how to treat animals, it is still something substantial.

Most social contract theorists devote very few pages to the animal issue, creating an impression of dismissal. The main part of morality is for humans only, and animals are just thrown a few scraps when the feast is over. But acknowledging a social dimension of morality that applies just to human beings doesn't have to be dismissive. If we do owe animals respect – even just respect proportional to the value of their lives – there are vast numbers of things we will have to stop doing, out of respect for them. It's no slur against animals that there are even more limits on what we can do to human "others," since we *both* owe them basic respect *and* live with them in a community under implicitly agreed upon rules.

The caveman's rationale is thus acquitted on all charges; it doesn't force us to step in and impede carnivorous animals. It doesn't force us to approve of human cannibals.

The Mini-Beasts

So far, so good, but another complexity looms over our tired, hungry caveman, a complexity about numbers. We are imagining him spearing one aurochs. If just one human life were saved by the beast's death, the killing would seem justifiable; all the better if many are saved. But what exactly is the acceptable ratio of aurochs killings to human lives saved? To think about this, we'll help ourselves to some hocus pocus.

Suppose the aurochs were half as big, so twice as many had to be killed to accomplish the same savings in human lives. Now make the aurochs even smaller, so it takes four to save the same number of people. Keep imagining the animals to be smaller and smaller, even to the point where they are mini-beasts, and hunting them involves scooping them off the ground instead of spearing them. Is there a "profligacy point," a point at which so many animals have to be killed to save one human life that respect no longer allows the killing? If so, what is that point?

This scenario is fanciful, but the numbers problem has direct relevance to our dilemmas in the modern world. Often what we have to decide is not whether one animal is worth killing to save one human being, or five or ten human beings, but whether vast numbers of animals are worth killing to save a few people. Medical researchers looking for a cure to a rare disease might be able to guesstimate that thousands upon thousands of monkeys will go into saving a small number of people. In some cases, the ratio might be even more lopsided. So we do need to know how to look at the mathematics of killing and saving. Should we agree that there's got to be such a thing as too much killing – some number of animal deaths that's an excessive price for saving one human life?

This is a hard question. As I put it in the last chapter, species can be very roughly ranged along a ladder. Individual human lives do have more value than individual aurochs lives, because they involve more valuable capacities. If that ranking meant there was an exchange rate, with one human life worth 100 aurochs lives, or something of the sort, then we could get a grip on the "profligacy point." If you kill more animals to save a human being than a human life is worth, then that's profligate … and disrespectful. But granting there's a ranking doesn't mean recognizing any exchange rate. If one human life has more value than one aurochs life, there's nothing that says that there must be an equivalence between one human life and 10, or 100, or 1,000, or any number of aurochs lives. And that's not a matter of speciesist prejudice. The same is true when two animal species are compared. Chimpanzee lives may have more value, typically, than squirrel lives. It doesn't follow that one chimpanzee is "worth" 10 squirrels, or 100, or 1,000.

The difficulty of the idea of an exchange rate arises on any view about the value of lives, but most obviously on the "capacity" view. The valuable capacities you get in a chimpanzee life you never get in a squirrel life, however many squirrels you add together. And what you get in a human life you never get in an aurochs life, no matter how many. That's at least some reason to look askance at the notion of equitable trading of lives for lives. Say that it's just happiness that makes a life valuable. Pretend chimpanzees are extremely happy, and squirrels only slightly happy. It does not seem true that one chimpanzee life is worth some number of squirrel lives, if you just put enough together. If you had to save one chimpanzee or a boatload of squirrels, it might make sense to save the chimpanzee; you might coherently think that that will give one individual a chance at a good life, which is better than there being lots of fairly low-quality lives.

So exchange rates are not available, and won't help us find the profligacy point, the point at which too much animal-killing is being done to save a human life. I would opt for a more parsimonious explanation why there really is some number of mini-beasts that are too many to sacrifice, for the sake of saving the caveman's life. Killing is disrespectful. It's got to be the case that doing it over and over again, a hundred, or a thousand, or a million times, is increasingly disrespectful. At some point, this mountain of disrespect becomes so high that it dwarfs the respect that the caveman rightfully feels for his own life and his own serious needs. The respectful caveman will think things have gone too far.

But when? After how many killings? Oddly enough, it doesn't seem possible to say. For this reason, it probably makes sense to concentrate, whenever possible, on other matters besides the ratio between multiple lives lost and multiple lives saved, when we are trying to decide whether hunting should continue, or a research project should be carried out, and the like. There are usually lots of other morally important questions. Hunting and research often inflict great suffering. Is it worth inflicting terrible suffering on a million monkeys to alleviate the suffering of one human being? As hard as that question may be, it's not as hard as asking how many lives are worth sacrificing to save one human life.

Compassion

Respect is a way of thinking and seeing that translates into ways of acting. But what about feeling? Imbued with respect and nothing else, there's a worry whether the caveman could be fully ethical. Out of sheer respect, he might take seriously what the aurochs takes seriously – the excruciating pain she is in after he throws his spear. But will he really rush in and respond, if he doesn't empathize? What will respect alone accomplish? Maybe not nothing, but not as much as respect accompanied by a supporting cast of emotions. At the very least, the caveman will be much more reliably ethical if he's equipped with the ability to feel. He'd better empathize, but after that he'd better sympathize. We want him to have respect, but also the three "c"s – care, concern, compassion.

All of these attitudes are interdependent. In fact, the sort of disrespect expressed in the thought that an individual is not fully human, or "just an animal," is one of the most effective sympathy inhibitors there is. The horrors imposed on African slaves in the US showed a lack of compassion, but the lack of compassion was only possible because of disrespect. The slaves were "just animals," the traders and slave owners thought. In fact, as if to reassure themselves of their innocence, slave owners created visual cues that reminded them that slaves were just animals. Marjorie Spiegel provides photo evidence in her strangely fascinating book *The Dreaded Comparison: Human and Animal Slavery*. There were shackles for cattle and shackles for slaves, branding for cattle and branding for slaves. And on and on.

The same short-circuiting of compassion took place during the Holocaust. One of the many self-justifying thoughts of the Nazis was that Jews were just animals – and especially unpleasant ones too. They were vermin, cockroaches, or even maggots. Sympathy is very effectively suppressed by disrespect.

If you can say some set of human beings are "just animals," when they clearly aren't, it's much easier to say that animals are "just animals." The result, as always, is to shut off compassion. In the 1950s Harvard psychologists placed dogs in a "shuttlebox," a divided cage with one side rigged to deliver severe electric shocks to the animals' feet. Naturally, the dogs jumped over the barrier to the other side. Then a glass partition was used to separate the two sides. The dogs kept on trying to avoid the shocks, smashing themselves against the partition over and over again while showing signs of distress like "defecation, urination, yelping and shrieking, trembling, attacking the apparatus, and so on." Finally, the dogs gave up and stopped trying. They passively submitted to the shocks. Additional experiments were done by Martin Seligman and his colleagues at the University of Pennsylvania, all involving the application of unpredictable and uncontrollable electric shocks to dogs, and thus was born (by quite a leap) the theory that *human* depression results from "learned helplessness."

If sympathy and compassion worked independently of high-level cognitive states like respect, then it's doubtful researchers could have brought themselves to do these experiments. The spectacle of dogs crashing into the glass barrier and then cowering on the floor, yelping and whimpering as they suffered shocks, would be overwhelming. At the very least, there wouldn't have been the willingness to subject another and then another set of dogs to the same excruciating experience, over nearly 30 years, despite the ever decreasing gains in insight.

Seligman is now a man devoted to happiness – at least, to human happiness. As the positive psychology movement's chief architect, he's authored many interesting books on the subject. In *Authentic Happiness*, one of his most popular books, he admits there was always something amiss with all those dog experiments. As it turns out, about one third of the dogs didn't actually give up and the same goes for humans; about a third will keep trying even when faced with insoluble problems. Even now, with his abundant enthusiasm for human happiness, Seligman's regrets are confined to the failure of the research to explain depression. He has nothing to say about the pain he pointlessly inflicted on animals. Well, why should he say anything? The dogs were just animals!

We've come a long way from thinking that African Americans are just animals. We have our levels of respect set in the right zone (most of us, anyway), so that compassion can flow freely. We know that Jews are not just animals, so books, movies, and new museums about the Holocaust bring tears to our eyes. But we're still saying that animals are just animals, with all the indifference, contempt, disgust, or even loathing that the phrase suggests.

Even animals are not "just animals." We owe them respect, and it's important that we also feel the compassion that's made possible by respect. Respect and compassion won't stop us from *ever* using animals to better our lives, but they force us to take nothing for granted. I've defended the caveman against an indictment that would say he erred, even though his life depended on hunting. The hunters of the Scarlet Wonderbird, on the other hand, are indefensible. It remains to be seen what else respect and compassion rule out, and what else they allow.

Dissecting the caveman's hunting problem has probably seemed utterly anachronistic throughout this chapter. Morality is for us in the civilized world, not for long ago people just trying to survive in an inhospitable world. Or is it? If there are rudiments of morality in animals, and moral instincts in us today – very basic patterns of thought and feeling that are universal – the point when our ancestors started to be capable of a moral response to the world must be in the remote past.

We even have some tangible evidence that Paleolithic humans felt something like respect for animals. They did cover the walls of caves (which they did not in fact live in, despite my playful use of the world "caveman") with pictures of animals and nothing else. The most famous site, the Lascaux cave in southern France, is a vast gallery depicting 60 species of animals painted on a grand scale, to look both powerful and beautiful.

It's debatable just what purpose these depictions served, and how they were used. Some say they had some religious significance and functioned in rituals. One author says animals loomed large in this community simply because of the centrality of hunting in their lives. I'm fond of the idea that the caves were like movie theaters serving the entertainment needs of Paleolithic teenagers. With the flicker of a huge fire, the herds of animals on the wall would have looked like they were in motion. Maybe they were the backdrop to a story-teller's tales and maybe the people supplied the musical score with chanting and singing.

Any interpretation of cave art probably contains an element of projection. We imagine these long ago people regarding the pictures as we would have. But whichever interpretation is preferred, it doesn't seem possible that Paleolithic people regarded animals as "just animals," as many of us do today. There is just too much grandeur in these pictures. Pre-modern people may very well have regarded animals with respect, or even with awe or even reverence. It may not be so wild to think that they actually did better than us, and resolved their predicaments with an awareness of the value of both animal and human life. If so, the fact that they killed animals to survive gives us no grounds for reproof.

So much for the most primordial dilemma. We rarely encounter it today. It's time to inch forward out of the remote past ever closer to the pressing problems that confront us today.

Part IV
Moral Disorders

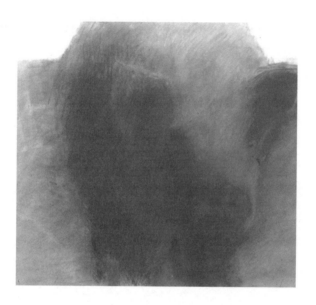

Somewhere along the way from Paleolithic survival hunting to modern factory farming, we went wrong. But where? Was the fundamental misstep recent or long ago? What part of our use of animals today must we change, and what can remain the same?

7

Going, Going, Wrong

The very raw relationship between human predators and animal prey changed gradually, disappearing thousands of years ago in some places, 50 years ago in others. Around the period from 10,000 to 7,000 BCE, the hunter-gatherer way of life started to be replaced by two other ways of life – nomadic herding and settled farming. A select group of mild and manageable animal species had come to play a critical role in human life. Farmers used the labor of domesticated cattle to plant and harvest and used manure to fertilize their fields. Both the farmer and the herder used cattle, goats, sheep, and pigs for milk and meat, leather and wool, and many other purposes.

Wild animals retain a way of life that's their very own, not modified under humanly devised conditions. A hunter meets his quarry as an independent power who can win or lose (unless, that is, the hunter's technology makes victory inevitable). Herders and farmers, on the other hand, give themselves total power over creatures that, over the generations, come to be increasingly mild and defenseless. The animals wind up no longer being independent "others" but property, and in fact the critical measure of a person's wealth. Was the new property status of animals an innocent change, or the root of all evil?

Hunter, Herder, Farmer

Once animals had been categorized as property, you might argue, all possibility of respect was out the door. We simply cannot combine the attitude that something is mine to buy and sell, preserve or destroy, with the respect deserved by something that has a rich life of its own. If this is correct, then restoring all due respect to animals today can only happen if a radical revolution takes place in our relationship with animals. The animal rights legal scholar and activist Gary Francione holds this position and believes that animals must be reclassified under law so that they are persons, not property.

Francione argues that the property status of animals under US law protects animal abusers from prosecution – when the abuser owns the animal in question. The problem is that great latitude is given to property owners. Courts too often presume that owners have an incentive to take good care of their animal property. Francione cites cases in which pet owners were prosecuted for abuse but still permitted to keep the pet. But this could change without wholesale recategorization of animals. Under ante-bellum law in the US, slaves were property *of a special kind* and in fact you could not gratuitously harm human property. Such laws were not enforced often, but they point to the possibility of continuing to classify animals as property, but strengthening animal abuse laws. In fact, animal cruelty law today is showing decreasing deference to ownership; increasingly animals are removed from the custody of abusive owners. It's true that the majority of animals in the US are lab animals or farm animals who are only minimally protected under the law, but the problem there is not property status, but the power of these categories over our thinking. Pets get considerable protection, lab animals little (mice, rats, birds, and cold-blooded animals none), and farm animals even less. (I'll come back to these issues in Chapter 8).

No doubt animals had to be classified as property for herding and farming to develop as secure and settled practices. A person couldn't be expected to invest his capital in planting a field if it was entirely possible that someone would come along and abscond with his ox before plowing time. A herder wouldn't carefully tend her sheep if she had to let them wander off in the night before shearing season. Treating animals as property is critical to herding and farming. So what we need to think about is the pair of practices together, not the property classification alone.

What was the rationale behind ending the hunter-gatherer way of life, and beginning to herd, farm, and therefore own domesticated animals? Was the benefit something that could justify not only taking the lives of other creatures, but dominating them throughout their lives, and giving them this new status as living property? Was it a benefit akin to survival, or something much more trivial?

The benefits were enormous, according to Jared Diamond, who explains that farming can make the plant and animal biomass on an acre of land 90 percent edible rather than 0.1 percent edible. With that much more food available locally, more mouths could be fed. A sedentary lifestyle became possible, and children started being spaced every two years instead of every four. Food surpluses built up so that not all hands had to be devoted to feeding the community. A division of labor became possible, and a leisure class could develop. Some members of a society could spend their time creating art, developing writing, educating children, making up stories, and – on the other hand – lording it over everyone else and fighting wars. The surplus food fed a leisure class of rulers, fighters, priests, artisans, and scribes.

Does all this make for a better way of life? Yes, if you think comfort, leisure time, knowledge, priests, and territorial expansion make life better. No, if you think equality, honest labor, and stunningly direct cave paintings make for a better life. Some will feel nostalgic for our hunter-gatherer days, but humankind actually opted for the first way of life. It's the stratified, technologically more advanced life that gave people a better chance of survival. All in all the practice of farming (and less so, herding) had serious advantages for human beings.

Admittedly, there's quite a bit of distance between killing an animal because otherwise you'll die fairly soon, and farming or herding animals because otherwise you can't play your part in a society that engenders a more comfortable way of life, specialization, writing, mathematics, and (oh, by the way) successful wars of aggression. It's not nearly as easy to give a seal of moral approval to the one as to the other. But it would be hard to say no to using animals for the whole bundle of advancements they helped to secure, to say that the advent of farming and herding was a step in the wrong direction.

Losing Our Balance

If not the only viable option, it's at least reasonable to hunt, farm, or herd wild or domesticated animals to supply yourself with necessities like meat and milk for food, leather and fur for warmth, bones as building material, and manure and labor for agriculture. The list of necessities obtained from animals is of course much longer than that. Traditional hunting and gathering Eskimos are a striking example. They used seal guts to create rain parkas and fishing lines, seal skins to create the sides of kayaks, bones for arrows.

And then, once an animal's life has been taken for necessities, why not make the most of it and let human ingenuity come up with uses for every last scrap of the corpse? If Eskimos killed whales to supply themselves with necessities, we would not even think of faulting them for also using whale blubber as a skin cosmetic. It's only a mark of cleverness and imagination that walrus ivory was carved into the shape of a "story knife," a pretty implement used by story-tellers to etch illustrations into the snow. It's impressive that they used seal guts as embroidery thread, so that parkas could be decorated with designs. If a life is to be taken, the more value we get out of it, the better.

When luxuries are obtained as byproducts of killing animals for necessities, it's one thing. When they are killed *just* for luxuries, it's another. The traditional Eskimo made the most out of taking the animal's life; by fully using the carcass, he was as unwasteful as possible and maybe even respected the animal more. Later commercial hunters who killed walruses just for their ivory were at the opposite end of the spectrum. The life of the walrus was squandered, because nobody can really think for the sake of a story knife, or ivory baubles, or pretty hair combs, it's really worth ending an animal's life.

And so here we have a very important type of going wrong. It consists of killing animals to obtain something that isn't worth the loss of their lives and their suffering. This is a problem of proportion or balance. What the human being gains is too small, considering the size of what the animal loses. In these cases, the disrespect paid to the animal can't be justified by human self-respect or respect for important human "others." The only option is to resort to thoughts that cannot be sustained in good faith. The animal's life has to be dismissed as having no importance, or a pretense must be made that the resource is really much more important than it seems.

One of the earliest practices that may appear to involve killing for a luxury is animal sacrifice. Animals were killed at religious altars by the ancient Greeks, Romans, and Jews. The animals lost their lives, and the gods gained some sort of satisfaction – if you believe what is written in Greek and Roman myth, and the Hebrew bible. If this is merely fictional satisfaction, then the real satisfaction was human, and surely goes under the heading "luxury." But whatever the truth may be, we needn't be detained by the issue, because this was really another case of animal death serving multiple purposes. In ancient Israel, animals weren't killed *just* to satisfy the divine commandments set forth in Leviticus and Deuteronomy. Animals used for food by all people were ritually slaughtered by a priest at an altar. God enjoyed the smell of the roasting animal, the bible reports several times (Genesis 8:21, Exodus 29:18, Leviticus 1:9, etc.), but the meat was eaten by all, with special allotments for the priestly class.

If it's possible to justify killing an animal to supply ourselves with necessities, then it's possible to justify the same thing to supply ourselves with a combination of necessities and luxuries. Since animals killed in temples were used as food – and quite possibly the extra protein was nutritionally important – the religious benefit, spurious or real, a necessity or a luxury, doesn't change the moral equation. We are still in the realm where disrespect for animals – killing them, butchering them, restricting their liberty – has a rationale in terms of our respect for our own serious interests. The luxury status of story knives and religious propitiation should not distract us from the basic fact that animal lives were not, in these scenarios, squandered for minor reasons.

But now ponder the Aztec art form known as the feather mosaic. Hundreds of birds had to be killed and defeathered to obtain the magnificent variety of colors in one of these masterpieces. Bartholomé de Las Casas, a chronicler of the Aztecs, writes that

> the activity in which they seem to excel over all other human intellects and which makes them appear unique among the nations of the earth is the craft they have perfected of representing with real feathers, in all their natural colors, all the things that ... other excellent painters can paint with brushes.

The Vienna Museum of Ethology still has an Aztec royal headdress in its collection, a present from Hernán Cortés to Charles V. It is made of 450 quetzal tail feathers plucked from 225 birds. The remainder of life was taken from an awful lot of creatures to get something nobody really, seriously, needed to have.

Elephants used to be killed entirely for their tusks, which made good piano keys and were carved into figurines and bas-reliefs that decorated private homes, churches, and temples. The milky white color of ivory may be lovely, but its extra loveliness over substitutes, like polished wood, seems awfully hard to assess as a plus worth ending an elephant's life for – if you're willing to give all due respect to that life.

Animal lives can be ended because some body part is needed to create a luxury good, but sometimes the incentive is not a thing but a pastime. Animals were killed by people, or given a chance to kill each other, in the Roman coliseum, for the sake of sheer entertainment. Nobody could seriously have said that the hour of excitement one spectator experienced while watching a man kill a lion was worth the loss to the lion of the rest of his or her life. Each one of them, if willing to take the lion's life seriously, would have recognized the disproportion between the loss to the lion, and the gain to himself.

Utilitarians will be impressed with the aggregate of pleasure that was enjoyed by thousands of people watching one man spend an hour fighting a lion to the death; 45,000–55,000 people filled the Coliseum. But how impressed should we be, considering that each and every person in the crowd would have had to admit that his or her piece of the total didn't really matter, and wasn't really worth the lion's life? If these spectators transcended absolute dismissal of the lion, flagrant speciesism, they all would have had to admit that, and the significance of the aggregate would have seemed dubious. In fact they might have said there was really nothing to aggregate.

Killing isn't, of course, the only harm to animals undertaken solely for the sake of luxuries. Denying an animal liberty by trapping it in a zoo is another harm that's hard to justify in terms of any serious, proportionate benefit. This is a hard thing for us to come to terms with when we've grown up with zoos. Modern zoos also have some new functions, such as housing injured animals, breeding animals for introduction in the wild, and maintaining a healthy population of endangered species as a safety net, in the event the species disappears in the wild. But the classic zoo is a place that limits the lives of animals in drastic ways, solely for luxury gains.

In the past, zoos have been the private haunts of powerful leaders, much like a sumptuous gallery of art or a collection of cars. Montezuma was a zoophile extraordinaire, housing (at the time) "the most extensive and well-managed animal assemblage anywhere in the world," says de Las Casas. The most impressive part of his zoo was an aviary where the birds of prey were fed 500 turkeys a day, and waited on by a staff of 300 people. But most odd was a special section for white plants and animals – white juniper trees, reeds, frogs, fish, and snakes. And strangest of all, white humans too. Yes, albino men, women, and children were part of the collection.

Another way of losing our balance is by getting necessities from animals, but killing more of them, when less will do. Plains Indians traditionally drove herds of buffalo off a cliff and butchered them by the hundreds in the pound below – in Blackfoot, a "piskun" (translation: deep blood kettle). Shepard Krech III's carefully researched book *The Ecological Indian* reports that the number of animals killed at one time could be in the hundreds, or even over a thousand. With each buffalo weighing from 700 to 1,200 pounds, the yield in meat could be as high as 240,000 pounds, if the buffaloes were fully butchered. But traders who witnessed the hunts in the early 1800s report that they weren't. Sometimes choice morsels – tongue, hump, fetus (!), and marrow – were consumed and everything else was left behind. The artist Paul Kane witnessed a Cree hunt in 1846 and wrote "the putrefying carcases (sic) tainted the air all around." He observed that Indians "destroy innumerable buffaloes, apparently for the mere pleasure of the thing. I have myself seen a pound so filled up with their dead carcases that I could scarcely imagine how the enclosure could have contained them while living."

Blackfoot compunctions about all that killing (see Chapter 1) were relieved by the thought that the buffalo master consented to the whole affair, and that buffalo spirits get reborn into other buffalo bodies. Similar notions were pervasive in other native American tribes. Compunctions apparently didn't trouble later commercial buffalo hunters like Buffalo Bill Cody, who slaughtered the animals by the thousands to meet the non-native market for buffalo hides. On the order of four million buffaloes were killed between 1871 and 1885, their bodies sometime left to rot and their bones strewn across the plains. It was as the slaughter started to augur extinction that Indians themselves started to complain about waste.

Our long ago forebears who hunted animals, then herded or farmed them, had innumerable reasons to do so. In ways they fully understood, and other ways they couldn't have consciously grasped, they advanced themselves by using animals. When they hunted non-wastefully, they could rightfully claim a balance between gains to themselves and losses to animals, or at least from a bird's eye view the balance is pretty clear. Thus, they could also have made a case that their disrespectful treatment of animals was necessitated by respect for themselves. Broadly speaking, they were still in the caveman's situation, unable to give maximum respect to both animals and themselves, and giving priority to their own good – in fact, the good of the party entitled to the most respect (as I argued in Chapter 6).

The elephant and rhinoceros hunters, the feather mosaic makers, coliseum spectators, zookeepers and buffalo hunters we've been considering are something else. To gratify any desire, no matter how deep or shallow, they were prepared to deprive an animal of life and liberty. There was no semblance of balance between gains (to humans) and losses (to animals).

Our job, if we want to make an honest assessment of ourselves, is to figure out who we are like – the balanced hunters, herders, and farmers? Or the coliseum spectators, the feather mosaic makers, the ivory hunters, who killed animals for reasons that paled by comparison to the value of their lives? Do we use animals just for luxuries, or for necessities? Do we kill as little as we can to obtain necessities, or more than we need to?

Animal Farm

In the developing world, animals are still used to plow fields in a great number of places, and manure is still critical for fertilizer. Milk is a critical source of protein in places without high protein plant foods. The sale of meat and milk is sometimes the only thing that allows parents to send their kids to school, because there is no other way to earn income. The central role of livestock in lifting people out of poverty is recognized by the anti-poverty organization Heifer International, which uses its huge budget to supply livestock to the poor around the world. For all intents and purposes, we still *are* the farmers and herders of long ago, if we live in some parts of the world.

But if you're reading this book, you're probably an inhabitant of the developed world. In industrialized countries, we don't need to use domesticated animals to plow because we have tractors. We don't use them for transportation, because we have cars. We don't need to fertilize fields with manure because we have chemical fertilizers. We don't need animals to keep our bodies warm and our feet dry. We have polyester that works as well or better. We don't need animals for eggs, milk, or meat, because we now understand that a plant-based diet is just as healthy, or even healthier (see Chapter 10).

We can support all of our basic aspirations without the use of animals. And that gives us a problem. Can we still justify what we take away from animals in terms of what we gain?

Of course, we do still get basics from animals – food, clothes, shoes. Those are the things we make out of animal bodies. But since we have alternatives, we must be more precise. What we really get are the specific types of food and garb *that satisfy us aesthetically*. We choose the leather shoes for their look, the chicken for the taste and the way it feels in our mouths. We choose eggs because they make delicious baked goods.

Can anybody seriously claim that self-respect and respect for human others propels us to kill animals for these purposes? Are these things really very important to us? On the face of it, they seem more like ivory piano keys and feather mosaics. These aesthetic benefits seem luxurious, not necessary.

But let's give meat-eating (and the like) all due consideration. Journalist Michael Pollan alludes to another part of our motivation in the bestseller *The Omnivore's Dilemma*. Through the wonders of the laboratory, we can convert petroleum into every conceivable form for wearing, and corn into every conceivable form for eating, but he and people like him prefer to maintain a more direct connection to the earth. For taste, look, feel, *and* elemental connectedness to nature, animals are still an irreplaceable resource.

Or maybe it's still more complicated, Pollan implies. There's an existential benefit to using animals for food and clothing. Doing so links us to our ancestors and our long ago forebears. Indeed, doing all these things links us to animals themselves. The prideful isolation of Western thinkers, who preferred to keep humans in a class by themselves, has a counterpart in the ethically pure isolation of human beings who don't make use of animals. Where every other wild animal lives in a complex ecosystem among a multitude of other species, we seem to separate ourselves from raw nature. In our isolation, we begin to look down on animals as savages without our ethical self-control, as barbarous parts of nature, which is said to be red in tooth and claw. If we value animals, we will want to recognize the animal in ourselves and "let him out." Chewing on a chicken drumstick, we keep ourselves a part of the animal world.

Of course, the herbivore does have a reply. For the person who has made the leap to a vegetarian diet, or always had one, a vegetarian meal may be just as elemental. It needn't be composed of laboratory-concocted substitutes. A vegetarian cuisine can simply be a good percentage of one of the world's largely plant-based cuisines, like Indian, Chinese, or Italian. Or it may be generated out of one of the great vegetarian cookbooks that has emerged in the last 25 years. Furthermore, there is existential satisfaction in knowing a meal involved no killing, no suffering, no blood – none of the things we find repellant when we actually face them head-on. And as for being a part of the animal world, there are other ways to do it. We're just as "animal" if we emulate herbivores rather than carnivores, and for communing with nature, there's always the peaceful option of a walk in the woods.

All that will fall on deaf ears, in many cases. The dedicated meat-eater wants to hang on to the aesthetic and existential plusses she's used to; the alternate food the vegetarian has to offer doesn't appeal to her and the benefits the vegetarian enjoys are beyond her ken. For the meat-eater's gains, can she justify imposing death on animals? If you take animals and their lives seriously, it's hard to say yes. It's hard to say why the modern meat-consumer isn't just like the ivory and horn hunters, coliseum spectators, and feather mosaic hunters. No doubt they too could embroider upon their basic rationales for killing. But the interests in all these situations just do not seem as compelling as the ones that motivated our hunter, herder, and farmer forebears, and still motivate people who use livestock to better their lives in the developing world today.

Creating and Destroying

It's hard to be impressed with the human interests that perpetuate the use of animals in the post-industrial world, even if they're familiar and understandable. But a defense of animal farming might still be made on different grounds. The ivory hunters and their ilk were pure killers. For every elephant (or rhinoceros, or quetzal bird, or buffalo) they killed, they left a gap. One less elephant. One less bundle of "good" of the sort provided by an elephant. But farmers and herders are not pure killers. They are also creators. As animals are killed and products sold, more animals are bred, so that the population stays the same or, if business is good, increases. So omnivores really have more to say on the question of balance. Offsetting the bad of killing are their own interests – admittedly not that compelling – but also the good of creating. Maybe they're in fine moral fettle after all.

The question, though, is whether the omnivore's moral math holds up under scrutiny. If it's a bad thing to kill a cow, can you cancel it out by creating a cow? In fact, we normally believe no such thing about killing and creating. If you learn that 1,000 people were murdered in the US today, and then learn 1,000 people were born, you don't think "no problem." The bad news is one thing and the good news is another. If one person is involved in both killing and creating – maybe she's a killer by night and an infertility doctor by day – we don't think the one effort annuls the other.

The reason creating people doesn't undo killing people is very simple. The people created aren't the same as the people killed. You can't make it up to X, who loses *his* life by being killed, by creating Y. To say it's otherwise for animals, you must point to some relevant difference between animals and people. What you must say, essentially, is that animals' lives aren't theirs, or aren't anything they have a right to, or an interest in. You have to say that killing Bessie puts an end to a stream of life, but it's just as well to get another stream going. One cow's pleasures and experiences are interchangeable with another's. In fact, you can think of cow experience as one big stream – much like the supply of milk that a herd of cows produce. The milk's all the same, and it matters not whether one cow is removed from the herd and another added. Although Daisy is not Bessie, she adds the same sort of ingredients to the collective cow-experience stream.

Now, you may be thinking we're ignoring some real-world details here – and we are. It hurts Bessie to be killed, and may also be uncomfortable for Daisy to be born. So switching out Bessie for Daisy pollutes the collective "stream of cow-life" temporarily. But let's ignore that detail. Is it really true that animals are interchangeable contributors to a collective stream, while human beings have separate lives (separate streams) and an interest in continuing to live their own individual lives?

Peter Singer argues that an individual's interest in continuing to live his own life turns on his preferences for his own future. You are 18 years old, and you want to go to college next year, want to get married some day, want to have three children. If you sit down and list all your desires for the future, you'll probably never stand back up – they are that numerous. Animals, on the other hand, are not easily credited with many thoughts about the future (see Chapter 4). They have no plans or preferences for next week or next month or next year. Or at most, maybe just the more sophisticated animals do, and they have thoughts just about the immediate future. But in any case, the death of an 18-year-old human stops millions of preferences from ever being satisfied, no matter how many other people are created. Creating other people doesn't undo the non-satisfaction of those preferences. The death of an animal, on the other hand, may stop no future-oriented preferences from being satisfied, or at most a few. If the collective stream of animal experiences stays full (and full of good experiences), there's no need to be troubled about the deaths (apart from issues about the manner of death). Singer certainly does see huge problems with meat-eating, because of the way farm animals are treated during their lives, but no clear-cut problem with the cycle of killing and creating.

All this is coherent, and you may want to sign on, but beware – this is a new-fangled way of thinking about life and death for animals. I doubt it's been *your* way before this moment, and going along with it just to defend meat-eating ought to make you nervous. We do take an animal's death seriously, as we see when we consider the animals we care about most – our pets. My cat Jerry (named for the philosopher Jerry Fodor), was hit by a car when he was about two years old. It pained me a lot to lose my cat, and no statistics about how a cat is born every six seconds in the US would have comforted me. I felt pained on Jerry's behalf, thinking it was a shame that he'd lost the chance to go on enjoying his life. If Singer's view is right, then

Jerry really lost nothing. He'd probably had no plans and preferences about the future, so there was nothing to fail to come to fruition. If another cat had been specifically bred to replace him, at the moment he died, making up for the happy cat moments he took with him, then nothing would have been lost – says Singer.

Now, I think this way of looking at animals is latently speciesist. It assumes the only sort of irreparable loss that can be caused by death is the loss of a chance to fulfill one's plans and preferences. But an animal seems to lose out by dying in a more primitive sense. Once Jerry had a future, and then he lost it. It was *his* future, even in the absence of any plans. Admittedly, the ownership talk – "he lost *his* life" – is not easy to clarify, but we need the concept for lots of reasons. If we don't have it, we can't say that death takes *her* future from a newborn. We are forced to see more of a tragedy when people die after obsessing about their futures, and less when they die after living in the present. Maybe the tragedy of death has some connection to an individual's plans and preferences, but stressing that connection to the exclusion of all else seems to leave us making the wrong judgments.

If dying takes away a future from an animal that's *his* (or *hers*), then the killing of an animal is a bad thing that cannot be annulled by the good of creating another. There's no automatic cancelation of destroying Bessie by creating Daisy. Of course, killing a cow is not an infinitely bad thing just because it *is* a bad thing. It's not a bad thing that can *never* be outweighed by *any* number of good things. But running a killing-*plus*-breeding operation is no automatic salve to the conscience. There's no automatic moral balance created by creating a new animal for every one that's killed.

The fact that animals are created by herders and farmers doesn't give us any solid solution to the balance problem. Still, the omnivore may insist, we live in a world where millions of animals get to mill about in the wide open pastures of west Texas, the lovely green hills of Wales, the mountainsides of the Himalayas. The multitudes of farm animals make the world buzz with animal happiness. If, with a wave of a magic wand, you could make them all go away, wouldn't the world be a more barren place? Wouldn't there be less happiness in the world? For all the killing that goes on, isn't the world a better place because of animal farming?

We get one impression when we focus on the endless killing – of male chicks as soon as they're born, of lambs at only a few months, of veal calves at six months, of chickens at seven months, and of cattle (in places where they are fattened in feedlots) at just over a year. And another impression when we look at a bucolic scene on a sunny day.

Would there be less happiness in the world with fewer farm animals? Not necessarily. As the population of domesticated animals has ballooned over the centuries, the population of wild animals has been shrinking (see Chapter 9). It's possible the covariation can move in the opposite direction too. With less consumption of sheep, there might be a return of woodlands and all the animals that fill them – deer, foxes, birds, frogs, rabbits.

Admittedly, it's hard to commit fully to that vision. We're accustomed to grazing animals dotting the landscape. And not just the animals, but the land itself, which has been sculpted by thousands of years of animal farming. This comes home to me whenever I spend time in the lovely British countryside, where most of the forests were long ago cleared away to make room for domesticated animals, and the land is crisscrossed by ancient stone walls and hedges that separate one farmer's sheep (and it is mostly sheep) from another's. There is a warmth to the landscape that's missing in places like Alaska, where you can drive for hundreds of miles without seeing barns, houses, or grazing animals. Farmland is part of our internal landscape, our sense of the way at least some of the world should look.

Bucolic scenes are warm and human. We'd miss them! The voice that tells us we cannot stop raising animals for food is insistent, but it's difficult to trust its pleadings.

How Now

Technological advances have brought us to a point where many of us no longer gain necessary things by killing animals, but aesthetic things: particular tastes, the sense of connection to the animal world, the sense of preserving traditions. The progress we have made, ironically, puts us in a position of having to go wrong, if we want to continue eating meat, wearing leather, etc.

But let's suppose you don't see it that way. You see the aesthetic gains as much more important than I've made them out to be, and you do think the gains balance animal losses. Or maybe you think that creating cancels out destroying. Unfortunately, you're going to have to contend with other ways you may be going wrong, even if (in your eyes) you're not losing your balance. If you recognize some very basic rights in animals but think we may continue to breed and kill them for aesthetic gains, you probably believe animals should be treated humanely even as they continue to be used to satisfy our aesthetic preferences. The problem is that for the most part, they're not.

Whether we can justify restricting the liberty of hens so that they provide us with their eggs, you can still be certain that stuffing them in cages, with each occupying no more than 48–72 square inches (that's less than the size of standard US typing paper), is not justifiable. If you're not quite sure about eating veal, it's got to be wrong to produce it by keeping animals in tiny stalls for the entire duration of their lives. Maybe, just maybe, you can justify continuing to eat beef, but it's another matter to defend the way cattle are treated in feedlots, where these ruminants stand around knee-deep in manure, being fed a completely unnatural diet of corn, hormones, antibiotics, and even cement, to get them to put on a huge amount of weight as quickly as possible.

Maybe bacon can be justified, but surely not the sow crate that's only just starting to be phased out in some parts of the US. It increases profits to put animals in pens 24 hours a day, where they can barely move about. But that way of rearing hogs is gratuitously cruel. We have no serious interests that could justify us in so totally disregarding a pregnant pig's serious interests.

If killing for food is acceptable, we still have to be concerned about the manner of slaughter. Some meatpacking plants are doing better now by adopting an auditing system designed by Temple Grandin, but we must wonder how gentle the process can be if cattle are killed at a rate of 400 per hour (as described by Eric Schlosser in *Fast Food Nation*). Clearly there's an ugly underbelly to the proceedings, as can be seen in a Humane Society undercover video that shut down one facility in 2008.

The problems of "how" are uneven. If you are eating meat in the US there's a huge chance that the animal that died to satisfy your appetite was treated as a thing, not a creature, and dispatched with minimal compassion. If you've gone out of your way to eat humanely raised animals by shopping at a store like Whole Foods, the problem of "how" is a bit less acute. The chickens were cage-free, but they did occupy giant barns housing upwards of 20,000 animals. If you spend an extra dollar or so, they were not only cage-free but free range, which means they had a chance to walk around out of doors. But that sounds better than it really is. As Michael Pollan discovered when he visited a big organic egg facility, the chickens are kept indoors for the first seven weeks, and by that point they're so used to their environment that they don't bother walking through the little door that leads to the out of doors. You should be glad that the cows that produced your milk aren't pumped up with bovine growth hormone, and are less likely to have endured over-engorged udders and repeated attacks of mastitis, but don't believe the picture on the carton. The cows spend most of their time indoors, hooked up to milking machines.

Whole Foods has the loveliest pamphlets. The Icelandic lambs in the pictures are outside in green pastures, not cooped up like the pigs that are packed into giant feed operations in the US. The New Zealand lambs look well-off too. The thing is, lamb is lamb. That is, it's baby sheep. These animals are killed at about four months (average natural life expectancy: 10–12 years), so there's no denying their lives are sharply curtailed.

Meat is not Green

We're very likely going wrong by continuing to raise and kill animals for merely aesthetic benefits, and we're surely going wrong by doing so inhumanely, most of the time. These are the problems that quickly meet the eye when we think about whether it's alright to eat meat. There's another set of problems that have only recently emerged. These are all problems of "collateral damage." They don't involve violations of animal rights and interests, but harm that lands on something else.

Some of the collateral damage is due to the high-tech way animals are now being raised for food. The hormones animals are fed to increase weight rapidly and increase profits wind up in our food supply. The estrogens in meat and milk are a suspected (but unproven) cause of early puberty in American girls, a concern because of both mental and physical consequences. More menstrual cycles over a lifetime mean a greater risk of developing breast cancer, for example.

Some of the collateral damage is due to the fact that killing animals is grueling work. Eric Schlosser has an eye-opening portrait of slaughterhouses (euphemistically known as "meat packing plants") and their impact on workers in his best-seller *Fast Food Nation*. Hours are long, work-related injuries frequent, and violations of labor laws ubiquitous. Many slaughterhouse jobs are filled by illegal immigrants who have to lie low and can't complain.

More recently it's become clear that meat is not good for the environment either. The UN's recent report *Livestock's Long Shadow* reports that grazing land plus feedcrop land, together, comprise 30 percent of the earth's land surface; 70 percent of all agricultural land is devoted to livestock and its upkeep. This is only going to become an even more serious issue because with increased affluence, the consumption of animal products rapidly increases. Right now, the amount of meat consumed is nearly three times greater in developed countries, compared to developing countries, but it's on the rise everywhere. In China, for example, meat consumption increased in the 20-year period from 1981 to 2001 by 29 percent in urban areas and by 85 percent in rural areas.

The large number of "food" animals has many effects. The most surprising one is that livestock account for 18 percent of greenhouse gases, "a larger share than transport," according to the UN report, which also opines that climate change is the most serious challenge now facing the human race. Some of that is due to deforestation to make room for pasture, and some due to the methane and other gases produced by flatulence, belching, manure, and urine. Of course, the world has natural pasture land. The grasslands of the western United States didn't have to be cleared for grazing. But often pasture land is created by cutting down trees – with a resulting increase in greenhouse gases that trees would otherwise absorb. The most obvious culprits are the most recent clear-cutters – the companies that are cutting down acres of the Amazon rainforest at alarming rates; 70 percent of formerly forested land is now pasture, and much of the rest is feedcrop land. But of course, the effect is the same whether an acre of trees was cut down yesterday or a thousand years ago. Some of the places we think of as naturally treeless really aren't. Great Britain was largely deforested in the middle ages, Haiti in the last hundred years, and other spots an hour ago. The result is the same – no trees to absorb greenhouse gases.

And where trees disappear, habitats for wild animals disappear as well. Beneath our notice, a war is going on today between livestock and wild animals, and the livestock are winning. If it is important for the world to contain myriad species of wild animals, then meat consumption must decrease (more on that topic in Chapter 9).

In the best case scenario, environmentally speaking, animals are pastured on natural grazing land from start to finish and then locally killed. That's the situation in New Zealand, where lamb is locally grown and slaughtered. There's little or no environmental cost to eating meat, over eating plant food, because local arable land is scarce. To replace meat with vegetables would mean flying in supplies from Australia or further away.

In the worst case scenario, animals are tightly packed into factory farms and separate land is used to grow their feed. The huge amount of waste produced in such places winds up in landfills and leeches into waterways.

And sad to say, in Western affluent countries when you sit down to dinner at a restaurant or at home, you're eating the product of the worst case scenario, unless you've gone out of your way to avoid it. For most of us, in the usual situations we find ourselves, meat is definitely not green.

Some recent statistics make the point in a new and striking way. We think of our choice of car as a critical one that can increase or lessen our contribution to greenhouse gases. The pressure is now on to buy a little hybrid Prius, and skip the roomy, family-friendly SUV. But a recent study shows that if every person in the US decreased meat consumption by just 20 percent, it would be as if we all drove a Prius (see Bittman in the Sources). Even if you do think the cost to animals is worth what we gain by eating meat, and even if you're not convinced that how we raise animals falls beneath reasonable humane standards, you still have a reason to eat less meat: for the sake of the planet.

By this point we've gone wrong in the way we treat animals many times over. We didn't go wrong when the earliest hunters decided to kill them to survive. We didn't go wrong when we started to treat animals as property, raising them as farmers and herders. I don't even think we went wrong when animals were sacrificed at ancient temples, or every time someone used an animal for a luxury product like a story knife. We went wrong when we started killing animals for nothing but luxury benefits, or killing them in greater-than-necessary numbers for necessities. Technological progress has put us in the affluent, industrialized world in a position where for most of us, most of the time, there is no necessity we must get from animals, and can't get in another way. Second, we've come to treat animals as things instead of creatures, making "how" a further problem. And third, lately it's becoming increasingly clear that our huge appetite for animal products is dangerous to our health and the health of our planet.

8

Science and Survival

There's something atavistic about laying hunks of meat out to cook over a fire. A holiday backyard barbecue feels like a trip back to our hunter-gatherer past. But for all that we feel like heirs of the primordial caveman, are we? He imposed suffering and death on other creatures to keep himself and his fellows alive, and today – with grocery stores packed with alternatives – we can't say that's what we're doing. Meat-eating today is only the heir apparent of meat-eating long ago. We are still (most of us) omnivores for a complex set of aesthetic and existential reasons, and that puts our behavior in another moral category.

There are other things we do to animals today that have a stronger claim to being the moral successors of primordial meat-eating. You don't need to eat a hamburger to stay alive, but medical research that's lethal to animals has kept human beings alive. The animal researcher is much more likely to be the caveman's true heir. It's the researcher who at least stands a better chance of sharing the caveman's innocence.

A caveman can be a true innocent – respectful of himself and his human fellows, respectful of the animals he hunts, but right to see that keeping himself and his fellows alive wins the day. A researcher could be guided by the same set of thoughts. He may respect the monkeys or mice in his lab and abjure speciesist disdain, yet see respect for human lives as requiring that experiments go on. He might juggle the various thoughts he has, and conclude that respect for people wins the day. Is the researcher's thinking just as innocent as the caveman's?

It surely depends on what's going on in his or her lab, and for what purpose. Survival hunting all fits a pretty narrow range of patterns, but experimentation is many things. Most of it goes on behind closed doors and has no clear image in our mind's eye. To say whether there's a moral defense of experimentation along the same lines as the defense of the caveman, we need to get a grip on a spectrum of research examples: from the good to the bad and the ugly.

The truth about animal research is hard to get your hands on. If you read books and websites that promote animal research, you'll learn everything you ever wanted to know about the benefits of the research – the discoveries, cures, drugs, vaccines, and procedures that we probably never would have had without it. Even if they're absolutely truthful about these benefits, the research advocates rarely disclose just what was done, and to how many animals, to achieve these benefits. Furthermore, they give you little sense of whether it might have been possible to get the same benefits with less animal suffering and death. The implicit message is that the benefits *must* be worth the costs, whatever they are; animals are that expendable.

On the other hand, books and websites that advocate for animals focus on experiments with the highest possible costs to animals (which are described in gruesome detail) but the fewest benefits. These experiments are morally repellant, but the reader is left wondering whether all animal research is like that. Some authors are responsible enough to admit that there are exceptions, but they are loath to give examples. If they know they're not being fair and balanced, the animal advocates presumably justify themselves by thinking their job is to make us skeptical; victims of bad animal research urgently need our help.

To think about the caveman analogy, we need to contemplate the closest thing to him – an example of a researcher doing experiments with life-saving potential, but lethal consequences for animals. For advocates, the experimentation that led to the polio vaccine is the showcase example of good animal research. If anyone wears the caveman's mantle of innocence, Jonas Salk does.

Vaccine Hunting

In 1952, there were 57,000 reported cases of polio in the US. Over 3,000 of the victims died and more than 21,000 were left with some degree of paralysis. Small outbreaks were reported in the nineteenth century, but incidence started to become alarming in the US starting around the turn of the century. A disease especially affecting children under the age of 15 (they were the victims, by 2 to 1), polio spread easily, especially in the summer months.

The virus entered the body by fecal-oral contact and incubated in the intestines before it was absorbed into the bloodstream and entered the central nervous system. Depending on the areas of the spinal cord and brain affected, the virus could cause partial or complete muscle paralysis, in the worst cases affecting breathing. Heart-breaking photos from the time period show children being kept alive in an "iron lung" – a body-sized ventilator that encased all but their heads. In fact, as I started writing this section, I glanced at a news website and learned of a woman who had endured 50 years in such a contraption following childhood polio, only to die of suffocation because of a power failure one day in May 2008. She had never been able to use a modern, portable ventilator because of a spinal deformity caused by the virus.

Even though the 57,000 cases at the height of the polio epidemic are not many more than the number of people killed on US highways yearly, it is easy to understand why the specter of this disease haunted parents every summer in a way that highway fatalities don't. They read about the latest outbreak in newspapers and saw the frightening pictures, and had no way to protect their children. It was a great day in 1955 when Jonas Salk announced plans to inoculate 400,000 children. The injected vaccine reduced susceptibility to the virus by 99 percent and all but eradicated the disease in developed countries.

Though the live virus vaccine developed by Albert Sabin 10 years later is now the vaccine of choice in developing countries, because it's orally administered, so easier (clean needles are not needed) and cheaper, Salk's vaccine is the one routinely administered in industrialized countries. Composed of inactivated virus but capable of triggering a strong antibody response, it cannot cause polio. The vaccine has saved thousands of lives, spared thousands of people a devastating disease, and granted millions of parents greater peace of mind. But those were the benefits. What were the costs ... to animals?

Most Salk enthusiasts don't know and don't care, or at least don't care to let us know. But a recent book about the research that went into the development of the polio vaccine is wonderfully transparent. As Jeffrey Kluger explains in *Splendid Solution*, animals played a role at every stage.

One of the first problems that had to be solved was how to obtain large quantities of the virus first for study, and then to create vaccine. Previously, influenza virus had been grown in eggs, but polio virus only seemed to grow *in vivo*, in central nervous system tissue. As early as the 1930s, monkeys were infected with large quantities of polio virus and then killed after symptoms developed. Virus was then extracted from their spinal chord tissues. If virus could be grown *in vitro*, it would be much easier to produce. Furthermore, there were concerns that virus grown in monkey nervous tissue could never be turned into vaccine, since that particular tissue had the potential to cause disease.

In the 1940s, John Enders discovered that the virus could be grown not only *in vitro*, but in many kinds of tissue besides nervous tissue. The seminal research, for which he won the Nobel prize along with two colleagues, involved growing the virus in kidney tissue, *in vitro*. The next step was testing the virulence of samples by injecting them into the brains of monkeys and waiting to see if symptoms developed. Luckily for Enders and the development of the polio vaccine, but not for the monkeys, symptoms did develop.

In the 1950s, the next stage was undertaken by a group of labs, including one run by Jonas Salk in the basement of the University of Pittsburgh's Municipal Hospital. First, 17,000 macaque and rhesus monkeys were used for purposes of typing virus samples. Thousands of samples gathered from polio victims had to be classified to determine whether any more types existed besides the three already identified. Kluger is candid about the procedure. After anesthesia the animal "would be stretched on a board. Its head would be shaved and a chin strap affixed to keep it stationary in the event of an involuntary flinch. A small hole would then be drilled in the skull and the virus would be injected directly into the brain." Why not just feed the monkey the virus? Monkeys aren't naturally vulnerable to the virus. Their immune system quickly fights it off. An oft-heard rationalization for animal research – that discoveries benefit both humans and animals – in unavailable here. Monkeys would never benefit from the development of the polio vaccine. They're born with all the protection they need.

After infection, the monkeys were watched for signs of illness. As the disease set in, they were scored for paralysis, with a number representing each limb. Some survived, presumably now immune to the first virus sample they had received. These monkeys were now "challenged" with a second sample; if they developed symptoms again, that showed the second sample contained a different type of polio virus than the first. As Kluger tells it, Salk found all this deliberate infecting of monkeys hard to watch. To reassure himself,

he would leave this lab and go up to the hospital's third, fourth, and fifth floors, where the wards of polio children lay. The children too were well and truly jailed – some in iron lungs, all of them in enfeebled bodies that had quit working as they should. It was the zero-sum nature of the virus game that the only way to prevent more blameless children from streaming into the upper floors was to sicken and kill the blameless monkeys in the basement.

The smaller macaque monkeys needed a few extra calories, which were provided by treats of fresh fruit. Salk thought of this as "a small adjustment of the moral scales but an adjustment nonetheless," Kluger writes.

When a vaccine had finally been developed, the monkeys played their final role. It was first tested on them. Interesting sidenote: the next group of guinea pigs were two groups of children living in "homes" for the mentally and physically disabled. Only then was the vaccine tried on higher-status groups – the students at a Pittsburgh prep school and Salk's own sons.

All of the researchers and lab workers who were involved in the research that led to the discovery of the vaccine had the goal of keeping people alive and paralysis free. They were trying to secure vitally important goods for human beings. So were our hunter-gatherer forebears when they embarked upon a hunting expedition. So are the researchers the moral heirs of the caveman who was acquitted back in Chapter 6?

There are many surface differences that distinguish the researcher from the caveman. Hunting strikes us as completely natural. The hunter and his prey are parts of the same ecosystem, caught in a web of relationships like birds have to insects and lions have to gazelles. The monkeys brought into the early polio labs were torn out of their natural environments and transported by plane around the world. When the polio researchers found themselves needing thousands of monkeys for typing the virus, they started breeding them at US monkey farms. These animals never had any real life to speak of, and certainly had not evolved to play a role alongside people in the manner of cows and sheep. Spearing an animal is a simple, direct, primal act, while strapping a monkey to a board, drilling a hole in his head, and injecting virus seems completely perverse. Research is clinical, detached, cold, unfeeling. Hunting is none of those things.

All of these differences surely do explain a difference in our emotional reaction to survival hunting versus vital animal research, but it's hard to attach deep moral importance to any one of them. The monkeys were transported across the world, but *that* can't be a decisive issue. There's something unnatural and repugnant about deliberately infecting a monkey with polio virus, but death by hunting is still death, and possibly even more painful. Things we find repugnant are often not morally questionable. Make yourself think about the details of gynecological or urological surgery – think about it graphically, get a vivid picture in your head. Unnatural, repugnant, to be sure. Quite possibly also cold and clinical and detached, especially for the support personnel who never meet the patient. These are reactions we push aside. They are *just* reactions.

You may say, more seriously, that the polio researchers were less certain to achieve the goal of saving lives, and that they had to sacrifice more animals in the process. In the 1930s, when a vaccine was far off, researchers couldn't have known the lethal experiments they were doing on monkeys had more than a very small chance of leading to any benefit. In the 1940s, when John Enders figured out how to grow virus *in vitro*, a vaccine was still very far off. Even the typing studies of the 1950s didn't have any certainty of saving lives or preventing polio. It wasn't until the very last round of studies, when the vaccine was tried out on monkeys, that the researchers could have believed the animals were clearly being used to lower risks to humans.

But there is uncertainty and inefficiency on the hunting side of the equation too. The animal might be hit by an arrow, but still may not fill any human stomachs if he winds up being impossible to track. In a dangerous world, one day's quarry may just forestall death by causes other than starvation.

There's one more issue that needs attention, the question of numbers raised in Chapter 6. If respect permits using one or a hundred animals for some legitimate purpose, it doesn't necessarily permit using a million. There is such a thing as profligacy, though we can't define it precisely. An estimated 100,000 monkeys died in the process of developing Salk's vaccine, a number we have to find appalling. But should we say "Too many"? "Not worth it"? The yearly number of humans saved from death was in the thousands, and the number saved from paralysis was in the tens of thousands. Animals died in large numbers, but there was a last animal death; without it, the human toll would have risen to staggering numbers, with no foreseeable end. If some research does seem profligate in its use of animals, I find it hard to make that assessment of this research.

It does not seem as if the differences between survival hunting and polio research go deep enough to place them in separate moral categories. Back in Chapter 6 we imagined the caveman standing by idly, unable to take the lives of animals, while his wife and children gradually expired. He seemed to be apportioning respect improperly, and not doing all that he should do. I have the same intuition about Jonas Salk. He could have anguished about infecting the monkeys in the basement, taken the elevator up to the hospital wards, and then refused to go on, out of deference for the monkeys. But he went back down to the lab and continued his work. Rightly, or so it seems.

Putting it with such simplicity and finality washes away the sense of regret and horror one has to feel about animal research, especially after seeing worst-case examples either first hand or in undercover videos (see PETA in the Sources). My sense of the situation is best expressed by saying the experiments were a necessary evil. The world did not provide Jonas Salk with another method of saving the next round of polio victims. Just as the caveman did not have a well-stocked grocery store where he could buy high protein alternatives to meat, Salk didn't have "tofu monkeys" – models of human disease without lives and a well-being of their own. He treated the monkeys in his lab with gross disrespect, but had no option that was morally better, all things considered.

At least the polio researchers weren't oblivious to the animals (on Kluger's account) – they didn't completely dismiss them as "just animals." As if reaching for a little bit of the impossible – full respect for both humans *and* monkeys – the lab chose one of the monkeys and made him a pet, letting him live out his life in peace. If only all the monkeys could have done so, and the polio-ridden children as well.

Horrible Harry

Another lab in the 1950s creates a very different picture of animal research. At the University of Wisconsin, psychologist Harry Harlow was also experimenting on monkeys. He wasn't killing them or infecting them with diseases, but rather putting them in situations that were supposed to simulate human environments.

In his earliest studies, infant monkeys were separated from their mothers and kept in bare cages with a choice between two wire mother-surrogates. One came with a bottle to feed from while the other was covered with soft terry cloth. The monkeys chose to spend only one hour out of the day with the bottle-mother, showing the importance of tactile comfort to rhesus monkeys, and therefore (by analogy) to human infants.

Harlow started to wonder how young monkeys would react to mother surrogates that were even less pleasant than the cloth-covered wire figure, so he created a variety of monster mothers. The following shocking passage from an article by Harlow and one of his colleagues is quoted in Peter Singer's book *Animal Liberation*.

The first of these monsters was a cloth monkey mother who, upon schedule or demand, would eject high-pressure compressed air. It would blow the animal's skin practically off its body. What did the baby monkey do? It simply clung tighter and tighter to the mother, because a frightened infant clings to its mother at all costs. We did not achieve any psychopathology.

However, we did not give up. We built another surrogate monster mother that would rock so violently that the baby's head and teeth would rattle. All the baby did was cling tighter and tighter to the surrogate. The third monster we built had an embedded wire frame within its body which would spring forward and eject the infant from its ventral surface The infant would subsequently pick itself off the floor, wait for the frame to return into the cloth body, and then cling again to the surrogate. Finally, we built our porcupine mother. On command, this mother would eject sharp brass spikes over all of the ventral surface of its body. Although the infants were distressed by these pointed rebuffs, they simply waited until the spikes receded and then returned and clung to the mother.

Of course, Harlow and his colleagues weren't zoologists trying to understand monkeys. They thought what they'd observed in monkeys shed light on human beings. They drew the conclusion that a human child will endure practically any abuse and still stay attached to his or her mother.

Polio research saved lives, and it's very hard to see how that result could have been achieved at lower cost to animals. What did Harlow's research achieve? That might seem obvious. The lesson drawn was that children need to be touched and held, and that they will continue to feel attached to a mother figure in spite of extreme abuse. These are clearly very important things to know. For handling cases of child abuse, it's critical for case workers to know that a child's clinging to his mother is not evidence that abuse has not occurred. Parents need to know that children want physical comfort even more than they want food.

But the crucial question is whether this research really did teach us these lessons and if it did, whether we could have learned the same lessons without doing such terrible things to young monkeys. It seems especially hard to believe that painstaking scientific research was needed to prove that parents should hold their children.

Deborah Blum puts Harlow's research in a very surprising light in her biography, *Love at Goon Park*. She offers quite a bit of evidence that childcare "experts" before Harlow often believed that touch was anything but beneficial. In orphanages, orderlies were expected to ... keep things orderly. Babies were not supposed to be touched for fear of spreading germs. We are used to extremely liberal hospital visitation policies today, but they are a recent development. In the 1950s, sick children were deposited in hospitals and prevented from seeing their parents more than once a day or even once a week. Child care manuals were full of dire warnings about spoiling children, and hugs and kisses were treated as sloppy indulgences.

It's hard to believe that no one was aware that children cling to abusive parents. Every parent knows that kids are quick to forgive a harsh scolding or spanking. We know that abused children will very often want to remain in the custody of their parents; that's a familiar part of the tragedy of child abuse. But let's give Harlow the benefit of the doubt. Maybe what we know now is not exactly what Harlow knew at the beginning of the 1950s. The question, then, is what role his experiments played in teaching the important lessons about attachment and abuse. Did they actually teach these lessons?

Nobody seriously thinks that rhesus monkeys are cognitively and emotionally just like human beings. The pattern of behavior observed in the monkeys couldn't possibly have led directly to conclusions about human children, without any additional information. I suspect the gap between data and conclusion was at least tacitly filled by theories of attachment that were current at the time. While Harlow was designing clever monkey experiments in Wisconsin, John Bowlby was studying attachment in the UK, based on observations at orphanages. Data had also been published about the way absence of touch, in orphanages, was correlated with higher disease rates. Many trends were pointing the way toward a new model of healthy parenting. The monkeys' affinity for abusive mothers must also have dovetailed with what was already known about abusive human mothers, for the researchers to have thought they were finding out about human psychology, and not just monkey psychology.

It surely would not be impossible to devise tests to determine the strength of a human infant or toddler's preference for food versus touch. And if it's abused children that need to be tested, the world is full of them. The attitude abused children have toward abusive parents could have been directly observed and carefully documented. But no, the scientific ethos of the time said the controlled, artificial study environment of the animal lab was the way to go, despite the problematic inference that had to be made: if it's this way with monkeys, it's this way with people. Harlow's studies did have one undeniable advantage. Who could possibly forget the pathetic image of the little orphan monkey clinging to the cloth-covered wire-frame mother? How utterly heart-rending that, in the absence of a real mother, the monkey would cling to so little! And who could forget the monkeys that continued to cling, even when the wire mother was turned into a monster? These images are more powerful than statistics about orphanages and abusive parents.

But if the teaching power of Harlow's research is the best that can be said for it, then we've come a long way from Jonas Salk. Salk's research yielded a vaccine that had the power to save thousands of lives. Harlow's research yielded an image – a touching, horrifying, pitiful image, and thus one that stays with every psychology student who runs into it in a textbook. It was an absurd image that corrected another piece of absurdity – the theory that parents should suppress the desire to touch their children, in the name of hygiene and discipline.

Harlow's image as an animal abuser was sealed by experiments he did on depression after the attachment and abuse experiments. He and his colleagues designed a literal "well of despair" – a vertical stainless steel well in which they placed young monkeys for up to 45 days. He carefully observed that the result was "severe and persistent psychopathological behavior of a depressive nature" continuing over nine months later. Could this seriously have come as a surprise to anyone?

Singer points out that Harlow inspired over 250 experiments in the US, involving over 7,000 animals. Every variation on the theme of deprivation, abuse, and isolation has been tried. You have to wonder how these scientists have been able to enlist the cooperation of so many students and colleagues over the years. Why did they all go along with so much pointless sadism? Stanley Milgram's famous obedience research, also from the 1950s, shines some light here.

Milgram created an ingenious set-up involving a punisher, a scientist, and a student. The punishers were 40 volunteers who had no idea what the experiment was really about. The scientist told the punisher he was supposed to deliver increasing electric shocks to the student every time the student gave the wrong answer to a test question. A label at the high end said "XXX warning, extremely dangerous!" Although they could see the student squirming, complaining ("Let me out of here!"), screaming, and growing faint, 26 delivered the maximum voltage despite the warning label. Of course, the students were just actors, and not really being shocked. What was really shocking was the willingness of the volunteers to impose suffering on the "students."

Milgram hypothesized that the volunteers imposed shocks because of the authoritative image of the scientist. The ingenious set-up led Milgram to that conclusion, but he could have reached it by noticing the animal research being done in psychology departments. Why did students and lab workers go along with Harlow's research plans? His authoritative image is part of the explanation, but of course there's another factor in the Harlow type of case, and one that explains why Milgram didn't even think to find it puzzling how students defer to animal researchers. Not only was Harlow an authority figure, but the subjects harmed in his research (and really harmed, not pretend harmed) were "just animals."

Into the Lab

Walk into an animal lab today, and what might you see? I tried to find out the answer first hand, but nothing came of it. Animal advocates have been protesting animal research in the US for decades now, even conducting raids on labs and freeing animals and harassing researchers and their families. The researchers are understandably afraid of letting anyone in the door. I tried to arrange a visit to a facility at Penn State University, but was told that would be impossible.

My image of the modern lab has to be second hand, pieced together from the writing of research-sympathetic authors like Larry Carbone, a lab veterinarian. His recent book *What Animals Want* is a helpful portrait of research labs and how they function. But my image is also indebted to unsympathetic sources like PETA, which have undercover videos to offer. In addition, I have made use of scientific reports of animal research and I've talked to people who work in animal labs.

My two case studies focused on research in which animals suffer a great deal, in one case for a reason that seems worthy, in the other not. Research varies enormously in cost to animals. For example, neuropsychologists have made some extraordinary discoveries about vision by studying monkeys, but without any cost in suffering or life. Monkeys are presented with visual stimuli while painless brain scans are used to identify the areas of the brain involved. But of course, research can be more invasive. Sometimes the visual stimuli are presented while the monkey's cranium is open and electrodes are used to record the activity of individual cells. This isn't painful during the procedure, but it's hard to imagine there's no suffering before and after. Another way to study the visual cortex involves presenting monkeys with images and then immediately killing them and looking at slices of their brains through a microscope. That could easily involve no pain at all, but "only" loss of life.

If you walked into an animal research lab at random, what you would be likely to see are cages full of mice, rats, guinea pigs, and rabbits, not monkeys. That's because something on the order of 95 percent of lab animals belong to those species. In one lab you'd see a study of the effects of mold-infested houses. Scientists would be exposing mice to various molds, then killing them and examining their lungs for damage. In another you might see a study of obesity. Researchers have looked at the role of the hormone leptin in strains of mice. Mice that lack leptin naturally eat too much and become obese. When given leptin injections, they stop over-eating and return to normal. In another lab, tumor growth and regression would be under study. Mice can be specially bred so that they develop tumors in specific organs. Then they are given various treatments to determine the effects on tumors, which requires killing and dissecting the mouse.

Medical techniques are tried out on animals before they're used on humans. You'll be grateful to know that, if you're ever lying on a gurney waiting to be wheeled into heart surgery. But you'll also have to thank the animals if you're ever on the verge of a cosmetic procedure. Silicone breast implants have been tested in rabbits. If it's smoother skin you want, you can rest assured that laser microderm abrasion has been tested on the skin of pigs. Every batch of Botox heading for a dermatologist's office is pre-tested in rats. All these animals either die as a result of research or they're discarded when they've outlived their usefulness.

It's hard to come up with exact numbers, but death is very often a part of research on animals, pain is often involved as well (but perhaps less often than death), and some research involves neither. Sometimes physical pain is deliberately inflicted as part of an experiment, like when painkillers are under study. Pain is generated, and then one cohort receives pain killers while the other doesn't. Of course, in the Harlow experiments, the emotional suffering of the monkeys was deliberately engineered.

In the 1950s when Salk and Harlow were doing their famous experiments, animal research was completely unregulated in the US. Every researcher was free to treat animals just as he or she pleased. In 1966, that changed. The trigger was concern of citizens for their pets. *Sports Illustrated* had published an article about a lost dog who wound up in a lab. Then *Life* magazine published a story about surplus dogs from pet dealers who wound up in labs, complete with pictures. In response to the public outcry, Congress passed the 1966 version of the Laboratory Animal Welfare Act (AWA), which put very minimal limits on labs that experimented on dogs and cats (only). To deal with the risk of labs using lost or stolen pets, they began requiring that dealers selling animals to labs have licenses. The 1966 Act also required animals to be housed and fed adequately before and after experimentation (though nothing was said about their treatment during experiments).

The AWA was amended five times between 1970 and 2002. The 1970 amendment expanded the act to cover all warm-blooded animals, except mice and rats, and to cover animals in circuses and zoos; still excluded were many venues like pet stores, pet shows, and rodeos. The 1970 amendment also took the critical step of regulating the way experiments are done, addressing the issue of animal pain; anesthetics now had to be used during surgery and analgesics had to be offered for pain relief.

Two raids on animal labs spurred the next set of reforms. Alex Pacheco of PETA had taken an undercover position at the lab of Dr. Edward Taub in Silver Spring, Maryland, where nervous system healing was being studied by means of macaque monkeys having the nerves to their arms surgically severed. Though the National Institutes of Health (NIH) had funded the study, there had never been an animal welfare visit to the lab, where Pacheco alleged hundreds of deficiencies in veterinary care. He had a chance to testify during 1981 congressional hearings. Then another lab was raided, this time by the shadowy Animal Liberation Front (ALF). The University of Pennsylvania head injury lab, run by Dr. Thomas Gennarelli, was using baboons to study head trauma during car crashes. The baboons were literally having their heads crushed in a crash-simulation device, and the proceedings were being filmed by the researchers themselves. The ALF broke into the lab and stole 64 hours worth of film, which PETA then reduced to a horrifying 26 minutes called *Unnecessary Fuss* (the name being borrowed from a phrase Gennarelli used to dismiss the whole affair). It took a great deal of further pressure from PETA, but the NIH finally withdrew funding, the head injury lab was closed, and the University of Pennsylvania was fined (the measly sum of) $4,000.

It was in the period following these exposés that Ronald Reagan signed the next amendments of the AWA into law. In 1985, the basic care standards were supplemented with requirements for dogs to have exercise and primates to have appropriate psychological enrichment. At the same time, new methods of oversight were introduced. Inspectors from the US Department of Agriculture (USDA) were required to make visits every year or two. Each facility was required to set up an animal care committee (IACUC – Institutional Animal

Care and Use Committee) composed of at least three individuals, including a veterinarian and an unaffiliated community member with an interest in animal protection. These committees are now standard at all US research institutions. They decide in advance whether lab facilities and plans for experimentation are compliant with AWA regulations. "Final approval of the grant, as well as local permission to obtain animals, rests on approval by the IACUC of that university," says Larry Carbone in *What Animals Want*. In addition, inspectors from the USDA are supposed to pay unscheduled visits to facilities.

For the most part, the AWA has been strengthened every time it's been amended. In 2002, prohibition of animal fighting was added. But not every change has been in the direction of greater protection. In response to a growing demand to cover mice and rats, a 2002 backlash amendment affirmed that mice, rats, birds, and cold-blooded animals were all excluded from all protections. Farm animals have never been covered by the AWA.

How much good has the AWA done for animals? Some scientists say there was never a need for regulation to begin with. Good research requires healthy, happy animals, they say, so the situation was fine before the regulations came along. The Silver Spring and University of Pennsylvania examples surely show that to be false. But it's not believable even apart from that irrefutable evidence. It's just not true that animals given enough space to thrive and enough pain relief to be comfortable always make better experimental subjects. Many animals are killed when their usefulness is over, and there is no gain for science in killing them less painfully. Some animals are surgically altered and then observed after recovery. As Carbone points out, it often makes no difference to science whether the recovery is painful or painless.

Clearly the AWA has progressively offered greater and greater protection to animals. The activists and legislators who worked for it, and those researchers who cooperated, have something to be proud of. So should we feel reassured that all is now right in research labs? Should we trust the existing regulatory structure to give animals all the protection they ought to receive?

Think of all the animals not covered at all by the AWA. The number of AWA-covered animals used in animal labs in 2001 was about 1.25 million. Unlisted animals are more numerous by a huge margin. It's hard to estimate, because the USDA keeps no statistics, but there are records of sales to be studied. Larry Carbone estimates 80 million rats and mice were used, in addition to the listed dogs, cats, primates, rabbits, hamsters, etc. Carbone reports that rats and mice in a typical lab will receive anesthesia and reason-able basic care, even though the law doesn't require it. But without the threat of lost funding and fines, it makes sense to think mice and rats are at risk.

AWA regulations stipulate living conditions for animals that are just shy of cruel. Animals are given "sufficient space to allow each dog and cat to turn about freely and to easily stand, sit and lie in a normal position and to walk in a normal manner." Cats have four square feet in cages two feet high. Dogs have cages that equal in length and width the length of their bodies, plus six inches. The height of the cage gives them six inches of head clear-ance. What dogs can't do in cages that size is wag their tails, jump up on their hindlegs, or run. Or anything else that dogs like to do, like explore, play, run after Frisbees, and enjoy human company.

Well, but it's all for a good cause. Or is it? The Humane Society estimates that 10–20 million animals per year (including both AWA-listed and unlisted animals) are used in labs for drug and product testing. Some of the drugs are no doubt vitally useful, but they include products like mascara, lip collagen, and Botox. Much testing is done to prove the obvious. Oven cleaner is fed to animals to find out just how bad for you it is. Some of the research has dubious relevance. Fabric protector is force fed to mice in amounts way beyond what any human would ever ingest to find out if it's carcinogenic.

Can we at least feel confident that medical research being done today is worthwhile? Peter Singer has an illuminating discussion of the dynamics of university research in *Animal Liberation*. Researchers are not pure seekers of truth and human betterment. They need to publish research papers to get tenure and maintain professional prestige. Studies that may have value at the beginning are repeated with subtle permutations, with constantly diminishing returns. It's reasonable to approach animal research with an inquiring spirit, and look head on at whether the cost to animals of any given experiment is really justifiable.

Yet, how can we really know the answer? As a layman and not a scientist, I am in no position to scrutinize great quantities of research and make a fair assessment of what's worth doing, despite the harm to animals, and what might be worth it, but could be done more humanely, and what really has no earthly justification. Why not, then, take it to heart that animal research is regulated by animal care committees staffed by researchers, veterinarians, and independent concerned citizens? Why not trust *them* to make the dif-ficult judgments?

Necessary Questions

Bernard Rollin teaches veterinary ethics at Colorado State University. He is a staunch advocate for animals, but not averse to working toward reform of existing practices, instead of toward utopian goals. In fact, he was involved in drafting the 1985 amendment to the AWA, and works closely with the animal care committee at his university. He complains that the AWA does not require research to meet the most basic moral standard: that it is worth doing, taking into account the costs to animals and the potential benefits to human beings. Asking that basic question is not within the purview of the animal care committees, a fact you can confirm by reading through the relevant portion of the statute (section 2143).

After 20 years of sitting on these committees, Larry Carbone also writes that they regulate not so much *what* research is done, but *how* it is done. They are nothing like human subject review committees, the very tough institutional boards that have to approve any research involving human beings. These committees require informed consent, making an exception only when informed consent is impossible (e.g. with children), research is vital and non-harmful, and consent of parents can be obtained. Animal research would be held to a much lower standard than human research even if committee members did have to consider whether the benefits are worth it, considering the cost to animals. But the animal care committees don't even have to ask that.

Of course, grant makers don't want to fund pointless research. You're not going to fund a university lab that conducts the sort of research we read about in the opening pages of Richard Adams' novel *Plague Dogs* – where dogs are submerged in water to the point of near-drowning, just to see how long it takes before resuscitation is impossible. (Why would we want to know this about dogs? How could the exact time before irreversible drowning be the same in humans as in dogs?) Federal research funds are limited, so funds will tend to get directed toward research that has more promise. But animal care committees are not under the same pressure to be selective, as Larry Carbone pointed out to me by email. There's literally no limit on the amount of research that they can approve, and no reason for animal care committees to set priorities, allowing more and less harm to come to animals depending on whether research will investigate cancer, or erectile dysfunction, or face lifts. There is pressure to carefully appropriate elite species that are in short supply – chimpanzees, for example, go into AIDS research, not face-lift research. But there's a literally endless supply of rodents, and no upper limit on the amount of pain and death that can be inflicted on them.

The committees do have to ask whether animals will be given proper housing and basic care, and whether they'll receive the sort of anesthesia and analgesia that's possible, given the limits of the experiment. The committee can say no if the *exact* same experiment has already been done (the regulations do give them that role), but not if the researcher has come up with a slight variation. But animal care committees are not charged with the fundamental moral question – whether it's worth doing A to animals in order to get B for humans. So relying on the committees to make necessary moral judgments would be senseless – that's not what they do.

Or so I was quite sure, before I read a book by two beleaguered defenders of animal research. P. Michael Conn is the associate director of the Oregon National Primate Research Center, and James V. Parker is the public information officer for the institution. They've been personally hounded and harassed by animal advocates, and they've got stories to tell that are worth reading. When I opened their new book *The Animal Research War* I was ready and willing to listen to their reply to the "half truths" they see coming out of the animal protection movement. But I was very surprised to read what they had to say. They claim that animal care committees *are* charged with assessing whether "the information sought in the experiments is important enough to the advance of medical knowledge to warrant the use of animals."

With Conn and Parker saying one thing and Rollin and Carbone another, I needed a tie-breaker, so I approached the administrator in charge of research ethics at a major US medical school. I explained that I was looking for guidance, since the literature is divided on what animal care committees actually do, and laid out the two accounts. The response I got was that the critics were "not very well informed." Animal care committees actually *do* ask whether experiments are worth doing, from a moral perspective, I was told. I didn't want the skeptical view to be dismissed so fast, so I emphasized that Rollin and his colleagues did help draft the 1985 AWA amendments, the ones that set up the IACUC system. Carbone, I pointed out, has served on animal care committees for 20 years.

My source insisted that animal care committees do tackle the basic moral question about the balance between costs and benefits. I was told they apply "The Sundowner Principles," and when I looked those up, I discovered a pretty impressive standard that speaks of respect for animals and the importance of judging whether harm to animals can be justified. The second of the three principles says:

> … where animals are used, the assessment of the overall ethical value of such use should include consideration of the full range of potential societal good, the populations affected, and the burdens that are expected to be borne by the subjects of the research.

If committees apply this principle, they're going beyond the requirements set forth in the AWA, but do they really apply this principle? I put the question to my informant, and was given all kinds of reassurances. The picture being painted was *so* rosy that I was starting to get worried. What part of this was the truth, and what part was public relations?

I went back to Carbone's book, and reread the relevant portions about animal care committees. He cites several studies of committee functioning that mesh with his experience: research projects are almost never turned down on ethical grounds, the studies show. But what about those "Sundowner Principles" the animal care committees supposedly apply? I asked Carbone for a reaction, by email. He wagered that maybe 3 percent of IACUC chairs have even heard of them and suggested I Google "Sundowner Principles" to find out how many schools include them on the webpages they provide to assist researchers and animal care committee. Answer: almost none. They're not even available at the research support pages for my source's medical school.

The right conclusion to draw is by no means that animal care committees do nothing important. Carbone emphasizes that they "have been enormously powerful in promoting animal welfare over the past fifteen years." Committees take the task of lessening burdens on animals seriously. But on the whole, it's questionable that they take a cold, hard look at costs for animals and how they balance with likely benefits for human beings. The requirement that they do so ought to be built into the AWA statute, which is after all the letter of the law on how animal research is regulated. It shouldn't be up to committees to apply or not apply such a standard, depending on the inclinations of the people who make it up.

Animal research is already held up to higher ethical standards in many other countries. In the UK, the Secretary of State for the Home Office makes an assessment before licensing research. A 1986 law stipulates that "the Secretary of State shall weigh the likely adverse effects on the animals concerned against the benefit likely to accrue." Stronger statutes than the AWA protect lab animals in Australia, Canada, Japan, Denmark, Germany, the Netherlands, Norway, Sweden, Switzerland, as well as the UK. It's not impossible to work toward a review process that gives more weight to ethics and animal welfare.

There's no saying for sure what sort of research would be rejected by committees that asked what is morally necessary. If that question became routine, and it was asked honestly, it seems significant change would be inevitable. Some research does seem necessary. Jonas Salk *had* to go back down to the basement to continue his research, like our Paleolithic hunter in Chapter 6 *had* to spear the aurochs to feed his family. Polio and starvation were powerful forces with which they had to do battle. But is it morally necessary to create obese mice? Is it morally necessary to inject rats with Botox, rabbits with silicone? So people can make their skin look smoother, is it really necessary to perform skin procedures on pigs? Animal care committees invested with the power to veto, on ethical grounds, might set priorities and attach more weight to some research goals than others. Research that is all equally respectable in the eyes of medical researchers today might come to be seen as ethically uneven, when animals are given all due respect. If serious judgments had to be made about what goals are worth the cost in animal death and suffering, animal care committees would surely make use of their veto power more often.

Nothing elicits admiration quite like the phrase "cancer researcher." We feel the greatest esteem and gratitude for the brainy, compassionate, dogged MDs and PhDs who make the cure for cancer their life goal. On the other hand, "animal researcher" elicits quite a different reaction. We are all animal lovers, at least in some part of our minds (a part that's typically not in full communication with other parts). We hate to think about what animals undergo in animal labs, and feel skeptical about the people who put them through it.

The two phrases had completely different associations for me until one day, at an embarrassingly advanced age, they suddenly got linked together. Aha! Cancer researchers in many cases *are* animal researchers! It is not possible for the first to be good guys and the second bad guys. I cannot feel general disapproval for animal researchers. But I can think they're a mixed lot. There are Jonas Salks and there are Harry Harlows.

The AWA has done a lot for animals, but it wouldn't have stopped a Harry Harlow. In fact, another isolation experiment was proposed by a Harlow student in 1990. He planned to separate 21 monkeys from their mothers at birth and raise them in near total isolation for four years. The goal was to observe which ones developed self-injurious behavior, and compare their surgically removed brains to the brains of those that didn't. That was supposed to tell us something about mentally ill human beings who injure themselves – even though the monkeys were (of course) neither human nor suffering from human mental illnesses. The university's animal care committee did not object.

In present form, the AWA is not all the protection that animals need. Probably no statute can be all they need and attitudes have to change pervasively. The speciesism that says animals are "just animals" has to be drummed out of us. We have to open our eyes even when we're looking at things that seem utterly normal. All that accomplished, I think we would be far more reluctant to experiment on animals and far more conflicted. Still, I think the caveman's justification for hunting does apply, *mutatis mutandis*, to the cancer researcher. If one is justified, so is the other – provided they both limit their predations to the strictly necessary.

Part V

Next

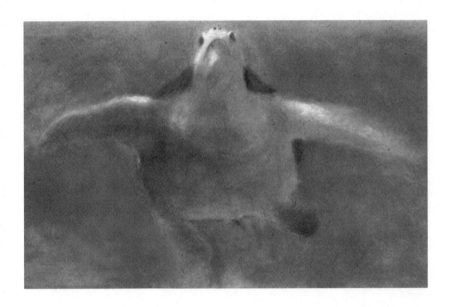

Something new is happening to animals today. The wild animals are disappearing, while the mild animals (the domesticated species we use for food) are becoming both extraordinarily numerous, and disturbingly ill-treated. What are the prospects for changing these trends?

9

Vanishing Animals

The plight of animals demands our attention. Individual animals, as I write this, are suffering in labs, overcrowded barns, and slaughterhouses. In the wild they're being squeezed out of their habitats and hunted for recreation. There's another sort of animal problem that's also urgent. Species are disappearing at a rapid rate. E. O. Wilson projects that 25 percent of existing species will be gone in 100 years if we go on polluting our environment, destroying animal habitats, and generating greenhouse gases at the present rate. Today there are just 5,000–7,000 tigers remaining in the wild. Polar bears are at risk because the arctic ice cap is shrinking. The rhinoceros is close to extinction, a victim of the demand for its horn, which credulous people covet as an aphrodisiac. If we don't make changes quickly, species that took millions of years to evolve will be gone forever.

The concern about species is not simply a concern about individual animals. When a tiger dies at the hands of a hunter, one creature suffers and stops living, whether there are 5,000 remaining tigers or a billion. The fact that there are few remaining doesn't cause a problem for the individuals being killed, beyond the problem of being killed, which they'd have anyway. There isn't the sort of problem for survivors that there is when people are threatened by genocide. It's excruciating to think your ethnic group is being decimated, but animals aren't tuned in to the decline of a species. At most, extinction can cause poignant problems for the last remaining members of a species, the ones left looking for conspecifics with whom to mate or carry out instinctive behaviors. But compassion for these few survivors is surely not what lies behind our huge concern about endangered species.

Animal rights organizations like PETA advocate for individuals, not species; the Sierra Club and the World Wildlife Fund focus on species, not individuals. In philosophers as well, the two concerns don't always go together. Peter Singer's book *Animal Liberation* has no chapters about endangered species, and neither does Tom Regan's book *The Case for Animal Rights*. Regan explains it like this:

> Because paradigmatic right-holders are individuals and because individuals
> do not acquire any further rights if they belong to rare or endangered species,
> the rights view does not acknowledge any privileged moral status on the part
> of members of rare or endangered species ... Moreover, to the extent that
> efforts to protect rare and endangered species foster beliefs and attitudes that
> place less importance on the value of plentiful animals, to that extent the
> rights view must lodge its strong moral dissent. All animals are equal, both
> the plentiful and the rare.

Conversely, some environmental ethicists give great weight to species and scoff at the notion that individual animals have rights. Of course, the two concerns can coexist. The primatologist Jane Goodall is passionately involved in saving chimpanzees from extinction, but also a devoted animal activist concerned with individual animals. The Humane Society is best know for its defense of individual animals, but also raises awareness about endangered species.

Supposing you do care about the serious problems of individual animals, and in the way I've suggested – with respect and compassion your guiding values, why care about species too?

Why Species Matter

If we want to do right by individual animals, I've argued, it's important for us to pay close attention to the sort of capacities that mark their kind. These capacities garner admiration and esteem, and ultimately respect. We must see what makes a chimpanzee different from a squirrel, before we can know our respect must be greater for the chimpanzee. We must see the difference between dolphins and tuna to see that there's a problem with killing tuna by any method, but a special problem with methods that accidentally kill dolphins as bycatch. A decision whether to use mice or dogs in an experiment (if the experiment is to be done at all) can't be made well unless we grasp the differences between mice and dogs.

Once we are tuned in to the characteristics of species and their power to evoke esteem and respect, it certainly seems natural to care whether there continue to be individuals of that kind. If chimpanzee capacities have value then it makes sense to want there to be chimpanzees. The fact that there are chimpanzees adds goodness to the world. The same ought to be said for animals that are less impressive. The fact that there are squirrels adds goodness. The fact that there are spiders adds goodness.

Of course, in nature there are interactions, so the difference an animal makes to the world derives both from its own assets and its impact. Bees add to the world because they have astonishing abilities, but also because they are a "keystone" species. Other species have assets, but a negative impact. A mosquito is a "good thing" intrinsically, but malarial mosquitoes lead to over a million deaths every year. Taking into account the intrinsic and instrumental good (and bad) associated with a species, we have reasons to care about species, though we will be more anxious to preserve some than others (and some we will want to destroy).

Thinking about the puzzle of species just this much and no more, you can see why it makes sense to care if an acre of forest is destroyed and replaced with an empty asphalt lot. That may eliminate a species (in *The Diversity of Life* E. O. Wilson explains that many species have astoundingly small niches), and thereby make the world a little worse. But that's not the sort of scenario we confront. Forests aren't cut down to make room for utterly empty lots. Often they're cut down to make room for more people or for the livestock that feed people. And therein lies a puzzle: if people have especially impressive assets, why not rejoice? Is it really better for the world to contain a huge variety of species than for it to be jammed with lots and lots of representatives of the "best" species?

We encountered some possible answers in Chapter 2. "It takes all kinds to make a world," say the plenitude thinkers. Without the frogs, chimpanzees, and spiders, the world would not be complete. The ladder of being would be missing rungs. Or: God created all the species (according to Genesis), *and saw that it was good*. There should be frogs, chimpanzees, and spiders and that is that. If none of that appeals, you could rely on a sense of beauty. Homogeneity is dull, variety is beautiful, and beauty is good. So the world really is a better place for there being vast numbers of species, instead of vast numbers of representatives of a few elite species. Certainly, diversity has a more mundane importance; a diversely populated biotic community is hardier, more capable of surviving threats that affect different species differently. Diversity tends to make for stability.

Each idea will have its fans, but the appeal to completeness strikes me as the most compelling. Say that I am creating a book collection – not a lending library that must cater to public tastes, but a collection. I may judge Tolstoy to be the best author, but I will surely not want the collection to contain nothing but Tolstoy. Even worse would be a collection consisting of *Anna Karenina* many times over. A collection is better for containing many kinds of good, instead of a huge amount of one kind.

Or perhaps I'm creating not a collection but a life – my own life. Perhaps I judge kindness or (more abstractly) morality to be the best good achievable. Knowledge is a separate and different good that's not quite as good, and self-expression is good too, but still lower in my estimation. To make my life as good as possible, it's not true that I will stuff it with kindness, and only kindness. Such a life would not be "complete" – it would not have all the important kinds of goodness. Overall goodness turns on a spectrum of goods, not just the greatest quantity of one good, even if it's "the best good."

If I'm not creating a book collection or my life, but a world … well, perhaps what that would be like exceeds our grasp. But if it's anything at all like creating in familiar situations, I will want all kinds of good to be included, not just human good, even if I think that's the best good. As I leaf through my catalog of possible worlds, it will be reasonable for me to pass by the one with 50 billion people and no other creatures (assume it's somehow a stable, hardy world), and select the one with a huge variety of species.

Now, we know that species evolved and did not appear *ex nihilo*. If you think evolution was the creation-method of a supreme being, you could coherently think the variety of species was intentional – a way of making the world better than it might have been. But if no deity was steering things, and the variety of species was merely a product of blind natural forces, it's still open to us to think of variety as a plus. You may still think "life is good" (as a popular line of T-shirts proclaim) and that one good thing about the world is the extraordinary variety of life – the fact that there are frogs and chimpanzees and spiders, and millions of other species, not just billions of representatives of one fine species.

Thinking about species this way comports with an intuition that many of us have. We think that the continued existence of tigers, as it might be, has "ultimate" importance. The world is better for there being tigers, and not merely better *for us*. I suspect that this is the sort of thinking about species that animates the most passionate wildlife activism, and the strongest sense of urgency about endangered species. But admittedly, some will find it intellectually impossible to sign on to the sheer goodness of tigers, and their power to make the world a better place. For naysayers, there are other rationales for worrying about species, though I think none quite as satisfying and motivating.

Man Is the Measure

The ancient pre-Socratic philosopher Protagoras said "Man is the measure of all things, of the things that are, that they are, and of the things that are not, that they are not." If we find it good that there are tigers, we must be projecting that goodness onto them. If we find it bad that there are no longer dodos, we must be projecting badness onto their non-existence. Tigers aren't *really* good, but good *to us*.

Tigers are good *to us* for a wide range of reasons. We grew up thinking of them as a part of our world. We read about them in story books and played with toy versions of them. We saw them in zoos and imagined them out in the wild. A world without tigers thus feels less like our world, the world we are used to. Tigers are good *to us* since they help make the world the home we are accustomed to. They satisfy our desire for familiarity. There must continue to be tigers in India, elephants in Africa, and polar bears in the Arctic, for this to be the world we know and love.

Could that understanding of the good of tigers fire up an activist to work hard for their preservation? Maintaining the familiar contours of nature doesn't seem like a mission that could ignite enormous enthusiasm. But the Protagorean approach can be developed in more inspiring directions. The trick is to see how our preference for species preservation might come from a deeper source than our desire for familiarity. Other species do great things for us. For one, they teach us lessons and give us food for thought. The study of animals tells us much about ourselves. If you're interested in male and female behavior, it's got to be illuminating to study rutting deer, attentive emperor penguin fathers, lions that kill cubs before taking over a pride. If you want to understand human sexuality, there's something to learn by studying pair-bonded birds and promiscuous bonobos. The varieties of animal behavior tell us something about ourselves whether by contrast or because there are commonalities. To understand the animal in ourselves, it pays to understand other animals.

And no, it won't do to let them die out, and study them in books. The vast majority of species, even including celebrity species like the lion and the emperor penguin, are not well understood. Their continued existence, in the wild – where instincts can play themselves out – is pivotal to learning how they live their lives.

Species are good *to us* because they teach us about ourselves, but also because their bodies do us good. This point won't appeal to animal rights advocates, but it's part of the thinking of environmental activists. If the rhinoceros horn really did produce an aphrodisiac (and humans had a deficit in that area), that would be a reason to conserve the species. We'd want to make sure that there would continue to be individuals to use as a resource far into the future. We do make valuable products using many plant and animal species that are now being threatened by the destruction of the Amazonian rain forest, and could make many more if they survive.

Perhaps the deepest version of the "good *to us*" way of thinking involves E. O. Wilson's notion of "biophilia." Wilson argues that the existence of a wilderness full of other species satisfies human desires that run much deeper than a desire for familiarity or a desire for knowledge and valuable resources. What we feel on a deep level is a desire for wildness itself, a desire for there to be creatures that are *other* than us, *not* tamable, *not* just useful in a crude sense. We want there to be other living powers in the world, other autonomous beings, other foreign ways of life. We don't want all the world to be like putty in our hands. On this interpretation, other species are good only *to us*, but they're good in a profound way, not in a shallow way. They meet a deep need, so that their disappearance must leave us not just a little uneasy, frustrated, or less amused, but deeply unsatisfied.

Biophilia, if it were something we all found in ourselves, would create a passion for species preservation, but I wonder if we really all do feel it. There's certainly a subpopulation that adores getting out in the middle of the woods, and thrills to the sight of an eagle or a deer, but what should we say to the person who is not moved by wilderness? What of people who are happiest at shopping malls, racetracks, and movie theaters? Should we say that they *should* feel biophilia, even if they don't? But then, why should they?

Try as we may to give depth to the Protagorean view of species, it is inevitably a view with limits. By definition it can't say that tigers matter *because tigers matter*: they are intrinsically good, and add to the good of the world. This thought gives *everyone* a reason to care about endangered species, and gives the activist the strongest inspiration. But we do well to pay attention to the Protagorean reasons as well. In our most hard-headed moments, we may find ourselves not quite sure a varied world is really the *best* world, or just the one we like best. And besides, multiple reasons are better than one. It may be true that tigers simply make the world a better place, and *also* true that they benefit us in many ways, both deep and shallow.

Mild versus Wild

Tom Regan worries that concern for endangered species will distract from concern for suffering lab and farm animals. Some environmental ethicists have the opposite worry – it's species, or ecosystems, or the biosphere as a whole, that matter most (for example, see Callicott in the Sources). The plight of domesticated animals is a distraction, they think. What we are now realizing is that animal agriculture has become a huge threat to wildlife. So people who care about domesticated animals and wildlife have reason to make common cause. Changes to agriculture are needed for the sake of all animals.

The destruction of forests is bad for our climate (see Chapter 7), but also bad for biodiversity. The leading cause of species endangerment is habitat destruction, and according to the UN report *Livestock's Long Shadow*, livestock and feedcrops are among the major causes of habitat destruction. So while some will enthuse about modern animal agriculture as a tremendous boon to animal populations, the truth is that as mild populations surge, wild populations dwindle, and whole species disappear. Recall Stephen Budiansky's view that farming does a favor to livestock species. I suspect it's no favor it all, as I argued in Chapter 1, but if it were a favor, we'd have to balance our enthusiasm with concern for the wild species that are being displaced.

Expanded animal agriculture is taking over more of earth's land surface, thereby crowding out wild animals in several different ways. First, there's the spread of animals over the earth's surface, as more and more land is used as pasture. These animals are mobile foragers who spend their lives under the open skies. Second, there is expanding animal agriculture on the new intensive model. Animals are housed in the smallest amount of space possible (which is good from the point of view of wild animals), but they have to be supplied with their feed. Half the cropland in the US is now used to feed animals who live out their lives inside of barns. Then there's animal agriculture on a mixed model. The standard procedure in the US today is for cattle to be pastured for about eight months and then transported to crowded feedlots for roughly another six months, where they are switched from a grass to a corn diet. Super-intensive feeding, together with hormones and antibiotics, are used to produce the largest possible animal in the shortest amount of time.

The impact on wild animals depends on the form of animal agriculture. Longstanding grazing lands are places where farm animals share living space with wild animals. The problem is that the livestock animals make overbearing roommates. The Sierra Club's brief is that they consume too much of the water in streams, and destroy riverbanks. The fences put up to keep one herd separate from another prevent necessary wildlife migrations. And when wild animals attack the intruders, private individuals and the US wildlife service steps in, killing 100,000 predators – mostly wolves and bears – a year. Intensive agriculture has a different sort of impact. The waste and chemicals generated by huge numbers of animals packed into a small space overload local streams and soils, affecting all organisms in the area.

Now, you may say, people have to eat. And if they didn't eat animals, they'd have to eat more plants. And so the land occupied by farm animals today would have to be occupied by crops, if the world's population lived on plant foods. So – the reasoning continues – what really threatens wild animals is too many people, not the farm animals we eat. But that's the wrong picture of agricultural land use. The total land it takes to feed a given human population is much greater if they are meat-eaters and much smaller if they have a plant-based diet. The extra land involved in meat-eating is due to the inefficiency of converting plant protein into animal protein, and then feeding animals to people. Much of the plant protein is "wasted" because it is used to sustain the animal's life until slaughter, and not just to build edible flesh. Some of the calories go toward putting flesh on a creature's bones, but some to the bones themselves, the fur, the basic bodily processes of respiration and maintaining body temperature. (The inefficiency varies with the animal: 21 pounds of plant protein are needed for a pound of beef while 8 pounds of plant protein are needed to produce a pound of pork.)

The growing human population is certainly part of what threatens bio-diversity today. Our shopping malls, roads, and housing developments have reduced the number of species that populate the world. Whatever we eat, huge tracts of land have to be devoted to our food supply. But if we have a meat-centered diet, we get in the way of wildlife much more than if we have a plant-centered diet. Whatever we eat, our growing numbers will increase the rate of extinction, but we are making that rate higher than it has to be by putting animal products at the center of our diet.

Wildlife organizations operate in a feel-good mode. They send out beautiful wildlife calendars (I have one on my wall that features three blue-footed boobies this month) and cultivate awe and love for the magnificent animals that share our planet. The organizations would risk alienating their supporters if they pointed a finger at us, but we're the ones who are expanding into animal territory; we're the ones who like malls and big houses on big lots. What's more, we're the ones who eat the animals that fill up ever more of the earth's surface. And that's something we can easily stop doing. Animal rights organizations urge us to decline the hamburger for the sake of the cow. But there's another reason to eat less meat (or none at all). With loss of habitat, species are going to disappear. You can decline the hamburger to save the cow, but just as reasonably, to save the tiger.

Culture Clash

How far should we go to protect a species? For many decades, Eskimos have been under pressure to change. They continue to hunt the bowhead whale in the Arctic Sea, even though there aren't many left – only around 10,500, according to the International Whaling Commission's estimate. There's also a problem on the individual level. Whales are particularly intelligent animals, with amazing abilities. The whales of Alaska somehow migrate all the way from Alaskan waters to Hawaiian waters in the spring. They seem to communicate with each other in song, and the females bond closely with their young. They have extraordinarily long lives, so what's gone when a whale dies is a repository of 130–50 years' memory. To learn more about whales is to find your respect for them increasing. Such a huge animal isn't easily killed, so there is no such thing as humane whale hunting. The whale is speared, but takes many hours to die.

Many Eskimos want to continue whale hunting because it's deeply entrenched in Eskimo culture. If the welfare of individual animals matters, and preserving species matters, does culture matter too, and does that give us human beings prerogatives that haven't yet been countenanced in this book? The cultural defense of whale hunting might be dismissed as entirely shallow, and without moral merit. After all, culture has been used to defend many egregious violations of human rights. It surely doesn't work as a defense of slavery that the culture of the antebellum south couldn't survive without it. It wasn't a good defense of slavery in ancient Greece and Rome that those societies couldn't have flourished if slavery had been abolished. Should we go as far as to say that culture isn't a good at all?

If you think of species diversity as a good, it's unlikely you will want to be that dismissive of culture. Some of the same reasons for valuing one are also reasons for valuing the other. A species is defined by some set of valuable capacities. Elephants, for example, have impressive abilities to bond together as families, take care of each other, remember the past, navigate long distances, and even (possibly) treasure the dead. Eskimo culture is associated with a set of strengths as well – e.g. resourcefulness, skill, artistry, perseverance. The same general kinds of reasons it seems good for elephants to go on existing carry over and apply in the case of Eskimo culture.

Culture also helps with a basic problem of human existence – too many choices. A culture provides the individual with a menu of possibilities. We pick from the housing, mating, food, and career possibilities on the menu, and don't have to ponder the pros and cons of every other conceivable option. Of course, some communities are more tolerant and porous than others. In most American communities, you can cast off the menu and pursue some countercultural way of life. But there's pressure to conform, enough so that most of us don't seriously have to entertain the full range of possible patterns of human existence.

The ways of a species may not improve the welfare of every single individual. In wolves, the alpha male mates with the females, while the rest don't have that pleasure or fecundity. There are cultures with similar patterns. Powerful men take multiple wives, leaving less powerful males forced to leave the community in search of mates, or resigned to permanent bachelorhood. We accept the ways of the species, without judgment, but it's reasonable to expect more of human cultures. A culture worth preserving must enhance the lives of individual members, giving each basic dignity and opportunities to flourish.

The survival or extinction of a culture also brings up more issues for the sheer fact that members of animal species can't contemplate their species identity, and members of cultures *can* contemplate their cultural identity. The threatened disappearance of a culture, whether through killing or assimilation is painful to survivors, while the dwindling of a species is beyond the ken of every animal but ourselves.

So the value (and disvalue) of culture is more complicated, but all in all, it would be odd to recognize species diversity as making the world a better place, but not value the multiplicity of cultures. The continuation of Eskimo culture has to be seen as *a* good. But an absolute good? A good that trumps all, even the extinction of the bowhead whale?

What we have here is a difficult conflict, with the good of species preservation *and* the individual whale's welfare pulling in one direction, but the good of cultural continuity pulling in another. The "simplifier" wants to resolve the problem by denying one or more of the goods that are apparently at stake. Eskimo defenders of whaling rights tend to do this, putting forth the not very convincing notion (see Chapter 1) that the individual whale "gives himself to the people." They insist as well that the species isn't really endangered, based on their own estimates of the remaining whales. Animal rights advocates and wildlife advocates sometimes do the opposite, trivializing the good of culture.

The tragic truth is that all the *apparent* issues at stake are real issues. Eskimo culture really does matter; the bowhead whale is an endangered species; each individual whale is clearly harmed by dying and by being killed in a slow and painful manner. So: to kill or not to kill? Any resolution will mean a loss of some sort.

Why not put up with the loss of a little bit of Eskimo culture? In fact, Eskimo whaling culture is not frozen in time. In *The Whale and the Supercomputer*, Charles Wohlforth describes his experience on a twenty-first-century Eskimo whale hunt. The hunters used aluminum boats. Communication between boats was accomplished with walkie-talkies. The whole community stayed in contact by listening to the radio. Whales were butchered with chainsaws, not knives, and whale meat was hauled away on sleds pulled by snowmobiles. If all of those changes could be made without serious damage to Eskimo culture, then why not compromise even further?

Many traditional practices have morphed from one thing into another, without total loss of continuity. The traditional African safari was a blood and guts affair. The wildlife lover took it for granted that the best way to look at animals was through the viewfinder of a gun. Counterparts of these hunters are now looking at animals through camera viewfinders. Is there no possibility of a successor whale-centered way of life, to replace the culture of whale hunting? It seems conceivable that looking and studying could replace killing and eating. In my mind's eye I see a whale research station in Barrow Alaska, a beacon to whale researchers everywhere. The whale continues to be central to the Eskimo culture, but as a celebrated species, not as meat.

But then what? Eskimos rely on subsistence hunting quite generally, not just on whale hunting. The genius of Eskimo culture has always been its power to make a good life in a harsh environment. Replace all forms of subsistence hunting with trips to expensive stores, where food is brought in by airplanes from hundreds or thousands of miles away, and you really do have a radically altered culture. You don't have the independent, resourceful way of life that Eskimos are justifiably proud of.

So is the best thing to stop the whale hunt but continue the hunting of plentiful caribou and salmon, because *some* form of subsistence is part of "what it means to be an Eskimo"? Putting myself in the shoes of people living in northern Alaska, I'm not happy with the idea of giving up the excitement and know-how involved in living off the land and sea. I don't think it can possibly be better to eat factory-farmed meat imported from the lower 48. The greens, grains, beans, and fruit that are part of a southern diet don't seem as if they must be the cornerstone of my northern diet. Giving up my customary connection to the land and my way of life is a lot to ask.

If all animal use vaporized over night, Eskimo culture would be altered a great deal. Subsistence hunting (but not necessarily for endangered species) is that integral to the Eskimo way of life. In other parts of the world, hunting or farming or herding have the same centrality. The "Reindeer People" of Siberia – carefully described in Piers Vitebsky's recent book by that name – would not be the same people if they gave up their nomadic, herding way of life. They would have to move to cities and take jobs with no connection to their history and traditions. Amish communities in Pennsylvania and Ohio couldn't go on with their nineteenth-century way of life if they stopped using horses to pull plows and carriages. The San People of the Kalahari desert couldn't have been the people they were, before assimilation extinguished much of their culture starting about 50 years ago, without being hunters. Cultural arguments could be used to defend the status quo in a wide variety of cases, but it could also be over-used. It's true that the bullfight is a distinctively Spanish cultural product, but who could truly say they'd lost a crucial chunk of their cultural identity by giving it up? I'm still an American, though I eat vegetable pie, not turkey, for Thanksgiving. I feel well-connected to Jewish traditions, though I use a lamb figurine instead of a shank bone on the seder plate for Passover.

Where cultural identity truly *is* at stake, is it a good rationale for continuing some animal-exploitative practice? Killing the aurochs to keep himself alive was justifiable for the caveman. Herding sheep to secure a safe and settled way of life was justifiable for our forebears. Killing monkeys to develop the polio vaccine seems defensible. But doing such things to preserve Eskimo, or Amish, or nomadic identities? What we have here is a delicate problem of weighing, with one genuine value pitted against another genuine value. Enthusiasts for animals will find the answer as obvious as enthusiasts for culture, yet completely disagree. I'd hope that successor options can be developed – the equivalents of my vegetable pie and plastic lamb, though it's not the way of the world that such tidy solutions are always available.

If you are feeling more animal-kind as a result of reading this book, you are probably thinking most about domesticated animals trapped in stalls, and lab animals being sacrificed for unnecessary research. Preserving endangered species isn't a question of kindness, since it's individuals that need our kindness, not species. But as we tune in to the magnificence of animals, we notice and appreciate what makes them different from one another. We have reason to want the natural world to remain splendidly varied. It makes sense to put the welfare of individual animals *and* the continuation of species on our list of serious concerns.

If we also add culture preservation to our list of concerns, we add yet another facet to the animal conundrum. We should do so, to countenance the full complexity of real-world situations. But let's not exaggerate. For most of us, our sense of ourselves and our way of life would not be threatened by moving in the direction of respect for animals both as individuals and as species. We can remain who we are while moving in new directions.

10

The Endless Story

Animal rights activists sometimes turn to the abolition of slavery for inspiration. At first there were only a few abolitionists opposing a giant, pervasive, and abhorrent institution. They were able to see the wrongness of slavery even when many couldn't. By campaigning for the end of the slave trade in the UK and convincing powerful people to take their side, they advanced toward their goal. Abolitionists in the US took on slavery even though it had been practiced for hundreds of years and permeated southern life. Fought over in a long, bloody war, slavery is something we all now recognize as a terrible mistake.

Some activists encourage us to see animal liberation as a similar struggle. They comfort themselves that they have the clarity of vision that the early abolitionists did, and look forward to the day when their goals will be achieved and everyone will look on their perspicacity with admiration. But I think the animal conundrum is something quite different from the question of slavery. The story of "animal liberation" is likely to be much more complicated.

The Animal Conundrum

The deep commonality that existed between African slaves and white citizens inevitably had to be recognized. Once you see that slavery is wrong, you see it plainly. When enough people had seen it, they had to take action. Slavery has now been eradicated, almost like a disease (but with occasional outbreaks still occurring in the modern world). The clear vision of its wrongness led to its demise.

There are commonalities between animals and people, but not like the ones between white master and black slave. You could see that slaves are just like you, but you can't see that mice are just like you. Mice are subjects of their own lives, but their lives are extremely different from ours. They are not persons, but neither are they rocks; they are in between. Chances are good that we will always debate the status of animals.

Some philosophers do see an absolute wrong in the exploitation of animals akin to the absolute wrong of slavery, but I argued against that outlook in Chapter 6. If the basic thing we owe to all creatures is respect, and using-merely-as-a-means is disrespectful, so, sometimes, is standing by idly. Doing nothing for your impoverished family when you could raise a goat, and doing nothing for AIDS patients when you could test drugs on mice, is not respectful to the family and the AIDS patients. Because animals really are very different from human beings, and there really *is* less to respect in a mouse or a goat than a human being, I've argued that it's OK to test the drug and raise the goat. But slavery is another matter. There isn't less to respect in an African slave than in his or her white owner. In every situation you can imagine, a person's best course is not to subjugate anyone as a slave. When there's that much consistency, we make a generalization – "Slavery is always wrong." But we can't make a similar generalization to the effect that using animals as resources is always wrong.

Part of the difficulty of simply stating what can and can't be done to animals is that respectfulness has fuzzy boundaries. My local vegan restaurant – the excellent "Spiral Diner" in Oak Cliff, Texas – does not serve honey. Bees work hard at making honey, which bathes their young in nutrients as they mature. We "steal" the substance and enjoy its delicious taste. I can detect a hint of disrespect in the practice, but is it so serious that we must bring it to an end? A friend of mine recently remarked that birdwatchers are a bit like stalkers, the way they pursue birds and spy on them with binoculars. Stalking people is disrespectful, but what about stalking birds? Must birdwatchers think hard about their hobby? To produce the marvelous series *The Life of Mammals*, David Attenborough's film crews surreptitiously invaded the space of animals in the wild. In one particularly fascinating segment, they drilled down into the burrow of a platypus – an egg-laying mammal – and inserted a periscope-like camera, giving viewers a chance to see a drop of milk emerge from the mother's skin for a blind, wriggling, tiny newborn. It's fascinating footage, but does this amount to a disrespectful violation of the private space of these animals? Is it disrespectful to use animals non-lethally, milking cows, shearing sheep, hitching an ox to a plow, and riding horses? Respect is not a perfectly crisp concept, yet it resonates. We do want to be respectful to animals, and we should be, but for the foreseeable future, there's bound to be some dispute over what a respectful person may and may not do.

The animal conundrum is not going to get resolved all at once, in a burst of moral clarity. It's going to keep bothering us and giving us new questions to answer. Yet I think some pieces of the conundrum do have a clear resolution. We need to do much better by farm and lab animals. We need better regulation of medical research so that all the research that's done can honestly be called "necessary." We need to protect wild animals from the vast herds we've created to feed ourselves.

What's going to bring about changes in these areas? And how can our moral insights make a difference?

Innovations, Alliances

There are whole categories of evil that we no longer inflict on animals. Artists and writers have depicted the suffering of horses forced to help us fight our wars, despite their total ignorance of the *casus belli*. E. L. Doctorow's novel of the civil war, *The March*, highlights the huge toll of Sherman's campaign in the south on the animals that carried men into battle, or carried wagon-loads of equipment and injured soldiers, or followed behind the column of soldiers as (literally) a walking food supply. The wear and tear on animals was so enormous that periodically the spent and injured were dumped into rivers or seas and fresh beasts were brought in as replacements. All this was phased out not because sensitive animal lovers challenged the abuse of animals in war, but simply because the engine was discovered, and trucks and tanks took the place of animals. Today there aren't many armed conflicts where animals play a role.

In peacetime, animals were everywhere used to pull plows and transport passengers. The sheep and cattle that milled around pastures all around the world were much better off than the horses that pulled people, goods, and farm equipment. Again, it wasn't moral outrage that changed things, but the sudden appearance of a new technology. Animals are still beasts of burden in many areas of the world, but at least in modern, industrialized countries, they are no longer.

Moral insight played little or no role in these changes. It didn't come first, and cause the changes. Yet, it does enter into the picture. Ironically, it's after a change that we're at liberty to say that the way we did things before was repugnant. The image of the spent animals being thrown out, if it were included in a movie version of Doctorow's novel, would surely horrify audiences. When a practice has been rendered obsolete by new technology, we don't have the sense of necessity swaying our thoughts any more. The insights into how terrible things *used to be* have the potential to gather new converts to the general cause of animals.

We've moved beyond the need to use animals for warfare and transportation. We've also reduced our need to use them for fiber. Mountaineers in photos from 50 years ago are bundled up in bulky natural fabrics, where today their counterparts are wearing polyester in many forms, though they still insulate their bodies with down. Again, no moral impulse has played much of a role, but just the march of technical progress. What once couldn't be done without animal byproducts can now be done even better with synthetics.

Today, animal exploitation is dominated by the use of animals for food. Every year 9.5 billion animals are killed in the US for food, and 218 million for all other purposes combined (including animal research, hunting, by animal shelters, etc.). How could the use of animals for food become obsolete? Well, we do have new products and know-how. There are innumerable vegetarian cookbooks that explain how to make delicious food without meat and animal byproducts. For people habituated to an animal-centered diet, there are meat, dairy, and egg substitutes made out of soy. And most perplexingly, we have the new idea of *in vitro* meat just above the horizon. This is animal flesh grown from animal starter-cells in the lab. The idea is to grow animal muscle without the rest of the animal. "Inputs" needed will be much reduced, since lab meat doesn't have bones and fur, doesn't keep itself warm and respirate. Lab meat also doesn't suffer from lifelong confinement and careless slaughter. Yes, to most of us today it sounds disgusting, but it's not impossible that our descendants in the third millennium will think *we* were disgusting for killing, disemboweling, and carving up the corpses of living creatures. They will take "manufactured" meat for granted, and look back in horror on "creature" meat. Well, maybe. One day, with greatly increased populations, earth will no longer support all the livestock that are needed to feed the world. A demand for manufactured meat may well develop; and research is under way to prepare for the day.

Meat-replacement innovations could be a long time coming. Meanwhile, those 9.5 billion animals a year, in the US alone, are enduring lives not worth living and facing painful deaths. What hope can there be for them?

One basis for hope is issue-alliances. Many people can barely hear a message about the mistreatment of farm animals, but are all ears on an allied issue like health. It's easy to be interested in a diet that promotes one's own health and longevity; harder to be convinced that your diet ought to be respectful and compassionate to animals. But fortunately, the healthful diet *is* the compassionate diet. Reducing meat and dairy products means reducing saturated fat, cholesterol, and possibly calories. And will you be robbed of essential nutrients? Here's what noted food science professor and author Marion Nestle had to say about Tony Gonzalez, a Kansas City Chiefs football player who switched to a vegan diet:

> Why anyone is surprised that people can do well on vegetarian and vegan diets is beyond me. Plant foods have plenty of protein and calories if you eat enough of them. If he is following a strict vegan diet – no animal products at all – he will need to find a source of vitamin B12 (it's made by bacteria and incorporated into animal tissues), but supplements work just fine.
>
> I just don't see this as any big deal. Many different dietary patterns promote health and this one can too. I suppose people will attribute any missed block or dropped pass to his diet, but cheeseburgers are not essential nutrients.

The conservative and conventional US Department of Agriculture also says, "Vegetarian diets can meet all the recommendations for nutrients" and adds that vegetarian substitutes for meat products are lower in saturated fat and cholesterol. Although dietary advice tends to be conflicted and ridden with fads, on the whole nutritionists are coming around to a consensus that we would do better for ourselves if we at least cut back on animal products, no longer making them the center of every meal.

Another important alliance has recently emerged. Animal advocates have long seen a natural alliance between animal concerns and environmental concerns. As I discussed in Chapters 7 and 9, the vast and growing livestock population feeds the world at a huge price in land and resources. That point has been made since Francis Moore Lappé published *Diet for a Small Planet* in 1971. But in the last several years the livestock population has been implicated as a factor in today's most alarming environmental trend – global warming. If people are disinclined to give up meat for the sake of the animals themselves, there's reason to hope they will cut back to slow down warming trends. Admittedly, this is tricky. Cutting back on meat consumption is just as "green" as buying a hybrid car (see Chapter 7), but the link to climate change is much harder to see. There's also much less visibility to personal dietary changes. We wouldn't want to assume people are motivated merely by image enhancement, but neither should we naively ignore the role that self-branding plays in personal decisions. What animal advocates have to hope is that a person walking into a steak house will start to seem (to himself and others) just as ungreen as a person driving a large SUV.

Just as moral arguments about animals can be more persuasive after innovations have altered our sense of the possibilities, so allied issues can give moral arguments a foothold. If you're convinced that too much meat is bad for your health *and* bad for the environment, it just may be possible for thoughts about animal welfare to sink in as well. The other issues may soften the conviction that animal products are an absolute necessity, thereby making room for a new concern about animals.

Public Activism

Better protection of animals isn't going to come entirely from moral insight, but insight surely has a role to play. A small band of committed and determined people can have an effect way beyond their numbers. The notorious Draize test used to be the procedure of choice for testing the effect of household products on the eyes. Rabbits were restrained in barbaric devices, as products from shampoo to oven cleaner were dripped into their eyes. Harry Spira's loud and public battle against Revlon in the 1980s led to the establishment of the Johns Hopkins Center for Alternatives. *In vitro* products mimicking the response of the human eye were developed for use in product testing. The Draize test has been largely phased out.

The same sequence of events, from insight, to advocacy, to change, has brought about changes in the treatment of farm animals in Europe and the US. Protestors have brought attention to the confinement of veal calves and gestating pigs. Negative publicity targeted against the McDonalds fast-food chain prompted changes in their suppliers and at slaughterhouses. Most recently some of the biggest pork and veal companies have decided to widen stalls. Publicity about caged laying hens has increased demand for cage-free eggs and saved at least a small subset of chickens from that miserable fate.

We live in a society where many people pride themselves in being animal lovers. In fact, in both Florida and Arizona, majorities have voted for referenda that would banish veal and sow crates. In 2008, California voters passed a referendum that will ensure a cage-free existence for all chickens. Animal legislation in the US Congress tends to receive massive attention from the public. Public pressure led to revisions of the Animal Welfare Act that have progressively given at least better protection to lab animals.

But how far should the activist go? The *Animal Research War* (see Chapter 8) paints an alarming picture of aggressive activism – harassment of researchers both at work and home, break-ins at labs, undercover video investigations, theft of animals, and even violence. The authors have no patience for people who complain about anything that goes on in any research lab, anywhere in the US, not even the completely peaceful complaining of academic philosophers. This attitude to debate only makes them look defensive, but are they right to decry every bit of anti-research aggressive activism?

Whatever you think of the rest of the tactics, animals do not have their own voices and need the help of undercover investigators. It's true that there are genuinely concerned researchers, lab workers, and veterinarians who do their best to protect animals, but they operate in a milieu where animal interests run a strong chance of being slighted. If all is well in the labs, videotapes will reveal nothing that embarrasses researchers, but if all is not well, the reality is that government inspections are infrequent, and insiders have "more important" things to worry about. Animal care workers can play an important role in the protection of animals not only by being good at their jobs, but as whistleblowers.

Personal Change

We each have the power to stop eating meat and other animal products, to avoid products that were tested on animals, and to phase out leather and fur from our wardrobes and homes. Or we can shift from the status quo to using animals *less*. We all look up to a moral saint who immediately does all of what is right, but very few of us are ruled by ethical considerations in quite so thorough a fashion. Reliance on animals is so deeply rooted in our pasts, our culture, and our habits that it's unrealistic to expect every conscientious person to succeed in an immediate and total makeover. For most people, being good is a work in progress, never to be completed.

I stopped eating veal about 25 years ago. PETA was leafleting in front of a Burger King in Boston (hard to believe, but they served veal parmesan on a bun in the 1980s). The facts and pictures made the decision very easy. Ten years later, after much thinking, reading, and vacillating, I gave up meat (except fish), thanks to an alliance of issues. There was the issue of wanting to do better by animals. But there was also the issue of wanting to live harmoniously with my new boyfriend, soon to be my husband. He was a vegetarian due to another alliance of issues. Yes, he wanted to do better by animals, but he was also concerned about health and about the environmental effects of meat-eating.

At the time, it was too much to contemplate giving up fish along with other meat, and I also saw a moral difference. Fish don't suffer the barbarities of factory farming, and some even live long lives in the wild. If you eat fish, restaurants are more manageable and friends and family find it much easier to be accommodating. Over time I've come to see that over-fishing is destroying marine environments and threatening populations of many species. Fish seem to die painful deaths when they are pulled out of the sea and bashed to death or left to suffocate. I still eat fish occasionally, but with an increasing sense that I should change. That moral insight may do the job, but there's an alliance of issues that's starting to make a difference. My daughter, now 12, decided to be a vegetarian at about age 6. It bothers her to see a dead fish on the table (whether whole or not) and she puts up a fight when I approach the fish counter. Respect for her sensibilities is increasingly keeping fish out of our diets.

Since I stopped eating meat, I've come to use cage-free or free-range eggs, and organic milk from more humanely treated cows. That means less animal exploitation, but not none (see Singer and Mason in the Sources section, as well as Pollan). I'm not unaware of the issue of the "invisible males." For every female chick who becomes a laying hen, there's an immediately suffocated male. The egg-eater is by all means complicit in all those deaths. For every female calf who goes on to produce milk, there's a male who becomes meat. I've written to some organic milk producers who tell me they don't sell their male calves to veal producers, but still, they're killed, and I know it.

I avoid leather as much as practicable – no leather upholstery or jackets or wallets – but don't strictly avoid leather shoes, if they're the only thing available. Fur is out of the question, but I do wear a little wool.

I tell my tale knowing that from the perspective of a scrupulous vegan, I'm not doing that well. The story is really meant for the reader who has given up nothing and can't imagine making the leap from total dependence on animal products to total abstinence. If the really important thing is the benefit to animals, do not scoff at reducing consumption as a positive step. The point is not to be perfect but to prevent (as much as you can) harm to animals.

But wait. If I'm convinced by the arguments I've made in this book, why not do more? Vegan pamphlets will tell you tofu products can take the place of milk, ice cream, eggs, and meat. Tofu is made out to be like the suitcase in the *Felix the Cat* cartoon I used to watch as a child: you can turn it into absolutely anything. It's all to the good that some people's experience validates this; good for them, but mine doesn't. Just as vegetables have their singular properties – you can't make a tomato out of tofu – animal products have their singular properties. My local vegan restaurant has good baked goods, but I'm not prepared to limit myself to substitutes all of the time. It's nothing to be proud of, but the milk in my cappuccino is something that I can't give up right now.

Then again, an excuse for giving up nothing might be waiting in the wings. Some argue that individual efforts cannot make a difference anyway. Not consuming animal products won't ever save a single animal, they say, because the huge animal industry is insensitive to tiny changes in demand. R. G. Frey makes this argument, using a very rough estimate of 25 billion animals killed for food per year, worldwide. Such a huge number can make a vegetarian feel awfully powerless. And Frey thinks they'd be right to feel that way. Even taken as a group, vegetarians are not numerous enough to make any difference at all to production quotas, he says.

In fact, reliable estimates are daunting. In *Livestock's Long Shadow*, the UN says 137 million metric tons of meat (2,200 lb per ton) were eaten in all developing countries combined in 2002. In developed countries it was 102 million metric tons. Demand in developing countries is expected to nearly triple by 2050, with most of the expansion coming in countries with fast economic growth, like China and India. In developed countries, where meat consumption starts off higher per capita and we are encouraged to cut back for a variety of reasons, demand will go up another 30–40 million metric tons by 2050 – according to current projections.

What should we make of the argument that vegetarians are powerless? The huge numbers have a psychological impact, but not simply the one Frey has in mind. The point of *Livestock's Long Shadow* is to warn us of the environmental devastation that looms in the future, as our planet is increasingly overrun by our herds. Our land, air, and water are at risk. In regions where meat consumption is highest, it is linked to obesity and to other health problems. With the quantities as vast as they are, there is a resounding imperative to *do something*. Clearly institutional and governmental interventions are going to be needed.

But what of the individual who wants to help the poor chicken living out her life in a small cage with five other chickens, or the veal calf stuck in a narrow stall, or the pig without enough room to turn around? Can you make a difference by not eating meat?

Making a difference means many things. What most vegetarians have at the forefront of their minds is the hope that one less chicken will be raised in abysmal conditions and killed painfully, as a result of their decision not to buy a chicken at the grocery store. But a "one less" difference is not the only difference that not buying the chicken could make. Killing and eating animals is disrespectful. This is an uncomfortable truth, especially for animal lovers who are accustomed to eating meat, but it's a hard thing to deny. It makes sense to suppose that this disrespectful activity places a limit on a person's degree of concern with animal welfare. We do our best to have the thoughts and feelings that match our deeds. And that could make meat eaters worse advocates for animals, by and large.

Peter Singer argues that vegetarianism does have this motivational rationale. Vegetarianism "underpins, makes consistent, and gives meaning to all our other activities on behalf of animals," he writes in *Animal Liberation*. My experience is that vegetarianism does keep animal issues on my mind on a daily basis. While you get used to it, it's hard to forget that you have a meatless diet when you live in a very meaty society. The effort to remain meatless keeps you thinking that animals matter for themselves and not just as means.

Singer also sees vegetarianism as a form of boycott that *can* reduce the number of animals bred, raised, and killed for food. Even if it doesn't succeed in bringing meat-eating to an end, like boycotting South African goods brought apartheid to an end, it can save many animals. But how is that? Isn't Frey's argument quite compelling?

Frey's argument is partly a sleight of hand. The "effect" is accomplished by bundling all the meat production in the world together. If there were one giant livestock corporation, raising and killing 25 billion animals a year, you really might have to feel impotent in its face. But there isn't one giant livestock corporation, any more than there's one giant computer corporation or cookie corporation. Like it matters to Apple Inc. whether you buy a Mac, or another company's PC, or revert to pencil and paper, it matters to Tyson Foods whether you buy chicken from them, or from another company, or vegetables at your farmer's market.

Of course, one Mac-rejection doesn't immediately translate into one less Mac being manufactured. If an anti-Mac campaign causes demand to drop a little, it won't necessarily make any difference to future production quotas. Just as many computers will be manufactured, and some will just sit around unsold. Likewise, an anti-meat campaign won't necessarily change Tyson's plans. Even knowing demand was down a little, they could very well produce the exact same number of chickens next time around. So buying one less chicken doesn't assure you of saving a chicken from being bred, cruelly housed, and indifferently killed.

On the other hand, at some point changes in demand do alter production quotas. As one person after another doesn't buy a chicken, the number of purchases may fall well beneath the expected range. The threshold for introducing a new, significantly lower production goal will have been reached. Now the breeder will be asked to supply 29,000 new chicks, instead of 30,000, to one of Tyson's massive feeding operations. The way production responds to demand has a rather surprising upshot. If you buy one less chicken, you will have no impact, *or* you will stand on the shoulders of everyone else who bought one less chicken. The only thing that's just about impossible is that by buying one less chicken, you will save one chicken!

Now, I think this is a pretty encouraging set of possibilities. It's not bad buying one less chicken and having no impact, but knowing that someone down the line could stand on my shoulders and save 1,000 chickens. My effort does contribute to that possibility. And it's not bad *at all* to hit the jackpot and be the person whose abstinence saved 1,000 chickens! Either way, there's no reason to feel that Tyson foods is insulated from my buying behavior.

Of course, saving 1,000 chickens is a drop in the bucket, in comparison to the 25 billion animals killed per year, if Frey's number is in the right ballpark. But we take pride in making small differences all of the time. If you send a check to Save the Children and alleviate poverty for a handful of children, you sensibly take pride in that, and don't let yourself be overwhelmed by the knowledge that there are millions of other children who need your help – or at least you should. But the immense numbers involved in both cases do tell us something important. Individual initiative needs to be supplemented by systemic change. But then we come back to the motivational role of vegetarianism. It does not seem psychologically possible to work ardently for change while not even trying to make our own personal behavior more respectful and compassionate.

———————

The goal for the abolitionists was to put an end to slavery, immediately, completely and with finality. Adopting the same approach, an animal advocate with superpowers would immediately end all animal research, despite the possible setbacks to human health. All animals would stop being used for labor, milk, fiber and meat, whether in the affluent world, where there are substitutes, or in parts of the developing world where there still often are not. The superpowered advocate might even go back in time and get rid of animal exploitation at the dawn of agriculture, and animal hunting in human prehistory. The entire course of history would be different, possibly with dire costs to human quality of life or even existence.

This is more than I can sign on for, but shouldn't we at least hope and aim for a day when we can treat animals without any disrespect at all, leaving them to their own independent way of life? That would mean developing substitutes so that an animal never has to be used for protein, for labor, for product testing, or research. It would also mean cultivating traditions and customs so that a people is never defined as "the reindeer people" (because they herd and kill reindeer) or the people of the whale (because the whale hunt is critical to their survival and way of life). It would mean creating new traditions, so that the centerpiece of our most meaningful celebrations no longer involved the killing of animals.

That is a day we should hope and aim for, and work toward, but it is very far in the future. In the meantime, we will find ourselves torn – pulled in one direction by respect for human beings, but in another by respect for animals. Sometimes we will choose our good over the good of animals, but sometimes we will give higher priority to animals. As we stumble toward the day when such painful choices needn't be made, the animal conundrum will continue to trouble us.

Annotated Sources

Introduction

Note: Factory farming is referred to in several chapters of this book. For details, good sources are the Humane Society website and the books by Scully and Singer listed below.

Alaska Department of Fish and Game, www.adfg.state.ak.us/pubs/notebook/ biggame/muskoxen.php. Source for muskox history.

Eisenhower, Chuck, "Nunivak Musk Ox with Bow and Arrow." www. outdoorsdirectory.com/magazine/alaska_musk_ox_hunt.htm. The grinning hunter.

Food and Agriculture Organization of the United Nations, *Livestock's Long Shadow: Environmental Issues and Options*. Rome: FAO, 2006. Provides a wealth of information about the environmental impact of livestock. Land use statistic: p. xxi.

Humane Society, www.hsus.org. Excellent source of information about factory farming, which I characterize only briefly at various points in this book.

International Whaling Commission, www.iwcoffice.org. The latest census of bow-head whales was conducted in 2001.

Scully, Matthew, *Dominion: The Power of Man, the Suffering of Animals, and the Call to Mercy*. New York: St. Martin's Press, 2002. For compelling reportage, there's no better source on the treatment of animals than this. The description of a modern hog farm in chapter 6 is unforgettable.

Singer, Peter, *Animal Liberation*. New York: Random House, 1975 (updated 1990).
    Required reading for anyone interested in the treatment of animals. Chapter 3
    is a detailed description of factory farming.

Chapter 1   The Myth of Consent

Bible, New International Version. www.biblegateway.com.
Budiansky, Stephen, *The Covenant of the Wild: Why Animals Chose Domestication*.
    New Haven: Yale University Press, 1999.
Campbell, Joseph, *The Masks of God: Primitive Mythology*. New York: Penguin
    Compass, 1976 (1st edn, 1959). "the animal is a living victim …": p. 293. "The
    buffalo dance …": p. 293. "the whole spirit of the feast …": p. 336.
Diamond, Jared, *Guns, Germs, and Steel*. New York: W. W. Norton and Company,
    1997. North American extinctions: pp. 46–7. For a contrasting view, see Krech,
    chapter 1.
Food and Agriculture Organization of the United Nations, *Livestock's Long Shadow:
    Environmental Issues and Options*. Rome: FAO, 2006. Land use statistics: p. xxi.
    Number of cattle and buffaloes, and sheep and goats: p. 53.
Humane Kosher Website, www.goveg.com/jsfkosher.asp. Site questions the humane-
    ness of kosher slaughter. Don't miss the interesting interview with the author
    Jonathan Safran Foer.
Judaism 101, Kashrut: Jewish Dietary Laws, www.jewfaq.org/kashrut.htm. Basic
    information about kosher slaughter.
Krech III, Shepherd, *The Ecological Indian: Myth and History*. New York: W. W.
    Norton and Company, 2000.
Sapontzis, Steven, ed., *Food for Thought: The Debate over Eating Meat*. Amherst, NY:
    Prometheus, 2004. Rod Preece's article about Native American traditions is
    balanced and thoughtful. See pp. 236–46.
Wikipedia. "Chickens": en.wikipedia.org/wiki/Chicken. "Pigs": en.wikipedia.org/
    wiki/Pigs. Source for statistics.
Wohlforth, Charles, *The Whale and the Supercomputer: On the Northern Front of Climate
    Change*. New York: North Point Press, 2005. The belief that whales "give themselves
    to the people": p. 30. Description of harpooning: p. 48. Whale lifespan: p. 21.

Chapter 2   The Order of Things

Aquinas, Thomas, excerpts from his writings on animals. In Regan and Singer,
    pp. 6–12.
Aristotle, *On the Soul*. In *The Internet Classics Archive*, classics.mit.edu/Aristotle/
    soul.html.

Aristotle, *Politics*. In *The Internet Classics Archive*, classics.mit.edu/Aristotle/politics.html. Nature provides living things with nutrition: Book 5, chapter 8. "Now if nature makes ...": Book 5, chapter 8. "Animals are better off ...": Book 1, chapter 5. Tame vs. wild animals: Book I, chapter 5.

Bentham, Jeremy, excerpt from *The Principles of Morals and Legislation*. In Regan and Singer, pp. 25–6. Quote is on p. 26.

Clarke, Desmond M., *Descartes: A Biography*. Cambridge: Cambridge University Press, 2006. Unlikelihood of marriage: pp. 131–2.

Cottingham, John, "A Brute to the Beasts? Descartes' Treatment of Animals," *Philosophy* 53: 551–61, 1978. An unorthodox interpretation of Descartes on which he didn't actually say that animals lack crude sensation, despite the way he was understood by his contemporaries.

Darwin, Charles, excerpt from *The Descent of Man* (chs 2 and 4). In Regan and Singer, pp. 27–31.

Descartes, René, excerpts from his letters. In Regan and Singer, pp. 13–19. "It seems reasonable ...": p. 18. "My opinion is not ...": p. 19. Some Descartes scholars say he's been misunderstood, and that he only meant to deny soul and thought to animals, not crude sensations. There are passages that seem to allow for more than one interpretation, but the passage in which he calls animals "nature's automata" is noteworthy. In his own time, he was understood as taking the position that animals literally feel nothing.

Fodor, Jerry, *The Modularity of Mind*. Cambridge, MA: MIT Press, 1983. Ground-breaking book on contemporary cognitive science and faculty psychology.

Food and Agriculture Organization of the United Nations, *Livestock's Long Shadow: Environmental Issues and Options*. Rome: FAO, 2006. Increased consumption of animal products in India: p. 10.

Gaffney, James, "Eastern Religions and the Eating of Meat." In Sapontzis, *Food for Thought*, pp. 223–35.

Kant, Immanuel, "Duties in Regard to Animals." In Regan and Singer, pp. 23–4.

Lovejoy, Arthur, *The Great Chain of Being: A Study of the History of an Idea*. Cambridge, MA: Harvard University Press, 1976. "it takes all kinds ...": p. 51. "Nor is the Disagreement ...": p. 234.

Nelson, Lance, "Cows, Elephants, Dogs, and Other Lesser Embodiments of Atman: Reflections on Hindu Attitudes Toward Nonhuman Animals." In Waldau and Patton, pp. 179–93.

Regan, Tom, and Peter Singer, *Animal Rights and Human Obligations*, 2nd edn. Englewood Cliffs, NJ: Prentice-Hall, 1989. A very useful volume for historical sources, but in need of updating.

Sapontzis, Steven, ed., *Food for Thought: The Debate over Eating Meat*. Amherst, NY: Prometheus, 2004. Excellent anthology covering the whole spectrum of views and issues about meat-eating, with a good balance of outlooks.

Singer, Peter, *Animal Liberation*. New York: Random House, 1975 (updated 1990). Chapter 5 is an interesting survey of Western thought about animals. For his interpretation of Descartes's views, see pp. 202–3.

Sorabji, Richard, *Animal Minds and Human Morals: The Origins of the Western Debate*. Ithaca, NY: Cornell, 1995.

Spencer, Colin, *The Heretic's Feast: A History of Vegetarianism*. New England: UPNE, 1995. "Descartes, the father of …": p. 201.

Stuart, Tristram, *The Bloodless Revolution: A Cultural History of Vegetarianism from 1600 to Modern Times*. New York: Norton, 2006. My discussion of Descartes is indebted to chapter 10, "Dieting with Dr. Descartes."

Waldau, Paul and Kimberly Patton, eds., *A Communion of Subjects: Animals in Religion, Science, and Ethics*. New York: Columbia University Press, 2006. Very useful, comprehensive collection of articles.

www.theivorybuddha.com. Religious artifacts made out of elephant ivory.

Chapter 3   Animal Consciousness

Baird, Robert M. and Stuart E. Rosenbaum, *Animal Experimentation: The Moral Issues*. Amherst, NY: Prometheus, 1991.

Bekoff, Marc, *Minding Animals: Awareness, Emotions, and Heart*. Oxford: Oxford University Press, 2002. My three quotes: pp. 100, 92, and 95.

Budiansky, Stephen, *If a Lion Could Talk: Animal Intelligence and the Evolution of Consciousness*. Darby: Diane Publishing Co., 1998.

Carruthers, Peter, "Brute Experience." *Journal of Philosophy* 86: 258–69, 1989. Distracted driving: p. 258. "Much time and money …": p. 268.

Carruthers, Peter, *The Animals Issue: Moral Theory in Practice*. Cambridge: Cambridge University Press, 1992.

Carruthers, Peter, "Animal Mentality: Its Character, Extent, and Moral Significance." In R. Frey and T. Beauchamp (eds.), *Handbook on Ethics and Animals*. Oxford: Oxford University Press, 2010. A different route to the same conclusion Carruthers reached in the earlier article and book: there's nothing about animals that compels us to be morally concerned about them. Fans will want to have a look.

Chalmers, David, *The Conscious Mind: In Search of a Fundamental Theory*. Oxford: Oxford University Press, 1996. Global availability is discussed on pp. 225–33.

Curtis, Stanley E., "The Case for Intensive Farming of Food Animals." In Regan and Singer, pp. 169–75. Curtis is a defender of factory farming who makes heavy use of the ignorance defense.

Damasio, Antonio, *Descartes' Error: Emotion, Reason, and the Human Brain*. New York: Picador, 1995. Attention and "enhancement": p. 197.

Dennett, Daniel, "Animal Consciousness: What Matters and Why." In Daniel Dennett, *Brainchildren: Essays on Designing Minds*, Cambridge, MA: MIT Press, 1998.

Descartes, René. See references for Chapter 2.

Gazzaniga, Michael, *Human: The Science of What Makes Us Unique*. New York: Ecco, 2008. Consciousness and the brain (including quotes): pp. 319–20. Pain as a shared experience: p. 169. Disgust: p. 174. People with congenital inability to feel pain: p. 182. Foresight in bonobos and orangutans: p. 54.

Gould, James L., and Carol Grant Gould, *The Animal Mind*. New York: Scientific American Library, 1994. Geese: pp. 22–3. Ticks: pp. 9–10. Toads: pp. 29–30.

Grandin, Temple, www.grandin.com. Information about slaughterhouses and other useful material.

Grandin, Temple, and Diane Johnson, *Animals in Translation: Using the Mysteries of Autism to Decode Animal Behavior*. New York: Scribner, 2004. "The fact that a fish …": p. 184. "I think injured animals …": p. 187.

Harrison, Peter, "Animal Pain." In Baird and Rosenbaum, pp. 128–39. This is an excerpt from "Theodicy and Animal Pain," *Philosophy* 64: 79–92, 1989.

Inside the Animal Mind, *Nature* series, produced for PBS by WNET, Channel 13, available on DVD (as *Animal Minds*) from www.pbs.org/wnet. Starting at chapter 7, Stephen Budiansky talks about consciousness, distracted driving, and the phenomenon of blindsight.

Microcosmos. Documentary directed by Claude Nuridsany and Marie Pérennou. Insects close-up, a must see.

Pepperberg, Irene, *Alex & Me: How a Scientist and a Parrot Uncovered a Hidden World of Animal Intelligence – and Formed a Deep Bond in the Process*. New York: HarperCollins, 2008.

Regan, Tom and Peter Singer, *Animal Rights and Human Obligations*, 2nd edn. Englewood Cliffs, NJ: Prentice-Hall, 1989.

Schlosser, Eric, *Fast Food Nation*. New York: Houghton Mifflin Harcourt, 2001. Chapter 8 is an unforgettable description of a slaughterhouse assembly – or disassembly – line.

Chapter 4   Dumb Brutes?

Bekoff, Marc, *Minding Animals: Awareness, Emotions, and Heart*. Oxford: Oxford University Press, 2002.

Clayton, Nicola, "Episodic-like memory during cache recovery by scrub jays." *Nature* 395: 272–8, 1998.

de Waal, Frans, *Chimpanzee Politics* (revised edn). Baltimore: Johns Hopkins University Press, 1998.

de Waal, Frans, *Primates and Philosophers: How Morality Evolved*. Princeton: Princeton University Press, 2006. Anthropodenial: pp. 59–67. Reciprocation: pp. 42–4. Fairness: pp. 44–9. Rats: p. 28. Consolation and empathy: pp. 33–6. "empathy is not an …": p. 41.

Dennett, Daniel, *Breaking the Spell: Religion as a Natural Phenomenon.* New York: Viking, 2006. "free floating rationale": p. 82.

Gazzaniga, Michael, *Human: The Science of What Makes Us Unique.* New York: Ecco, 2008. Foresight: p. 54. The study was done by Nicholas Mulcahy and Josep Call.

Gilbert, Daniel, *Stumbling on Happiness.* New York: Knopf, 2006.

Goodall, Jane, *In the Shadow of Man.* New York: Houghton Mifflin, 1971.

Gould, James and Carol Gould, *Animal Architects: Building and the Evolution of Intelligence.* New York: Basic Books, 2007. The explanation of how we determine the direction of sound is on p. 50. Kohler's famous insight studies: pp. 280–2. Beaver dam repair: pp. 266–8. "Each web is a custom production": p. 57.

Haidt, Jonathan, *The Happiness Hypothesis: Finding Modern Truth in Ancient Wisdom.* New York: Basic Books, 2005. The study by John Bargh is discussed on pp. 13–14. "everything you do": p. 14.

Hauser, Marc D., *Wild Minds: What Animals Really Think.* New York: Henry Holt, 2000. My discussion of the mirror test is indebted to chapter 5. "I don't think the mirror test …": p. 101.

Hauser, Marc D., *Moral Minds: How Nature Designed Our Universal Sense of Right and Wrong.* New York: Ecco, 2006.

Hauser, Marc D., "Are Animals Moral Agents?" In Waldau and Patton, pp. 505–18. The selector–receiver experiment: p. 507.

Heinrich, Bernd, *Mind of the Raven: Investigations and Adventures with Wolf-Birds.* New York: Harper Perennial, 2007. This paperback reprint of the 1999 hardback has an "update" at the back about the fishing line study. There's a segment about the study in the video *Inside the Animal Mind.*

Inside the Animal Mind, Nature series, produced for PBS by WNET, Channel 13, available on DVD (as *Animal Minds*) from www.pbs.org/wnet.

Kant, Immanuel, "The Categorical Imperative." In Singer, pp. 274–9.

March of the Penguins. Documentary directed by Luc Jacquet, 2005.

Masson, Jeffrey Moussaieff and Susan McCarthy, *When Elephants Weep: The Emotional Lives of Animals.* New York: Delta, 1995.

Pinker, Steven, *The Language Instinct: How the Mind Creates Language.* New York: William Morrow and Co., 1994.

Ridley, Matt, *The Origins of Virtue: Human Instincts and the Evolution of Cooperation.* New York: Viking, 1997.

Rogers, Leslie J. and Gisela Kaplan, "All Animals are *Not* Equal: The Interface between Scientific Knowledge and Legislation for Animal Rights." In Sunstein and Nussbaum, pp. 175–202. The point about dogs recognizing their own smell is on pp. 176–7.

Rowlands, Mark, *The Philosopher and the Wolf.* London: Granta, 2008. The chimpanzee penis example is on p. 70. Rowlands attributes it to Richard W. Whitten and Andrew Byrne, *Machiavellian Intelligence*, Oxford: Oxford University Press, 1989.

Singer, Peter, ed., *Ethics*. Oxford: Oxford University Press, 1994. Anthology of classics in ethics, with a section about proto-morality in animals.

Stich, Stephen, "Do Animals Have Beliefs?" *Australasian Journal of Philosophy* 57: 15–28, 1979.

Suddendorfer, Thomas and Janie Busby, "Mental time travel in animals?" *Trends in Cognitive Sciences* 7(9), 2003. Criticism of Clayton's claims about episodic memory in animals.

Sunstein, Cass R. and Martha C. Nussbaum, eds., *Animal Rights: Current Debates and New Directions*. Oxford: Oxford University Press, 2004.

Waldau, Paul and Kimberly Patton, eds., *A Communion of Subjects: Animals in Religion, Science, and Ethics*. New York: Columbia University Press, 2006.

Zimmer, Carl, "Time in the Animal Mind." *New York Times,* April 3, 2007. Covers Clayton's studies as well as brains of rats during REM sleep.

Chapter 5   The Lives of Animals

The Ant Bully. Animated film directed by John Davis, 2006.

Coetzee, J. M., *The Lives of Animals*. Princeton: Princeton University Press, 1999. "The value that is lost …": p. 90.

DeGrazia, David, *Animal Rights: A Very Short Introduction*. Oxford: Oxford University Press, 2002. The "sliding scale model": pp. 34–7. "animals deserve consideration …": p. 36 (box). "we cannot responsibly …": p. 37.

DeGrazia, David, *Taking Animals Seriously: Mental Life and Moral Status*. Cambridge: Cambridge University Press, 1996.

Humane Society. www.hsus.org/hsus_field/hsus_disaster_center/disasters_press_room. Information on animal rescue during disasters, including extensive coverage of the Katrina fiasco.

Kazez, Jean, *The Weight of Things: Philosophy and the Good Life*. Oxford: Wiley-Blackwell, 2007. See chapters 4–6 for discussions of happiness, desire fulfillment, and the capacities that make a life go well. "The good life" for animals is discussed at the end of chapter 6.

The Life of Mammals. BBC TV documentary starring David Attenborough (available on DVD).

Nussbaum, Martha, *Women and Human Development*. Cambridge, MA: Harvard University Press, 2000.

Nussbaum, Martha, *Frontiers of Justice*. Cambridge, MA: Harvard University Press, 2006. Nussbaum has an interesting, cautious discussion about equality on pp. 380–4. My discussion of the elderly and incapacitated was inspired by remarks she makes on pp. 357–66.

Rogers, Leslie J. and Gisela Kaplan, "All Animals are *Not* Equal: The Interface between Scientific Knowledge and Legislation for Animal Rights." In Sunstein and Nussbaum, pp. 175–202. "guard against, or …": p. 196.

Singer, Isaac Bashevis, "The Letter Writer." *The New Yorker*, January 13, 1968.

Singer, Peter, *Animal Liberation*. New York: Random House, 1975 (updated 1990). "ideological camouflage": p. 186. The claim that all animals are equal: chapter 1, especially pp. 6–9, 15. In this chapter he does not use the term "egalitarianism"; in fact, he disavows it in *Practical Ethics*, p. 24. I use the term because there's no other convenient, simple appellation for Singer's principle of equality – i.e. the principle that equal interests should receive equal consideration.

Singer, Peter, *Practical Ethics*, 2nd edn. Cambridge: Cambridge University Press, 1993. Singer's account of the value of a life is stated in terms of preferences instead of desires, as befits his own moral theory – preference Utilitarianism – but there's little that separates the two concepts, and much of Singer's discussion is couched in terms of desires.

Steinbock, Bonnie, "Speciesism and equality." *Philosophy* 53: 247–56, 1978. I am indebted to Steinbock for the point that there's a connection between how much a pain matters and the value of the sufferer's life.

Sunstein, Cass R. and Martha C. Nussbaum, eds., *Animal Rights: Current Debates and New Directions*. Oxford: Oxford University Press, 2004.

Wikipedia, "Animal Rights and the Holocaust." en.wikipedia.org/wiki/Animal_rights_and_the_Holocaust. See for details about the PETA exhibition, "The Holocaust on Your Plate."

Wolfson, David J. and Mariann Sullivan, "Foxes in the hen house: Animals, agribusiness, and the law: A modern American fable." In Sunstein and Nussbaum, pp. 205–33. On p. 206 they claim that 266 chickens are killed per second. That makes roughly 6 million chickens every 6 hours. See their footnote 2 on p. 226 for the way they arrived at 266 per second.

Chapter 6   Caveman Ethics

Note: The social contract tradition's position on animals is a matter of dispute. Below, I briefly identify the way various philosophers understand it. See Carruthers, Nussbaum, Regan, Rowlands, Scanlon, and Warren.

Appiah, Kwame Anthony, *Experiments in Ethics*. Cambridge: Harvard University Press, 2008. On Kantian respect: pp. 136–9.

Baird, Robert M. and Stuart E. Rosenbaum, *Animal Experimentation: The Moral Issues*. Amherst, NY: Prometheus, 1991.

Carruthers, Peter, *The Animals Issue: Moral Theory in Practice*. Cambridge: Cambridge University Press, 1992. Contractualism is discussed on pp. 98–121.

Carruthers' view is that the social contract excludes animals, and therefore we have no obligations at all to them.

DeGrazia, David, *Animal Rights: A Very Short Introduction.* Oxford: Oxford University Press, 2002. The "sliding scale model": pp. 34–7.

Guthrie, R. Dale, *The Nature of Paleolithic Art.* Chicago: University of Chicago Press, 2006. Controversial – and beautiful – book challenging the orthodox view that cave art had religious and ritual significance.

Kant, Immanuel, "Pure Practical Reason and the Moral Law." In Singer, *Ethics*, pp. 123–31.

McCarthy, Cormac, *The Road.* New York: Knopf, 2006.

Mulgan, Tim, *Understanding Utilitarianism.* Stockfield: Acumen, 2007.

Nussbaum, Martha, *The Frontiers of Justice: Disability, Nationality, Species Membership.* Cambridge, MA: Harvard University Press, 2006, pp. 325–407. Nussbaum's view is that animals are excluded from "the social contract." For that reason and others, she sees social contract concepts as insufficient for understanding ethics and animals.

Regan, Tom, *The Case for Animal Rights.* Berkeley: University of California Press, 2004 (first published 1983). Lifeboat case: pp. 324–5, 351–3, 385–6. Regan sees animals as being excluded from any social contract, but considers that tradition generally inadequate for understanding ethics.

I should say a little more about my interpretation of Regan on survival hunting. Regan never discusses ordinary survival hunting, but he does take up a variation on the lifeboat case. Now it's not sinking, but rather everyone is starving. All will die unless one is eaten. The people could eat the dog or the dog could eat the people. Regan gives the people permission to do the eating. This tells us nothing about ordinary survival hunting, where hunter and prey are not "in the same boat": in the scenario I discuss, there's plenty of grass for the aurochs, but the hunter is starving.

It becomes crystal clear what Regan would say about Mr. Caveman when he imagines a really strange lifeboat case. Four men are on a boat with one dog, and they have plenty to eat; nor are they sinking. The problem is that one of the people has a life-threatening brain disease and a vial of untested medicine. Would it be all right to somehow infect the dog with the brain disease and use him to test the medicine? No. Unlike in the first lifeboat case, this dog doesn't naturally have the man's problems and shouldn't be made to shoulder them. Regan would have to say the same about Mr. Caveman. It's his problem that he's starving and he has no right to make it the aurochs' problem.

Regan, Tom and Peter Singer, *Animal Rights and Human Obligations*, 2nd edn. Englewood Cliffs, NJ: Prentice-Hall, 1989.

Rowlands, Mark, *Animals Like Us.* London: Verso, 2002. Rowlands' view of the social contract differs from most; he argues that animals would be given rights under the original contract. That is so, he thinks, because the contractors would have to make decisions in ignorance of their race, gender, *and* species. They would make agreements that protect all species, he argues, if they didn't know whether they were human or non-human.

Scanlon, T. M., *What We Owe to Each Other*. Cambridge, MA: Harvard University Press, 1998. Animals are discussed on pp. 177–89. Scanlon holds that animals are excluded from the narrow, contractarian aspect of morality, but there is more to morality. "Responding appropriately to the value of other creatures is part of morality in the broad sense …" (p. 181).

Schweitzer, Albert, "The Ethic of Reverence for Life." In Regan and Singer, pp. 32–7.

Seligman, Martin E. P., *Authentic Happiness: Using the New Positive Psychology to Realize Your Potential for Lasting Fulfillment*. New York: Free Press, 2002. Doubts about learned helplessness experiments: pp. 20–3.

Singer, Peter, *Animal Liberation*. New York: Random House, 1975 (updated 1990). The Harvard learned helplessness studies are explained on pp. 45–8. "defecation, urination, yelping …": p. 48. Singer gets that phrase from an article written by the researchers themselves.

Singer, Peter, ed., *Ethics*. Oxford: Oxford University Press, 1994.

Spiegel, Marjorie, *The Dreaded Comparison: Human and Animal Slavery* (revised edn). New York: Mirror Books, 1997.

Warren, Mary Anne, "Difficulties with the Strong Animal Rights Position." In Baird and Rosenbaum, pp. 89–99. Warren distinguishes between strong and weak rights. Strong rights are contract-based and only possessed by rational, self-interested individuals. Animals can still possess weak rights – weak in the sense that they are more easily overridden. Warren's position has been a key influence on my own thinking about animals.

Chapter 7   Going, Going, Wrong

Belozerskaya, Marina, *The Medici Giraffe: And Other Tales of Exotic Animals and Power*. New York: Little, Brown, 2006. "the activity in which …": pp. 148–9. The Aztec royal headdress: pp. 148–9. "the most extensive …": p. 147. Montezuma's zoo: pp. 147–54.

Bible, New International Version. www.gateway.com.

Bittman, Mark, "Rethinking the Meat Guzzler." New York Times, January 27, 2008. This is the source for the Prius statistic.

Connolly, Peter, and Hazel Dodge, *The Ancient City: Life in Classical Athens and Rome*. Oxford: Oxford University Press, 1998. Coliseum: pp. 190–207.

Diamond, Jared, *Guns, Germs, and Steel*. New York: W. W. Norton and Company, 1997. Farming increases edible biomass: p. 88. Benefits of farming: chapter 4. Deforestation of Haiti: chapter 11.

Diamond, Jared, *Collapse: How Societies Choose to Fail or Succeed*. New York: Viking Penguin, 2005.

Food and Agriculture Organization of the United Nations, *Livestock's Long Shadow: Environmental Issues and Options*. Rome: FAO, 2006. Land use statistics: p. xxi. Increasing meat consumption: p. 15. Increased consumption in China: p. 8. 18% of greenhouse gases, "a larger share than transport": p. xxi. Deforestation in Amazon: p. xxi.

Francione, Gary L., "Animals: Property or Persons." In Sunstein and Nussbaum, pp. 108–42.

Friedman, Richard, *Who Wrote the Bible?* Summit Books: 1987. For the meaning of animal sacrifice, see pp. 90–1. Friedman writes, "The function of sacrifice is one of the most misunderstood matters in the Bible. Modern readers often take it to mean the unnecessary taking of animal life, or they believe that the person who offered the sacrifice was giving up something of his or her own in order to compensate for some sin or perhaps to win God's favor. In the biblical world, however, the most common type of sacrifice was for *meals*. The apparent rationale was that if humans wanted to eat meat they had to recognize that they were taking life. They could not regard this as an ordinary act of daily secular life. It was a sacred act, to be performed in a prescribed manner, by an appointed person (a priest), at an altar. A portion of the sacrifice (a tithe) was given to the priest. This applied to all meat meals (but not fish or fowl)."

Gandhi, Renu and Suzanne M. Snedeker, "Consumer Concerns about Hormones in Food." envirocancer.cornell.edu/Factsheet/Diet/fs37.hormones.cfm. Overview of issues about hormones in milk and meat, with main message being that "evidence does not exist" to answer questions about health impact.

Grandin, Temple, "Recommended Animal Handling Guidelines and Audit Guide for Cattle, Pigs, and Sheep." American Meat Institute Foundation, 2005 with 2007 updates. www.grandin.com/RecAnimalHandlingGuidelines.html.

Heifer International, www.heifer.org.

Humane Society, www.hsus.org. A reliable source for information about factory farming. "HSUS Investigates Slaughterhouse" is at video. hsus.org.

Krech III, Shepherd, *The Ecological Indian: Myth and History*. New York: W. W. Norton and Company, 2000. Buffalo hunting yields: p. 132. Parts eaten: pp. 133–5. "the putrefying carcasses …": p. 134. Indians begin to worry about waste: p. 140.

Pollan, Michael, "An Animal's Place." *New York Times Magazine*, November 10, 2002.

Pollan, Michael, *The Omnivore's Dilemma: A Natural History of Four Meals*. New York: Penguin, 2006. Chapter 9 is an eye-opening look at "big organic" farming, including "humane" egg farming, which differs less than you'd think from mainstream egg farming. The little door that chickens don't walk through: p. 172.

Schlosser, Eric, *Fast Food Nation*. New York: Houghton Mifflin Harcourt, 2001. "400 per hour": p. 173.

Scully, Matthew, *Dominion: The Power of Man, the Suffering of Animals, and the Call to Mercy*. New York: St. Martin's Press, 2002. See chapter 6 for an unforgettable description of a contemporary intensive hog farm.

Singer, Peter, *Animal Liberation*. New York: Random House, 1975 (updated 1990). See chapter 3 for a detailed description of factory farming as it affects each commonly eaten species.

Singer, Peter, *Practical Ethics*, 2nd edn. Cambridge: Cambridge University Press, 1993. For his careful stance on the replaceability of animals, see pp. 119–34. On infants losing their futures: pp. 181–91.

Singer, Peter and Jim Mason, *The Ethics of What We Eat: Why Our Food Choices Matter*. New York: Rodale, 2006. (Original title was *The Way We Eat: Why Our Food Choices Matter*.) See chapter 8 for the reality behind "humane farming," which turns out to be impressive in some cases, but disappointing in others.

Sunstein, Cass R. and Martha C. Nussbaum, eds., *Animal Rights: Current Debates and New Directions*. Oxford: Oxford University Press, 2004.

University of Alaska Museum of the North, www.uaf.edu/museum. Material about Eskimo use of animals is based on my visit in 2007; the website is informative too.

Wikipedia, "Unnecessary Fuss." en.wikipedia.org/wiki/Unnecessary_Fuss.

Chapter 8   Science and Survival

Adams, Richard, *Plague Dogs*. New York: Knopf, 1978.

Altweb, Johns Hopkins School of Public Heatlh, altweb.jhsph.edu. Organization dedicated to finding alternatives to animal research, but not to immediately abolishing it. Highly recommended as a source of information about both animal experimentation and alternatives.

Americans for Medical Progress, www.amprogress.org. Organization dedicated to promoting animal research.

Animal Welfare Act, www.aphis.usda.gov/animal_welfare/publications_and_reports. shtml.

Associated Press. "US woman dies in iron lung after power failure." www.msnbc. msn.com/id/24859306/

Baird, Robert M. and Stuart E. Rosenbaum, *Animal Experimentation: The Moral Issues*. Amherst, NY: Prometheus, 1991. Useful anthology of articles for and against animal research.

Bernstein, Mark, *Without A Tear: Our Tragic Relationship with Animals*. Urbana: University of Illinois Press, 2004. In chapter 5 Bernstein argues that it is generally not possible to extrapolate from animal "models" to the human case. His examples are interesting even if he doesn't fully prove his thesis.

Blum, Deborah, *Monkey Wars*. Oxford: Oxford University Press, 1994. The 1990 isolation experiment, proposed by Gene Sackett, is discussed on p. 99.

Blum, Deborah, *Love at Goon Park: Harry Harlow and the Science of Affection*. Chichester: John Wiley & Sons, 2002. See chapter 2 on avoidance of touch as practiced in orphanages and hospitals, and recommended by childcare experts.

Carbone, Larry, *What Animals Want: Expertise and Advocacy in Laboratory Animal Policy*. Oxford: Oxford University Press, 2004. Number of animals used in labs: p. 26. Space requirements: p. 101. The limited scope of IACUCs: pp. 181–4. Quotes about IACUCs are on p. 183. A very rich source of information about the world of animal research, from a lab vet's perspective.

Conn, P. Michael and James V. Parker, *The Animal Research War*. New York: Palgrave Macmillan, 2008. "the information sought …": p. 139.

Kluger, Jeffrey, *Splendid Solution: Jonas Salk and the Conquest of Polio*. New York: G. P. Putnam, 2005. "would be stretched …": p. 116. "he would leave …": p. 117. "A small adjustment …": p. 117.

Lauerman, John F., "Animal Research." *Harvard Magazine*, 1999. On the web at harvardmagazine.com/1999/01/mice.html.

Michigan State University School of Law, Animal Legal and Historical Center, www. animallaw.info. Source for history of the Animal Welfare Act. The act is provided there in full, and in summary. Great source of information about animal law.

Oshinsky, David, *Polio: An American Story*. Oxford: Oxford University Press, 2005. Polio statistics: p. 161.

PETA (People for the Ethical Treatment of Animals), www.columbiacruelty.com. Undercover video of a Columbia University animal lab.

Rollin, Bernard E., "Some Ethical Concerns in Animal Research: Where Do We Go Next?" In Baird and Rosenbaum, pp. 151–8.

Singer, Peter, *Animal Liberation*. New York: Random House, 1975 (updated 1990). "The first of these …": p. 33. Bowlby's attachment research: pp. 32–3. Harlow's well of despair: pp. 34–6. 250 experiments involving 7,000 animals: pp. 34–6. "the Secretary of State …": p. 77.

Sundowner Principles (NASA Principles for the Ethical Care and Use of Animals – Sundowner Report), www.iacuc.ucsf.edu/Links/awSundwnr.asp.

Chapter 9   Vanishing Animals

Callicott, J. Baird, "Animal Liberation: A Triangular Affair." *Environmental Ethics* 2: 322–38, 1980. Classic expression of the view that animals do not count as individuals, but only as contributors to environmental "wholes." Callicott has since softened his position.

Food and Agriculture Organization of the United Nations, *Livestock's Long Shadow: Environmental Issues and Options*. Rome: FAO, 2006. See chapter 5, "Livestock's Impact on Biodiversity." Pollution from intensive farming: pp. 209–11.

International Whaling Commission, www.iwcoffice.org. The latest census of bowhead whales was conducted in 2001.

Kazez, Jean, *The Weight of Things: Philosophy and the Good Life.* Wiley-Blackwell: 2007. On creating a life with all the important kinds of goodness, see chapters 5 and 6.

Marshall Thomas, Elizabeth, *The Old Way: A Story of the First People.* New York: Farrar, Straus, Giroux: 2006. Sensitive description of San hunter-gatherer ways.

Pollan, Michael, "Power Steer." *New York Times Magazine,* March 31, 2002. Eye-opening account of the life of one steer.

Regan, Tom, *The Case for Animal Rights.* Berkeley: University of California Press, 1984. "because paradigmatic right-holders …": pp. 359–63.

Sierra Club, www.sierraclub.org/grazing. Good source on impact of livestock on grazing lands, especially in the American west.

Singer, Peter, *Animal Liberation.* New York: Random House, 1975 (updated 1990). Inefficiency of feeding plant foods to animals: pp. 264–5.

Vitebsky, Piers, *The Reindeer People: Living with Animals and Spirits in Siberia.* London: HarperCollins, 2005.

Wikipedia, "Tigers." en.wikipedia.org/wiki/Tiger. Source for tiger statistics.

Wilson, Edward O., *The Diversity of Life,* new edn. New York: Norton, 1992. 25% of species gone in 100 years: p. 342. Biophilia: pp. 350–1. Unmined riches: chapter 13.

Wohlforth, Charles, *The Whale and the Supercomputer: On the Northern Front of Climate Change.* New York: North Point Press, 2005. Whale lifespan: p. 21. Whale hunting with modern conveniences: chapter 1.

Chapter 10 The Endless Story

Altweb, Johns Hopkins School of Public Heatlh, altweb.jhsph.edu.

Bittman, Mark, "Rethinking the Meat Guzzler." *New York Times,* January 27, 2008.

The Blue Planet: Seas of Life. Superb BBC documentary narrated by David Attenborough (available on DVD). For reasons to be wary of eating "seafood," see the informative extra, "Deep Trouble: a compelling exploration of man's impact on the Earth's oceans" (on vol. 4: "Tidal Seas, Coasts").

Conn, P. Michael and James V. Parker, *The Animal Research War.* New York: Palgrave Macmillan, 2008.

Doctorow, E. L., *The March.* New York: Random House, 2005.

Food and Agriculture Organization of the United Nations, *Livestock's Long Shadow: Environmental Issues and Options.* Rome: FAO, 2006. Meat consumption statistics: pp. 15–16.

Frey, R. G., "Utilitarianism and Moral Vegetarianism Again: Protest of Effectiveness." In Sapontzis, pp. 118–23.

Humane Society. www.hsus.org/farm/camp/victories.html. Changes in the treatment of farm animals spurred by animal advocacy.

Humane Society. www.hsus.org/farm/multimedia/gallery/layers/male_chicks.html. Disturbing truths about male chicks.

The In Vitro Meat Consortium, invitromeat.org.

Kazez, Jean, *The Weight of Things: Philosophy and the Good Life*. Oxford: Wiley-Blackwell, 2007. Chapter 8 grapples with "moral saints" and the question of how good we have to be.

Lappé, Francis Moore, *Diet for a Small Planet*. New York: Ballantine, 1971. (Revised edns published in 1975, 1982, 1991.)

The Life of Mammals. BBC TV documentary starring David Attenborough (available on DVD). For the platypus scene, see vol. 1: "A Winning Design." An extraordinarily informative series.

Nestle, Marion, "Can a Big Guy Play Football on a Vegan Diet?" www.thedailygreen.com/healthy-eating/blogs/healthy-food/marion-nestle-food-vegan-45012808.

Norcross, Alastair, "Puppies, Pigs, and People: Eating Meat and Marginal Cases." *Philosophical Perspectives 18: Ethics*, 2004. Response to "ineffectiveness" argument is on pp. 32–3.

PETA (People for the Ethical Treatment of Animals), Victories for farm animals spurred by animal advocacy. www.goveg.com/f-american_veal_association.asp.

Pollan, Michael, *The Omnivore's Dilemma: A Natural History of Four Meals*. New York: Penguin, 2006. Much disappointing news about large-scale "humane" farming, and a possibly too-rosy picture of tiny, local organic farms.

Sapontzis, Steven, ed., *Food for Thought: The Debate over Eating Meat*. Amherst, NY: Prometheus, 2004.

Singer, Peter, *Animal Liberation*. New York: Random House, 1975 (updated 1990). Singer's response to the "ineffectiveness" argument is on p. 163.

Singer, Peter and Jim Mason, *The Ethics of What We Eat: Why Our Food Choices Matter*. New York: Rodale, 2006. (Original title was *The Way We Eat: Why Our Food Choices Matter*.) Chapter 9 delivers the bad news about seafood. See chapter 8 for the reality behind "humane farming," which turns out to be impressive in some cases, but disappointing in others.

Sunstein, Cass R. and Martha C. Nussbaum, eds., *Animal Rights: Current Debates and New Directions*. Oxford: Oxford University Press, 2004.

USDA, mypyramid.gov/tips_resources/vegetarian_diets.html.

Vitebsky, Piers, *The Reindeer People: Living with Animals and Spirits in Siberia*. London: HarperCollins, 2005.

Wise, Steven, "Animal Rights, One Step at a Time." In Sunstein and Nussbaum, pp. 19–50. Comparison of the treatment of slaves with the treatment of animals, by a legal scholar and animal advocate who has also written on the history of slavery.

Wolfson, David J. and Mariann Sullivan, "Foxes in the hen house: Animals, agribusiness, and the law: A modern American fable." In Sunstein and Nussbaum, pp. 205–33. Statistics on animals killed for various purposes are on p. 206.

Acknowledgments

Thank you very much to my husband Peter Groves, for all things supportive and for reading the manuscript, offering critical feedback, and discussing all sorts of strange things over the dinner table.

Thanks very much to Ruth Talman Kazez, who read an early version of the manuscript and weighed in on whether it was hopeless or not. I appreciate the encouragement. The artwork in the book is hers. All pictures are large mixed-media canvasses, except the first, which is a drawing. It's got to be the case that growing up in a house full of animals, and with pictures of animals on the walls, made this book possible. Thank you to Emil Kazez too, for passing along a philosophical temperament.

Robert Howell, Steve Sverdlik, and Alastair Norcross generously commented on several chapters of the book. I appreciate Larry Carbone's taking the time to answer my questions about animal care committees. I also appreciate the input of the anonymous research administrator mentioned in chapter 8. I decided on anonymity for the sake of candor and because I truly am grateful for the time this individual gave me.

Students in my animal rights classes over the years have been a huge help. I don't just mean the animal advocates, of which there are just a few in every class. I've found it illuminating to talk to students with every possible attitude toward animals, from utmost compassion to total dismissal.

At Wiley-Blackwell, thank you to Anna Oxbury for great copyediting (and some much-appreciated fact checking), Liz Cremona for producing a good-looking book, two anonymous referees, and especially to philosophy editor Nick Bellorini.

Thanks, finally, to Becky and Sammy, my two animal-loving children, for being good humored about the book-writing business, and for your great ideas for titles. The way you stand up for animals is an inspiration to me.

Index